CW01111172

Iurii Trifonov (1925–81) is known primarily as a writer of Soviet urban life. This study, however, takes as its starting-point Trifonov's interest in history and the passage of time, and attempts to show how this interest informs all his writing, from his earliest, Stalin Prize-winning period to the self-consciously modernist later works. The theme of time is expressed in several ways in the course of Trifonov's creative evolution. In his early works he merely reflects the abiding ethos of his age, that of Stalinism and then the thaw. In his works of the 1960s and 1970s he integrates a sense of history into his exploration of the cynicism and opportunism characteristic of the Brezhnev period. Trifonov's use of flashback, memory and multiple narrative viewpoints is crucial here, as is his interest in decisive events of Russian history, such as the assassination of Tsar Aleksandr II, and the Russian Civil War. In his later works, Trifonov emphasizes the interconnectedness of human life and history, with the individual as 'the nerve of history', linking epochs, places, civilizations. Trifonov discerns patterns and analogies in history, and develops a language of hints and allusions with which to combat the repressive censorship of his time. He upheld the concepts of truth and justice when *glasnost'* was unknown, and where 'historical expediency' was all-determining.

CAMBRIDGE STUDIES IN RUSSIAN LITERATURE

IURII TRIFONOV

CAMBRIDGE STUDIES IN RUSSIAN LITERATURE

General editor: MALCOLM JONES

Editorial Board: ANTHONY CROSS, CARYL EMERSON,
HENRY GIFFORD, G. S. SMITH, VICTOR TERRAS

Recent titles in this series include:

Dostoyevsky and the process of literary creation
JACQUES CATTEAU
translated by Audrey Littlewood

The poetic imagination of Vyacheslav Ivanov
PAMELA DAVIDSON

Joseph Brodsky
VALENTINA POLUKHINA

Petrushka: the Russian carnival puppet theatre
CATRIONA KELLY

Turgenev
FRANK FRIEDEBERG SEELEY

From the idyll to the novel: Karamzin's sentimentalist prose
GITTA HAMMARBERG

'The Brothers Karamazov' and the poetics of memory
DIANE OENNING THOMPSON

Andrei Platonov
THOMAS SEIFRID

Nabokov's Early Fiction
JULIAN W. CONNOLLY

A complete list of books in this series
is given at the end of the volume.

Iurii Trifonov:
unity through time

DAVID GILLESPIE

Senior Lecturer in Russian
School of Modern Languages and International Studies
University of Bath

CAMBRIDGE UNIVERSITY PRESS

Published by the Press Syndicate of the University of Cambridge
The Pitt Building, Trumpington Street, Cambridge CB2 1RP
40 West 20th Street, New York, NY 10011–4211, USA
10 Stamford Road, Oakleigh, Victoria 3166, Australia

© Cambridge University Press 1992

First published 1992

Printed in Great Britain at the University Press, Cambridge

A catalogue record for this book is available from the British Library

Library of Congress cataloguing in publication data
Gillespie, David C.
Iurii Trifonov: unity through time / David Gillespie.
p. cm. – (Cambridge Studies in Russian literature)
Includes bibliographical references and index.
ISBN 0 521 41947 6 (hardback)
1. Trifonov, Iurii Valentinovich, 1925–81 – Criticism and
interpretation. 2. Time in literature. I. Title. II. Series.
PG3489.R5Z67   1992
891.73′44 – dc20   92-7312   CIP

ISBN 0 521 41947 6 hardback

Contents

Preface		*page* ix
Introduction		1
1	From Moscow students to the Turkmenian desert (*Studenty; Utolenie zhazhdy*)	14
2	Moscow life, 1966–1975 (*Obmen; Predvaritel'nye itogi; Beskonechnye igry; Dolgoe proshchanie; Drugaia zhizn'*)	47
3	The house on the embankment (*Dom na naberezhnoi*)	99
4	Terrorism, Civil War and the present (*Neterpenie; Otblesk kostra; Starik*)	123
5	Time and place (*Vremia i mesto; Ischeznovenie*)	160
	Conclusion: unity through dislocation (*Oprokinutyi dom*)	194
Notes		208
Bibliography		225
Index		245

Preface

This book has come about as the result of several years' work on Trifonov's texts which began as I was completing my doctoral thesis in 1984–5. The thesis concentrated on the work of the 'village writers' Valentin Rasputin and Vasilii Belov, but as work on it drew to an end in the summer of 1984 I became equally interested in the 'urban prose' of Iurii Trifonov. I was struck by the fact that most critics wrote only about the writer's depiction of urban life and mores, whereas I became increasingly interested in the historical and temporal dimensions of his world. This book attempts to fill what I perceive to be a large gap in Trifonov criticism, although worthy full-length studies have appeared in the last few years both in the USSR and the West.

Consequently, much preliminary work, in particular in compiling the bibliography, was carried out in the Lenin State Library and the Academy of Sciences' Library, both in Moscow, and in the Academy of Sciences' Library in Leningrad, in the Spring of 1982 and the whole of the academic year 1984–5. Further work was done in the library of Khar'kov State University in the Ukraine in August 1990 and March 1991. Part of this study has already appeared in article form: 'Time, History and the Individual in the Works of Yury Trifonov', *Modern Language Review*, 83, 2 (April 1988), 375–95; 'Unity through Disparity: Trifonov's *The Overturned House*', *Australian Slavonic and East European Studies*, 5, 1 (1991), pp. 45–58.

In the notes and bibliography I have chosen to use the abbreviations M and L for publications in Moscow and Leningrad respectively. The bibliography alone contains full publication details of Trifonov's works and criticism; details of references in the notes have been kept to a minimum. Unless otherwise stated, all quotations from Trifonov's works are taken from his four-volume collected works, Iurii Trifonov, *Sobranie sochinenii v chetyrekh tomakh*, published in Moscow by Khudozhestvennaia literatura in 1985–7, with volume and page number incorporated into the main text (full bibliographical details are in the bibliography). All translations are my own. The Library of Congress system of transliteration has been used throughout. Words and phrases in square brackets indicate my own insertions in quotations, usually for reasons of elucidation.

I would like to thank friends and colleagues of the British Association for Soviet, Slavonic and East European Studies, and the American Association for the Advancement of Slavic Studies, for their interest, advice and encouragement, in particular Bob Porter, Frank Ellis, Kathleen Parthé and Gerald Mikkelson. I would also like to thank the staff of the School of Modern Languages and International Studies at Bath University, especially Bill Brooks and Roberta Tozer, for their help in tracking down background information relating to Trifonov's interest in French and Italian history. Special thanks are reserved for Chris Williams, for his invaluable assistance in transferring texts to computer disk, and to Louise Roberts, for her immense patience and fortitude in deciphering what was often an almost illegible manuscript.

The book is dedicated to Anna, in the hope that one day she may read it.

Introduction

When Iurii Trifonov died suddenly on 28 March 1981 at the age of fifty-five following what should have been a routine kidney operation, he was at the height of his success as a writer, and one of the most discussed Soviet writers, both in the USSR and abroad. A quick glance at the bibliography at the end of this monograph confirms that even before his death there had been much critical discussion of his work, and evaluation and comment have continued unabated into the 1990s. On the whole, he has been treated with a mixture of indulgence, hostility and suspicion by Soviet critics, at least until his death, and considerable interest from Western and *émigré* critics in his narrative technique and the 'half-truths' about Soviet history and society he manages to convey. Indeed, it was not until Gorbachev's policy of *glasnost*' in the arts beginning in 1986 that his hitherto unpublished fiction was made available to the public, with the appearance in December of that year of his short story 'Nedolgoe prebyvanie v kamere pytok' ('A Short Stay in the Torture Chamber'), part of the *Oprokinutyi dom* ('The Overturned House') cycle published in 1981. January 1987 saw the publication of his unfinished novel *Ischeznovenie* ('The Disappearance'). From 1987 until 1990 there has been much further publication of Trifonov texts, letters, memoirs and other documentary materials. Critical interest in him has also been considerable, and is now more appreciative than during his lifetime.

Iurii Trifonov is important as a Soviet writer not only for what he wrote, but also for what he was. As the son of a purged Old Bolshevik he tried to examine and interpret the times he lived through, the phenomenon of Stalinism and its psychological consequences for his generation. He is a precursor of those writing in the heady days of *glasnost'* who are free to expose and catalogue the crimes of Stalin and his confederates. Trifonov's interest in history emerged in the dark and dangerous years of Brezhnev's cultural freeze, now called the years of 'stagnation', and even if he had wanted to, he could not be as forthright and challenging as writers practising under the conditions of *glasnost'* are.

Iurii Valentinovich Trifonov was born in Moscow on 28 August 1925, the son of Valentin Trifonov, a prominent Bolshevik and hero of the Revolution and Civil War. Valentin Trifonov had joined the Party in 1904 at the age of sixteen, took an active part in the revolutions of 1905 and 1917, and spent several years in Tsarist exile. Valentin and his elder brother Evgenii were born in the Verkhne-Kundriuchenskii village of the Don region, of Cossack descent. From the age of seven, when his parents died, Valentin moved to the town of Maikop. It was there that he first organized strike action, and in 1905 he and Evgenii took part in the armed uprising in Rostov. He was arrested in 1906, and from the age of seventeen to twenty-six was in Siberian exile. Several times he tried to escape. In February 1917 he was one of the few Bolsheviks in St Petersburg at the time of the Tsar's abdication, and in July and August the same year was helping to organize and lead the Red Guard in the Vasil'evskii district of the capital. He later helped mould the zealous but poorly trained Red Guard into the more disciplined and professional Red Army. Valentin's subsequent career in the Civil War is an illustrious one: he took part in major campaigns across the land, fighting in Tsaritsyn, organizing the Don Cossacks, and pushing back the advancing Czechs in the Urals. In short, Valentin Trifonov was a committed Bolshevik of impeccable revolutionary credentials whose dedication to the cause reflects the idealism of those fighting to create a new world. After the Civil War Valentin represented the fledgling Soviet state in several responsible posts abroad, including China and Finland.[1] His subsequent fate also reflects that of Lenin's comrades-in-arms: he was arrested in June 1937 and never seen again, one of thousands of Old Bolsheviks to perish under Stalin.

Iurii Trifonov was only eleven years old when he last saw his father, a circumstance which helps explain the sudden and often violent disruption of childhood and loss of innocence in his later fiction. Iurii's mother was arrested shortly afterwards, and spent eight years in camps and exile before returning to Moscow in 1946.

Following the arrest of his mother Iurii and his sister Tania were legally adopted by their maternal grandmother, T. A. Slovatinskaia, and they moved out of the large house inhabited by the families of top-ranking government officials on Bersenevskaia Embankment (the 'house on the embankment' he was to later describe in detail). Until the beginning of the War they lived on the outskirts of Moscow, on Bol'shaia Kaluzhskaia (now Leninskii Prospekt), and in 1941 they were evacuated to Tashkent. Iurii went to school there from 1941 to 1942, and then he returned to Moscow to work as a labourer and fitter in a factory making radiators for warplanes, and as a part-time fireman.[2] It was while he was working in the factory that he applied to enrol in the Gor'kii Literary Institute. He submitted some short stories and poems as proof of his talent, and, believing his gift to be primarily a poetic one, was surprised to learn that his poems were rejected, but that his prose particularly impressed Konstantin Fedin. He enrolled part-time in 1944, and in 1945 transferred to a full-time course, graduating in 1949.

In 1947 he published his first short story in the newspaper *Moskovskii komsomolets*. This was followed by other short pieces in 1948, and in 1950 he achieved his first success with *Studenty* ('The Students'), a novel based on his graduation diploma which was later to be awarded the Stalin Prize. It took him eighteen months to complete. Here again Fedin helped him, recommending the novel to Aleksandr Tvardovskii, the new editor-in-chief of *Novyi mir*, the country's foremost literary periodical. The novel was phenomenally successful, and the October and November 1950 issues in which it appeared were sold out almost immediately. The Communist Party newspaper

Pravda published a favourable review of it, and Mosfil'm wanted to film it. Trifonov was later to reflect on the reasons for its success.

The best books of the late 1940s, he asserts, were about the War, books by Grossman, Kazakevich, Viktor Nekrasov, Vera Panova. Other books were considerably duller, less authentic. Yet 'readers wanted books on the life of today that they knew ... There was a genuine reading famine.' *Studenty* contained 'some everyday truth, there were details that were reminiscent of real life. And not in a different time and place, but in Moscow, here and now.'[3]

Thereafter he became a full-time writer and journalist, which he was to remain until his death. As the son of an executed 'enemy of the people', however, he still had to face dangers. He had concealed the truth of his parentage in his enrolment forms for the Institute, but after he had won the Stalin Prize it was discovered. He was no longer a student, but was still a member of the Institute's Komsomol organization. He was threatened with dismissal from it, which would have prevented him from joining the Writers' Union and so becoming a professional writer. Eventually he was merely 'severely reprimanded'.[4] He was only accepted into the Writers' Union in early 1957.[5]

After *Studenty* Trifonov wrote two plays, produced in 1952 and 1954 in the Moscow Ermolova Theatre. Neither was a great commercial or artistic success. *Molodye gody* ('Years of Youth') was an adaptation of *Studenty*, and the later *Zalog uspekha* ('Guarantee of Success') concerned the life of Moscow artists, a milieu he got to know through his recent marriage.

In 1951 he married Nina Nelina, a singer at the Bol'shoi Theatre whose father, Amshei Markovich Niurenberg, was an artist who in his youth had known Marc Chagall in Paris. (Amshei Markovich acts as the prototype for Georgii Maksimovich in *Drugaia zhizn'* ('Another Life', 1975) and Iona Aleksandrovich in *Oprokinutyi dom* ('The Overturned House', 1981).) Despite his marriage, and the fact that his daughter Ol'ga was born in 1951, Trifonov spent much time in the early 1950s travelling, at first to the Kuibyshev Hydro-Electric Station on the Volga, and then to Central Asia. In 1952 he visited his sister Tania, who had been working as a botanist in the Turkmenian desert since 1951, in order to gather material on the building of the Great Turkmenian Canal. After the death of Stalin in March 1953 this project was suddenly stopped, and Trifonov was left with a manuscript of one hundred and twenty pages about a project which was no longer considered viable. After all, he mused, who would publish a story about a construction project that had been closed down? With the failure of his excursions into the theatre, and not having published anything new since *Studenty*, by 1954 he was poor and depressed. Tvardovskii refused to give him an advance for a new novel, and rejected the manuscript of *Zalog uspekha*. This was a time of personal crisis for Trifonov, and can be seen reflected in the writer Rebrov's own lack of success in *Dolgoe proshchanie* ('The Long Goodbye', 1971). The affair led to a cooling of relations between him and Tvardovskii that was to last until 1966.[6]

Throughout the 1950s Trifonov continued to travel to Turkmenia to collect material on the building of the Kara-Kum canal project, the successor to the Great Turkmenian Canal. In 1959 he published some short stories set in Turkmenia, focusing on the tensions involved in modernizing a backward culture and the new post-Stalin political climate. These themes of construction, irrigation and the thaw eventually bore greater fruit with the publication in 1963 of *Utolenie zhazhdy* ('The Quenching of Thirst').

Trifonov agreed with the division of his creative development into three stages by the German Ralf Schröder: the first being the period of his Stalin Prize award; the second his 'word pictures' (*slovesnaia zhivopis'*) of the late 1950s and 1960s; the third his 'thinking prose' (*mysliashchaia proza*) and 'polyphonic novel of consciousness' of the late 1970s and early 1980s.[7] These periods also coincide with the changes in his publishing outlets: *Studenty* was published in *Novyi mir*, while his works of 1959–65 appeared in the then lack-lustre *Znamia*. He published his 'Moscow stories' of 1966 to 1975 again in *Novyi mir*, while the works of his last few years were published in *Druzhba narodov*, edited by his friend Sergei Baruzdin.

However, these categorizations concern mainly literary form; in terms of theme and subject-matter, and in particular the treatment of time and history, there are two periods. The first is the 1950s and early 1960s, up to the publication in 1965 of *Otblesk kostra* ('Fireglow'); the latter period embraces everything from that work until *Ischeznovenie*. Both *Studenty* and *Utolenie zhazhdy* are typical works of the prevailing political and cultural ethos. It is with *Otblesk kostra* that Trifonov moves away from writing as an external response to events towards a sense of time and history as personal, individual experience. *Otblesk kostra* is a historical study of the revolutionary and Civil War exploits of Valentin Trifonov and his brother Evgenii; it is above all a son's rehabilitation of his father. It is also a record of injustices perpetrated by the Reds during the Civil War, and an indictment of Stalin's crimes.

In 1964 Trifonov renewed his acquaintance with Tvardovskii when both almost simultaneously became the owners of neighbouring *dachi* in Krasnaia Pakhra just outside Moscow, and in 1966 Trifonov once more began publishing in *Novyi mir*. At first he published some short stories, and then in 1969 *Obmen* ('The Exchange') appeared, and Trifonov once more became a much discussed writer. Here, as well as in the works that soon followed – *Predvaritel'nye itogi* ('Preliminary Stocktaking', 1970) and *Dolgoe proshchanie* – he portrayed Moscow *byt*: the grey, everyday lives of ordinary residents of the capital, focusing on their personal morality, or the lack of it, and the aspirations for material betterment associated with life in the big city.

Trifonov notes that the December 1969 issue of *Novyi mir* which contained *Obmen* was the first in a long time completely untouched by the censor. This was a bad sign, the lull before the storm, as the wolves were now gathering to force the dismissal of Tvardovskii, the publisher of Solzhenitsyn, and emasculate the country's leading liberal journal.[8] Trifonov was heavily involved in the campaign to protect the journal and its esteemed editor from conservative attacks, alongside Grigorii Baklanov and Boris Mozhaev, and it was through the latter that he made the acquaintance of Aleksandr Solzhenitsyn. Solzhenitsyn was expelled from the Writers' Union in 1969, and awarded the

Nobel Prize for Literature a year later. As a result of the Western publication of *The Gulag Archipelago* Solzhenitsyn was arrested and deported in 1974. By then *Novyi mir* had ceased to be a major force in Soviet literature. The journal's editorial committee was disbanded in February 1970, and Tvardovskii handed over the reins as editor-in-chief to V. Kosolapov. Tvardovskii was ill by this time, and he died in December 1971.

The critical reaction to Trifonov's 'trilogy' was largely favourable: most critics, such as B. Sokolov and M. Sinel'nikov, were content to see the works as a satire on modern forms of *meshchanstvo*, the dreaded Russian condition that is a mixture of materialism and philistinism. Others were more astute. Iurii Andreev and Grigorii Brovman saw that Trifonov offered an unsettling picture of 'a hermetically sealed small world' of individual conflicts which eclipsed the greater reality of the life of society going on around them. In her own study of these reactions, Anne Hughes characterizes the *bol'shoi mir* as 'the arena in which the struggle to build communism is taking place and everything that the artist depicts in his work must be related to this struggle and to its necessarily triumphant conclusion'.[9] In eclipsing this world by concentrating on individual characters and personal feelings, Trifonov was seen as subverting socialist realist aesthetics. The reader's attention is distracted from the greater tasks of society in the period designated as 'advanced socialism' (*razvitoi sotsializm*), where the 'scientific and technological revolution' (*nauchno-tekhnicheskaia revoliutsiia*) was taking place. The picture the reader gets of reality is thus unrepresentative, and the educative function of the literary work is neutralized.

For example, after a positive appraisal of *Obmen*, the editors of the theoretical journal *Voprosy literatury* passed the following judgment:

But in the two latest stories (especially in 'Dolgoe proshchanie') there is the distinct feeling that the author's field of vision does not take in all the links that connect the characters to the greater world, and several of them – sometimes extremely vital ones – are not explored as they should be. And it seems that the world inhabited by the characters of 'Predvaritel'nye itogi' and 'Dolgoe proshchanie' has become artificially 'hermetically sealed'. This, incidentally, denies the author the opportunity to give adequate expression both to the force in society that constantly opposes and does battle with *meshchanstvo*, and to one of the characteristic features of the modern *meshchanin*: his mimicry, to which he must resort every time he comes into contact with people of a different world outlook, and with the greater world beyond mere 'domestic' concerns.

The editorial went on in similarly turgid style to criticize the lack of a 'moral ideal' in *Dolgoe proshchanie*, and the author's failure to depict in that work the 'social and moral forces that determine the development of our society and which lead the offensive against survivals of the past and *meshchanstvo*'.[10] It did not, though, say what these 'forces' were.

In his reply the author denied that he was writing about *meshchane*, or about positive and negative characters in general; he was simply writing about ordinary people and trying to express his own vision of society and the diverse, often paradoxical forces that make it up. Nevertheless, the same accusation is made against him some years later, after the publication of *Dom na naberezhnoi* ('The House on the Embankment', 1976). Following a hostile review of the work in *Literaturnaia gazeta* in May of that year, Georgii Markov, the First Secretary of the Soviet Writers' Union, and therefore the single most powerful voice in literary affairs, singled out the work for criticism at the Sixth Soviet Writers' Congress in June:

> ... the thematic and structural basis of the novel (*povest'*) is essentially so enclosed within the author's chosen form that neither the characters nor the readers are always able to discern with due clarity the presence of forces capable of alleviating the hopelessness (*besvykhodnost'*) of some lives and situations. In cases like these not only the question of form and genre, but also the philosophical outlook of the author are open to question.[11]

With the appearance of *Drugaia zhizn'* ('Another Life') in 1975 and *Dom na naberezhnoi* in 1976, Trifonov moves towards a more complex narrative style, involving multiple temporal planes and several narrative voices. Both these works are fundamentally concerned with questions of historical interpretation, and how an individual can integrate the past in his present life. Flashback and memory are important structural principles, and continue to be so in the fiction of Trifonov's latter years.

The five above-mentioned works published between 1969 and 1976 have been labelled by critics the 'Moscow stories [*povesti*]', because they deal ostensibly with the life of Moscow's intelligentsia, and concentrate on everyday struggles and squabbles. In 1973 Trifonov also published a historical novel, *Neterpenie* ('Impatience'), about the 'People's Will' (*Narodnaia Volia*) revolutionaries of a hundred years ago and their assassination of Tsar Aleksandr II in 1881. With the publication in 1978 of *Starik* ('The Old Man'), and its contemporary setting and use of flashback and memory to recreate the early years of the twentieth century and the Civil War, we can trace Trifonov's historical theme stretching from the present day, back to the years of Stalin, then to the Civil War and Revolution, and coming to rest with the Populists of the late nineteenth century. Trifonov is increasingly interested in the development of Russian radicalism from the terrorism of a hundred years ago to the Revolution and Civil War, and then through to the Stalin terror. All the time, as in *Otblesk kostra*, he is searching for the meaning of his father's life, a life of ideals destroyed by the system he created. However, as we shall see, Trifonov's historical enquiry goes further back into the centuries, to analyse the roots of Russian autocracy and fundamental questions of the relationship of people and power, freedom and tyranny.

Starik was Trifonov's last piece of fiction to appear in his lifetime. His collection of short stories entitled *Oprokinutyi dom* ('The Overturned House') appeared posthumously in July 1981, followed in October and November the same year by the appearance of *Vremia i mesto* ('Time and Place'). *Ischeznovenie* could be published only in 1987. These last two novels both contain many elements and strands from Trifonov's previous work, as if the writer were trying to find a synthesis of his own life and work in order to paint a multi-layered picture of his society and establish his own place and role in time. It is also as if the writer is assessing his own development as a writer and as a person, aware that his own creative evolution is perhaps a reflection of the changes in Soviet society and literature over three decades.

Trifonov's preoccupation with time and history must be seen largely as a consequence of being the son of Valentin Trifonov, a man close to the 'fire of history' who passionately believed in the Bolshevik cause from an early age. In Trifonov's works there are many characters who occupy positions of eminence, only to fall from grace. Indeed, his plots revolve around the struggle of two types: tyrants who rule by force or coercion, and their victims. This is true both of his historical works, and those which are set in present-day Moscow. The tyrants have their confederates and assistants, eager to ingratiate themselves in order to gain material benefit or status; the victims have their friends and family, who offer simple human sympathy, support or understanding. Ultimately his works are about the struggle of the human, the personal, with the anti-human, the impersonal.

But the author's preoccupation with the workings of time is also connected with his living in a society which has seen tumultuous change in seven decades. As he has said, if rather obliquely:

I am extremely interested in the problem of time, for it is a category that changes life. Even if these changes are not always discernible, since we live in the flow of time and, as they say, large things are better seen at a distance. But to feel these changes while living from day to day, to be able to communicate how change takes place, this means showing how today is different from yesterday and from the day before, how it differs from what it was ten years ago. This I see as one of the main tasks of a Soviet writer.

Sometimes you don't notice or feel the changes going on around you. But you have to be able to see them.[12]

The key to understanding Trifonov's works, both in terms of theme and structure, is *slitnost'*, the word he uses to describe the interconnection of all strands of life, the totality of experience, the interweaving of past and present. The word in Russian means 'unity' or 'merging', and it, or its adjectival, verbal or adverbial cognates, recurs in his writing to a remarkable degree.

Slitnost' determines the dynamics of his writing, for Trifonov's world is one where the great and the small, past and present, the individual and the collective, coexist and interact. As he says:

A man carries within himself, whether he realizes it or not, everything he has lived through, or everything he has been forced to live through. He can't shake off the burden of the past. It sits inside him. Therefore I try, when I depict a man, to draw out all his inner layers, all the layers that have become entangled inside him, merged together [*slilis'*] in a single whole. As a writer I am, so to speak, bound to understand what he carries from the 1940s, what from the 1960s and what is totally new, what dates from today. Therefore I believe that for a writer who describes today's life, the form of the novel of consciousness is very, very useful.[13]

Slitnost' is a sense of unity in which everything and everyone are interconnected and part of a continuing process. Trifonov tries to give 'as multifaceted and intricate a picture as possible of the entire layer of circumstances in which man lives', to depict 'relationships both at work and in the family, with friends and with parents, attitudes to money and to women – in short, a whole layer of circumstances'.[14] Thus he wishes to give his reader 'a sense of the incessancy of life,... the impression of pulsating life'.[15]

The effects of the past are ever-present, and the shifting political and social background of the 1950s, 1960s and 1970s is an important consideration in his works. For Trifonov's treatment of time is largely conditioned by time's treatment of him.

Trifonov, then, is trying to interpret his society from an objective and critical standpoint, in as much as this is possible given the conditions of censorship and repression at the time. The nature of his criticism is a controversial issue: critics are still divided as to whether he was an opponent of the Soviet regime who masked his real feelings behind allusion and half-truths, or whether he was a critic who may have attacked Stalin's misuse of power, but who remained loyal to the fundamentals of Soviet rule. Whatever the case, he succeeded in creating a narrative discourse rich in interpretation and meaning. On the role of the writer, he would merely quote Herzen: 'We are not the doctors, we are the pain.'¹⁶ That is, like Lermontov, Chekhov and others, he refused to provide answers to the ills in his society, he simply depicted these ills and their consequences.

There is, of course, a long tradition in Russian literature where the writer becomes historian: Karamzin, Pushkin, Tolstoi all attempted to interpret the course of Russian history, even the historical process itself, and the relationship of the ruler to the ruled. After 1917, and in particular after the formulation in 1934 of socialist realism, history had to be justified to conform with ideological criteria, and writers were called upon to legitimize the Bolshevik takeover and to point the way to the bright vistas of a Communist future. In recent years, however, writers such as Rasputin, Mozhaev, Belov, Tendriakov, Abramov and many others have, like Trifonov, tended to look back, rather than forward, in order to fill in the gaps, the 'blank spots', of Soviet history. In so doing they have discovered an alternative history, one different from that promulgated by their rulers, and one based not on class conflict or economic relations but on the suffering and the sacrifices of millions of ordinary people.

These authors, known as the 'village writers' (*derevenshchiki*), have much in common with Trifonov. Although he was at pains to distance himself from them, and in his fiction sometimes parodied their motifs, he nevertheless acknowledged a certain kinship. He was particularly drawn to the work of Vasilii Shukshin and Valentin Rasputin. In an interview with Lev Anninskii shortly before his death he furthermore denied that the city was an 'unnatural' phenomenon, as some 'village writers' and their sympathetic critics have asserted. He pictured his city in rural terms, affirming that his 'natural world of the city' was like 'a forest', with its own 'trees, ravines, cliffs, and ditches'.¹⁷ It is no accident that in many of his works Trifonov refers to the city as 'a forest', which itself becomes a metaphor for life and the struggle to find one's path in it.

On another level, Trifonov does for Moscow what the *derevenshchiki* do for the village: he gives it historical roots and lineage, so that past and present are never far from each other, and draws portraits of its dominant characters. Like them, he is writing about his home, and about childhood. But while for the 'village writers' the village is a place equated with stability and harmony, and the purity of childhood, Trifonov's home in the city is disrupted, 'overturned', the family unit torn apart by the death of the father, childhood bliss abruptly brought to an end.[18] The theme of the home and the chronotope of the house are constant throughout Trifonov's fiction, but the home is only in his earliest, most optimistic work a happy one, and the house is a place of trial and conflict.

Trifonov is difficult to categorize as a writer. He is both a socialist realist, because he depicts social relations between individuals and the changes in their environment as they progress through life ('society in its revolutionary development'), and a modernist, with complex narrative patterns and a multi-layered discourse. He does not, at least in his mature fiction, point to any great resolution of conflicts in the future. Rather, his concentration of the process of time and the individual's perception of it become fused with his later 'stream of consciousness' writing. The purpose of this monograph is itself an exercise in practising *slitnost'*: both to disentangle the various strands and layers of his writing, and to assess the totality of his work and its significance for the Russian and Western reader.

CHAPTER 1

From Moscow students to the Turkmenian desert (Studenty; Utolenie zhazhdy)

Studenty is separated by thirteen years from Trifonov's second novel, *Utolenie zhazhdy*. Though the period of time between the two novels is considerable, and the attitudes that set them apart even more marked, they have one thing in common. In this the early phase of his career Trifonov was following the traditions of socialist realist writing, and writing to order. Under Stalin writers were required to portray the life of society in a one-sided and artificially optimistic manner. Under Khrushchev writers were expected to support the policy of 'de-Stalinization' by rebelling against such schematization, and by affirming the emergence of a 'new', more humane morality.

Studenty is very much based on Trifonov's own experiences in the Literary Institute in the late 1940s, and *Utolenie zhazhdy* combines the elements of thaw literature, with its critical reappraisal of the Stalin years, and the typical Soviet construction novel. Trifonov is thus here reflecting, but not interpreting, his times, in line with the prevailing political ethos. Nevertheless, both novels contain elements that are peculiar to Trifonov's view of his society and which we recognize in his later writing.

Studenty was last published as a separate edition in 1960, and in his last decade the author was at pains to dismiss it, saying that it belonged to the period of the first stage in his literary development, and was 'completely different' from his more mature works.[1] This is hardly a surprising statement, especially when we learn from Vadim Kozhinov that the novel, which sold more than a million copies between 1950 and 1960, was discussed at 'hundreds' of student meetings, became 'a weighty factor in the "literary situation" recreated in *Dom na naberezhnoi*, and led to the dismissal of academics branded as 'Kozel'skii's' (Professor Kozel'skii is the main 'negative' character in the novel).²

Studenty describes the life of a section of the students of Moscow's Literary Institute (although in the novel it is a teacher training institute), the upwardly mobile bright young things who are to benefit from Stalin's social reorganization. Vera Dunham has commented on the novel: 'The affluence of the rich is taken for granted. The author neither approves nor disapproves. One finds no note of criticism of the ways of the privileged. That is the point: affluence has entered the fare of the mass reader.'³ Conversely, its sister work of quarter of a century later, *Dom na naberezhnoi*, describes a society much darker, more sinister, where relationships and emotions are exploited to the utmost for personal gain.

Studenty is set in Moscow, like most of Trifonov's fiction, and like most of his later writing, the image of the city looms large throughout the novel. Indeed, it could be said to be one of the protagonists, for over the three years of the narrative Moscow's physical presence is stressed. It thrives as its streets teem with people and buzz with transport, it changes as old houses and districts are pulled down and new buildings and suburbs take their place. But Trifonov is describing what he sees and hears on the surface; there is as yet no sense of the interconnectedness of life, of the deep strands that bind people to places and which run through time.

The novel's central character is Vadim Belov, returning to his home in Moscow after five years, some of which has been spent fighting at the front. We join the novel in 1946, and the first pages recount Vadim's joy at being back in his home city and his recognition of once-familiar places as he walks through the centre:

Moscow. He was walking through Moscow! Here he had known and remembered everything since he was a child, here was his home, that simple human home that soldiers at war would recall, each one his own. At midnight in a forest outside Vienna and in the wild hills of

Hingan he would remember Zamoskvorech'e, Iakimanka, the granite river banks and the old lime trees in Neskuchnyi garden...

And now everything had come back to him. Everything, everything his memory had stored so carefully. In that detached house over there, by Spaso-Nalivkovskii, he had worked in the Leninskii district Fire Brigade during the first year of the War. And he had only been sixteen years old! Now the house bore the sign it had borne before the War: 'Kindergarten No. 62'. From open windows peered the shiny leaves of an India rubber plant, and songs poured forth from radio sets. (I, 23–4)

Belov's path takes him from the Bol'shoi Kamennyi bridge and the Udarnik cinema past the Kremlin on his right and towards the Lenin Library, before leading him in the direction of Red Square with Gor'kii Street and the Hotel Moscow to his left. Belov's return to the heart of his native city is described with loving care, as is the joy he experiences when recalling and then explaining to a stranger how to get from Red Square to the Tret'iakov Art Gallery on foot. From the very outset, then, there is a strong sense of the physicality of Moscow and particularly the historical heart of the city, and it is significant that the author returns here four hundred or so pages and three narrative years later to bring the novel to a close. It is Belov's – and Trifonov's – home, and the author displays an awareness (still in his mid-twenties) of the power of memory. Here Belov's subjective memory of his home is at one with the objective reality of Moscow, and he is only pleasantly surprised to be corrected by a passer-by on the existence of a new Metro station.

Moscow is indeed a participant in these opening pages. Real streets are passed through and named (Gogolevskii Boulevard, Korovii val, Polianka, Frunze Street, and many more). The new is added to the best of the old, and the two coexist in harmony: alongside the institute Vadim is to attend a new building is being constructed, as are the Palace of Congress in the Kremlin and the new university complex on Lenin Hills. This is a quintessential socialist realist picture of reality, where Moscow developing and growing is a politically charged synecdoche for the development of the country as a whole. The future is built in symbolic icons of Party leadership and an enhanced education for thousands of young people. In this picture of reality past, present and future are part of an ideological continuum, and it is exactly here that the disruption of time is to be perceived in his future works.

The narrative style of this novel is not, however, entirely dissimilar to that of the later Trifonov. Events in the past are quickly summed up through the recollections of a character, as when Belov recalls his father going off to war (where he is to be killed), and his own service as a fireman, before being evacuated with his mother to Tashkent and then going into the army. Belov is a typical Trifonov hero in that he shares many biographical details, especially from his childhood, with his creator. A fundamental, but necessary, difference is that Belov's father was killed in the War; it would have been impossible to state that he had been executed by the Soviet security forces. Similarly, the passage of time is related retrospectively: in a later chapter Belov takes his fellow-student Lena Medovskaia, whom he is courting, to the theatre, and afterwards in an internal monologue recounts the events that led up to the invitation a week before. Further examples of this occur when Belov reads through his diaries of his childhood and the early part of the War, as if he is trying to recapture those lost years. Elsewhere an unseen third-person narrator informs us of events that have taken place outside the narrative focus. Here we can see the seeds of Trifonov's later mature style. Nevertheless, memory here is used merely to fill in the background, the author is content to set a scene or give us relevant details about various characters.

Belov is about to enter a teacher training college to study literature when the novel begins, and the first three chapters very quickly cover his first two years as a student and his friendship with his childhood friend Sergei Palavin, a budding writer. The remaining chapters dwell on his third year and the conflicts that develop. We recognize this rapid acceleration and then deceleration of narrative time as a feature of Trifonov's later writing.

As the novel progresses we are introduced to Belov's fellow-students and teachers in the institute. Apart from Palavin, intelligent, gifted and ambitious, the students include Petr Lagodenko, a former sailor and, like Belov, a war veteran, Andrei Syrykh, a former factory worker and his sister Ol'ga with whom Belov eventually develops what looks to be a long-term romance, the flighty Lena Medovskaia, with whom he initially falls in love but who later drifts toward Sergei, and Spartak Galustian, a Komsomol activist. There are many others who come in and out of the narrative focus, but these are the characters who play an important part in the development of the plot. The staff include the professors Kozel'skii and Krechetov, teachers of literature, and Sizov, the Dean of the Faculty.

The plot is straightforward and, as a work of Stalinist socialist realism, on the surface holds no surprises. The students progress through their studies and prepare for their examinations before the fourth and final year of their course, after which they will go forth into the world and contribute to the post-war rebuilding of society. Early on Belov's worries go no further than wondering whether to wear a tie in which to take Lena to the theatre, and Palavin reminds him that it is not fashionable nowadays to fasten the lower button of one's suit jacket. The lives of these young people are naive and optimistic, but also affluent, as Lena's father allows her and Belov to go to the theatre in his chauffeur-driven car. These are the material riches the young can expect in Stalin's Russia, if they maintain their ideological loyalty. As illustration of their commitment, one chapter is devoted to a description of the zeal and solidarity felt by the students as they help lay gas pipelines on the outskirts of Moscow on a December *voskresnik*, day of unpaid and voluntary labour. Belov is appointed the work leader because of his army experience, and is inspired by the sense of purpose and the exhilaration of physical labour. The others (with the exception of Lena and Palavin, who excuse themselves) are similarly infected by the collective effort, and they all work themselves into a sweat despite the cold weather. At the end of the working day even the woman who sells them beer has eyes that are 'bright and shining', just like the hopes and prospects of this, the young generation that has known no-one but Stalin as their leader.

The young Trifonov already has a sharp eye for the changing face of Moscow:

> The building site was situated on a narrow, winding street that had miraculously survived as part of the old suburb. About forty years ago this region was populated by impoverished families of the gentry, small shopowners and artisans fallen on hard times. After the Revolution great factories grew up here, old streets were pulled down and levelled, and new ones built. Moscow was stretching out further to the west, and there, in the west, a new Moscow was growing, a Moscow of multi-storey housing blocks, huge shops, squares and public gardens, a Moscow that the Metro and trolleybus brought within ten minutes of the centre. And this part of Moscow, which was to all intents and purposes the outskirts, in no way resembled the outskirts; rather, the narrow, winding streets that remained tucked away behind the new houses were more worthy of the name, although they were considerably closer to the centre and comprised the heart of the city. Moscow was pushing outwards, spreading beyond its former boundaries, and not only westwards but in all directions, and this astonishing displacement of suburbs was evident everywhere. (I, 161–2)

Here there is enthusiasm for the growth of the city as the justification of official teleology, the discarding of the old and the unnecessary, and its replacement by the new and the dynamic. The synecdoche is evident: the 'small' reality is but a microcosm of the 'large' life of society. But at the same time the passage ends on a slightly ambiguous note, as past and present stand uneasily side by side.

Not surprisingly, the novel glorifies Stalin's Russia and the symbolic achievements of Soviet society. The students set up a literary circle with a local factory, thus consolidating the symbolic link between the intelligentsia and the working class. Andrei Syrykh is the key functionary here, for he had worked in this factory, his father is working-class, and it is with considerable enthusiasm that he establishes links with the workers. In the factory itself the older and younger generations share the same ideals and have the same goal, as embodied in old Mikhail Terent'evich and his son Andrei, so symbolizing the togetherness and continuity of the 'great family' under Stalin.[4] The atmosphere among the work-force is friendly and business-like, everyone knows his place and shares the dignity of manual labour. The sense of political purpose and commitment is very strong, so that the novel paints a rosy picture of people under Stalin's leadership working together harmoniously and devotedly towards the common goal.

Byt here is described in rosy colours, in terms of whether Lena should wear a brooch or a necklace, and her observation that perfume scent stays longer if it is put behind the ears. This is a smug, self-satisfied, confident attitude to life, as Geoffrey Hosking observes, 'the red carpet that leads into the future, its smoothness and attractiveness a proof that it is indeed the highway to magnificent prospects'.[5]

The students are similarly infused with faith in the cause. In their rooms they meditate on the nature of happiness in life, and come to the inevitable conclusion that happiness resides in working for the benefit of society and the good of all. As they later raise their glasses to greet the New Year, they pronounce a life-affirming toast to the new world and to fighters for Communism everywhere. Indeed, the 'positive' characters Belov, Lagodenko, Syrykh and Galustian become indistinguishable as personalities and merge into a single composite image of the political functionary: they talk about the same things, agree on the right topics and praise the same people (for example the educationalist and writer Makarenko).

Trifonov is also at pains to legitimize Stalinist culture: when Vadim's mother falls ill her choice of recuperative reading is Veresaev (though we are not told whether this is his fiction, autobiography, or literary criticism), and later the poet Isakovskii is deliberately mentioned in the same breath as Shakespeare, as presumably the socialist realist heir to the bard's crown. Koreans and Albanians study in Moscow and relate to their Soviet counterparts the international situation, how life was terrible in their home countries before their respective 'revolutions', and how lucky they are now to have a socialist form of government. The students' visit to the Tret'iakov Gallery reinforces these points: they see pictures depicting different stages of Russian history and culture, such as Vereshchagin's 'Before the Attack at Plevna', whose theme is the Russian liberation of Bulgaria from the Turks, and the same artist's 'Surprise Attack', about the Tsarist conquest of Central Asia. The choice of these two pictures is not fortuitous, as they give historical justification to the internationalist 'myths' of Stalinist (and post-Stalin) presumptions, respectively the 'fraternal assistance' rendered by the Soviet government to other countries, and the 'single family' of Soviet peoples under Russian tutelage. Belov muses further on the unity of history in the paintings of Russian artists:

It was as if all of Russia was here, the great history of our homeland: here there were Vaznetsov's epic heroes, the hazy morning of the execution of the *strel'tsy* military corps, the snow-topped Shipka, the silent melancholy of the Vladimirka road, the weary nags by the last tavern, and the proud, pale face of a man dying in the gloom. And then an October sky, a sailor with cheek-bones forged of iron, the victorious sabres of the First Cavalry Army and Vladimir Il'ich in his study, creating a great state... (I, 94)

In contrast with his later idea of *slitnost'*, history and peoples here are united only through ideology. The message is clear: the victory of the Bolsheviks and Lenin's creation of the new socialist state is the culmination of centuries of Russian history, and it is the Russian people who have forged the new socialist brotherhood of nations, peoples and countries. This sense of historical continuity is revised in Trifonov's later works.

Studenty offers a touchingly naive and simplistic picture of life where political commitment takes precedent over ordinary human feelings and emotions. The main characters are sketched schematically and in black-and-white terms, we are left in no doubt who are the positive characters and who are negative, and human relationships are reduced to a series of opposing world-views: Palavin and Belov, Lena and Ol'ga, and Kozel'skii and Sizov. Each of these pairings deserves attention.

Belov, as we might expect, is a model Soviet citizen in the Stalinist mould. Palavin, though, is not. In the course of the narrative he becomes increasingly preoccupied with his own narrow selfish aims, and he has no qualms about the methods he uses to achieve them. He is opportunistic and cynical in his manipulation of people: he courts Kozel'skii as he aims to win the prestigious Belinskii prize and later, after the old man has fallen from grace, prepares to denounce him at a Faculty meeting. Palavin's eventual downfall is twofold: both in terms of his personal ambition and ideology. Firstly, as he sees himself as a writer of some promise, he suffers a shattering setback when he reads his short novel (*povest'*) to a meeting of students, with some workers from the factory's literary circle present. The work is roundly criticized by those present, but the criticism from the worker Balashov is especially damning:

'The trouble is not that the author does not know the factory, or that he has only a vague idea of factory management,' said Balashov. 'The trouble lies in the fact that comrade Palavin's story seems to have been written according to a recipe. He has insufficient knowledge of both the life and the people he wrote about, the only thing he did have was a scheme. And this scheme he put down on paper, but without any people. Is this Tolokin of yours actually like a real worker or Komsomol member? Everything he says is very correct, as it is in the newspapers, but you don't believe him, because he doesn't come alive, he's just made of cardboard. The author should have spent more time with his friends in our factory. Then, perhaps, it would have turned out all right. But what have we ended up with? Hack work, sheer rubbish, pure and simple...' (I, 330)

Balashov's attack is greeted with applause, and Palavin is crushed. His true fall, that is, the exposing of his personal and ideological 'incorrectness', only occurs later. Belov learns that he has abused and exploited the feelings of Valia Gruzinova, a student who is in love with him, in order to obtain a copy of a dissertation on Turgenev written by Valia's cousin, a postgraduate studying at Moscow University. It transpires that Palavin has plagiarized this work in order to write an essay which is later published. He is momentarily disgraced, his cynical opportunism apparent to all. Belov stresses the link of the social and the private spheres when he comments on Palavin's behaviour to Galustian: 'It seems to me that careerism and selfishness are two sides of the same coin. You see, a person who is selfish like this in his private life cannot be honest in his public life either. Can't you see the link?' (I, 339). Once more the private world becomes a synecdoche for the public.

But Palavin is not irredeemable. Because he has been born and brought up under the Soviet system, and is a product of it, he can be reintegrated into it through the efforts of the collective. Belov and Palavin had been the best of friends as children, but whereas Belov had grown into an earnest and responsible young man, Palavin's character has been decisively influenced by the 'strange, uncomfortable and incorrect' atmosphere in the family: his parents had quarrelled endlessly, his father was morose and taciturn, and Palavin had been brought up and spoiled by his mother, under whose 'bourgeois influence' he had fallen. But, as Belov reflects further: 'Sergei could not become a complete "panamist" or a "hopeless piece of meat", because all around him there were healthy people and a vast and durable life. He had become a minor "panamist"' (I, 348).[6]

Lena, who is now in love with Palavin, then appeals to Belov to help Palavin return to the bosom of society: 'Without the collective he will perish, that much is clear,' she cries (I, 378). Sure enough, Palavin is given moral support by his comrades, and through collective action, namely team sport, the great Soviet panacea. He is recalled into the institute's volleyball team, and his strikes are a vital contribution in their eventual victory in the tournament final against a team of chemistry students. At the end of the novel he and Belov are again friends, and Palavin has mended his ways. Belov largely takes the credit for Palavin's 'rehabilitation'.

Within Trifonov's cast of charaters Palavin is a very interesting case. He is undoubtedly talented, but he is also cynical and with an eye for the main chance. He is an aberration in Soviet society, not a typical product, but he is one that can be healed. In Trifonov's later works there are similar characters, but their cynicism is triumphant, and they inflict considerable damage on those with originality, talent, or just sheer kindness.

Lena and Ol'ga are similarly contrasting psychological types. Their respective spiritual make-up can be judged by their emotional allegiance: Lena supports Palavin, and Ol'ga and Belov are increasingly seen together. They are viewed by the author solely in terms of prospective wife-material. Lena is superficial and vain, but, more importantly for Belov, she takes no interest in the students' political activities, such as their links with the factory and laying the gas pipeline. Furthermore, she is not particularly clever. Ol'ga, on the other hand, has a mind of her own that belies her tender age (she is a mere seventeen). When Belov first meets her at a New Year's party at the institute, she impresses him with her cool intelligence as she immediately sees through Palavin's arrogance and self-assurance. In short, she is everything Lena is not: quick-witted, politically aware, spontaneous, sincere: the perfect partner for such an upstanding and eligible young man as Belov.

The clash between Kozel'skii and Sizov, though, is a different matter, and much more substantial for the book's ideology. Both men are about the same age, both born in pre-revolutionary Russia. Kozel'skii, unlike Sizov, has not been able to commit himself to the new order, nor has he made any attempt to adapt himself to it. We know he is a representative of an 'alien' culture because he has a bust of Schiller in his flat, and he also has a preference for brandy. (It is surprising that a character so obviously 'backward-looking' as Kozel'skii survived the 1930s.) In an early chapter Lagodenko (supported by Belov) criticizes the old professor as a 'formalist' who is 'indifferent' to Soviet literature. A judgment like this from a character with such impeccable ideological credentials as Lagodenko does not augur well for the old professor. Kozel'skii and Sizov have known each other for over forty years, they studied in St Petersburg and lived on Vasilevskii Island, but were then separated by the events of the First World War, Revolution, and Civil War. During the last war Sizov fought at the front but Kozel'skii stayed in Moscow. Clearly they are on opposite sides of the ideological fence: Sizov has a good revolutionary record, is at one with the new generation, but Kozel'skii is an individualist, alienated from the new world and eventually cast out of it. Following students' criticisms he is dismissed from his post and forced into retirement.

In a later telephone conversation with Palavin, Kozel'skii admits that he has reappraised his values in the light of what has happened to him and what has been said of him, and hopes to be allowed back into the institute. His defeat, therefore, is total. He admits not only that his lifestyle, but that also his values were false, and he begins to embrace the values of the new society.

A key chapter involves a conversation between Sizov and Kozel'skii, as the latter is about to leave his post. Sizov informs Kozel'skii that the latter's guilt is not so much in the 'labels' attached to him, as they are merely the flavour of the moment, the 'consequences' of a more serious malaise. More important is the fact that Kozel'skii has never believed in anything strongly enough to fight for it, he has never committed himself to anything and has acquired, according to Sizov, 'a comfortable scepticism' which involves no obligations. Sizov accuses his former colleague of being interested in nothing but material prosperity. His whole life-style is 'incorrect', therefore, and his liking for tennis is symptomatic: it is an individualist game, whereas volleyball, through which Palavin returns to the fold, requires teamwork and collective responsibility. Kozel'skii clearly falls into the anti-formalist trap of the late 1940s. As Sizov says to him: 'If you like, you are that professor in Chekhov for whom Shakespeare's works are not important, but the footnotes' (I, 267).

This scene, however, is not without its ambiguities. When Kozel'skii leaves Sizov's office, he fires his parting shot: 'By the way, Miron, let me admit something to you... All my life I have had the feeling that you have envied me. Evidently I was wrong' (I, 271). But is he? Kozel'skii has had considerable academic success, whereas Sizov has been a mere administrator. This idea is not developed, for a positive character such as Sizov cannot be seen to be capable of such moral betrayal, but it is significant that Kozel'skii has written a book whose title is *The Shadow of Dostoevskii*. The analogous situation in *Dom na naberezhnoi* also has its Dostoevskian side, where denunication and betrayal are seen within a context of 'everything is permitted'. The implication that the ideologically irreproachable Sizov is merely getting his revenge on his former friend because of the latter's success adds a darker perspective to what is otherwise a clear-cut conflict between 'progressive-minded' and 'backward-looking' elements.[7]

Furthermore, this is not the only ambiguity in the novel. The relationship between literature and truth is also addressed, albeit obliquely. At a meeting of the literary circle of the factory with which the students establish links the electrical engineer Shamarov reads out a short story he has written based on his wartime experiences. In it two Soviet soldiers (Shamarov and his friend Nikolai) go behind the enemy lines and capture a German officer. As they then try to cross the river to get back to their own lines the German twice tries to drown himself, but they get him across to the other side and successfully give him artificial respiration before getting back to base. Their mission is thus accomplished. But this socialist realist literary representation is different from what actually happened, as Shamarov himself then reveals. In the actual situation he and his friend were spotted crossing the river, a flare was fired and, with the enemy shooting at them, Nikolai gave in to normal human feelings, perfectly justifiable in the extreme circumstances, of fear and panic, wanting to free their prisoner and try to escape alive. He was shot, and went to the bottom. Shamarov admits that he, too, was terrified, but 'of course, you can't describe that as it was in real life' (I, 297).[8] There are further hints in the novel that art and truth are at odds. At Lena's house her mother shows off an as yet incomplete portrait of her daughter. The fact that the picture is not finished enables the author to say that Lena is, of course, better in real life and, indeed, 'everything is better in real life' (I, 312). Under the conditions of socialist realism, it should be the other way round.

Socialist realist method is discussed in another passage in the novel which is illuminating from the point of view of Trifonov's later development. Over lunch one day Krechetov tells the hopeful writer Palavin how he should write: 'The main thing is to be bold and make generalizations, don't rummage around in minor details. That's the trouble with novice writers – you get carried away with mundane trivia, memoir rubbish and anecdotes. That is always a diversion. And you should stick to the straight and narrow' (I, 65). It is exactly the 'mundane trivia' and 'memoir rubbish' that Trifonov is to concentrate on in his later works, focusing on the 'minor details' of personal lives and eschewing 'generalizations'.

Shamarov's story sticks to the 'straight and narrow' of socialist realism under Stalin, but thereby removes the truth from art, as he is himself aware. Socialist realism encourages a falsification of reality, a real event is shorn of its rough edges in order to conform to rigid ideological criteria.

The novel comes to an end with the Victory Day Parade of 9 May, which reminds Vadim of the year 1944. Everyone and everything come together in the Parade: students, factory workers, students from Albania, North Korea, exiled Spaniards, and also Lena and Sergei. All conflicts are now resolved (there is even the hope that Kozel'skii will be reinstated), and all the elements of progressive mankind march as one with the progressive Red Army on to Red Square, the heart of the capital of the world's most progressive country:

The nearer they got to the centre, the slower the column moved. At the Arbat they again had to come to a stop. Next to them was a large column of young people, another institute, probably, or maybe the university. Everywhere the air was filled with songs being sung in different languages, both with and without musical accompaniment. A few short, dark-haired students were singing a very familiar song loudly, but Vadim could not make out the words... Ah yes, they were Spaniards, singing '*Bandera roja*'! They were joined by young Russians, the words may not have been familiar, but everyone knew the tune. And only the Albanians evidently knew the words, because they immediately picked up the song with gusto. (I, 402)

The lives of these people are inexorably bound up with the greater reality around them, the personal is merely a composite part of the political. The novel's explicit aim is to glorify the belief and certainty in the cause as these young people study and prepare for adult life in the hub of the socialist world, Moscow: the city where ideology is determined and where history is made.

It is not difficult to see that the novel is of limited interest in purely literary terms: the plot is straightforward and the telling of it simple; the 'positive heroes' are barely individualized, and in human terms Trifonov's characters are unbelievable as either primitively sketched types or as mouthpieces for what is deemed the correct outlook on life. The vital life of society that Trifonov portrays so vividly in his later works is here relegated to the background.[9] *Studenty* affirms the symbolic myths of Stalinist socialist realism: the solidarity of workers and intellectuals, defeat of alien elements, reintegration of recalcitrant elements through collective effort, the internationalist spirit of socialist brethren across national borders, correlation of the personal (the 'small' reality) and the political (the 'greater' reality), and the triumphant celebration of positive characters contributing to the building of socialism.

The novel also contains several features that recur in Trifonov's later writing: the physical presence of a Moscow undergoing change; past and present side by side as time moves forward; a preoccupation with the figure of the writer and the role of literature and art in society and history. We also have motifs of recollection and memory. At the same time there are hints of darker things: the death of the father and a disrupted childhood and family (Belov's *alter ego* Palavin also suffers from a broken home: his mother and father are divorced), careerism and betrayal. The vital ingredients are there, but the author is not yet free of the influences of his environment: he has not yet risen above the 'flow' of time to discern its patterns or effects. In later works these motifs come together more cohesively, where moral and ethical questions of ends and means characterize life in the present, and where Trifonov's search for his father is combined with the desire to establish truth and justice. Not least, of course, the novel is of considerable interest because the author was to return to the plot and characters a quarter of a century later in *Dom na naberezhnoi*, where 'the shadow of Dostoevskii' looms larger and darker.

Before the publication of *Utolenie zhazhdy* in 1963, Trifonov published some short stories set in Turkmenia. These are worth studying, as they can be seen as stepping-stones on the writer's path towards the novel. Trifonov himself claimed that they contained the 'embryo' of what he was looking for, and what he was to develop more fully in his novel.[10]

In 'Posledniaia okhota' ('The Last Hunt') the author presents the conflict of the old and the new in the character Sapar Meredovich, a local bureaucrat with a penchant for hunting desert antelopes illegally and accustomed to immunity from prosecution because of his connections. The arrival of a new game inspector, though, threatens to put an end to the cruelty and arbitrariness of his clandestine activity, a sign of the 'new' age of humanism after Stalinism. Significantly, this is Trifonov's first work of fiction where the treatment of helpless animals is to be interpeted directly as an allegory of the human condition.

New and old are juxtaposed in other works of this time. For example, in 'Staraia pesnia' ('An Old Song') two songs, an old one about love and a new one about the new canal, are heard together on a train journey: past and present exist side by side. The realia of Turkmenia are observed and noted with an eye for technological progress and narrative diversity: first- and third-person viewpoints, Turkmenian wrestling, desert wildlife, the canal – all serve not only to set an exotic scene, but also to highlight how the contemporary world differs from the old, and how the writer himself is developing and becoming aware of the potential of narrative discourse. The desert as a metaphor for the spiritual and moral barrenness of Stalinism is made explicit in the story 'Doktor, student, i Mitia' ('The Doctor, the Student and Mitia'), as the student of the title speaks of the good guys and the bad guys to his two travelling companions as they drive across the sandy wastes: 'Yes, we're not only fighting the desert, but people like Petukhov, careerists, self-seekers who have come here to make a tidy sum for themselves. That is much more difficult. And I, for instance, am no good for this kind of fight. Savchenko, though, is. And sooner or later he'll get rid of that scoundrel, just as he would a rotten stump of wood, you'll see.'[11]

The best of Trifonov's Turkmenian stories is 'Pesochnye chasy' ('Clock of Sand'), where the author-narrator reflects on history as he visits the now-forgotten grave of a former general of the Arab conqueror Omar. He is advised to ask a local resident for information (*spravka*) about the grave, but the resident then responds with his own interpretation of what a '*spravka*' should mean: a certificate which would entitle him to a pension, and which he does not have. The play on the semantic and thematic divergence of this most Soviet of words points out the gulf in understanding between the Moscow intellectual and the Turkmenian peasant. But this gulf is also an ideological one: a sense of history is being lost in the banal struggle to attain some material security and respect in the present. It is precisely this, that people have to struggle to get what should be theirs as a right, that reveals the nature of this society and the power that rules it. And it is because people have to devote so much time to getting by in the here and now that they do not have the time to reflect on less transitory things, and so the past is eroded and ultimately lost. This story more than any other of this time reveals Trifonov's growing interest in the connection of past and present: here the struggle with the everyday, the banal, prevents a true appreciation and understanding of the importance of the past.

Utolenie zhazhdy was written between 1959 and 1962, and if *Studenty* can be seen as a novel typical of the time in which it was written and published, with supposed enemies unmasked and committed young people working happily towards the radiant future, then *Utolenie zhazhdy* bears the corresponding marks of its time, Khrushchev's thaw. Because the central character, like the author, is the son of an 'enemy of the people', the novel is clearly in line with the 'de-Stalinization' of the late 1950s, which was meant to expose the injustices of Stalinism. It is also a novel about construction, with the plot reduced to the formulaic production novel conflict, that of which production method is best for the achievement of 'the plan'. The novel, however, marks the coming of age of Trifonov as a writer of fiction, with its wealth of detail on construction methods, exotic description of the flora and fauna of Turkmenia and above all its complex and sometimes subtle narrative shifts.[12]

The author uses both third- and first-person narrative viewpoints in the novel, thus expanding the range of narrative possibilities and giving the reader differing perspectives on characters and events. The 'I' is Petr Koryshev, a journalist through whom we see both the political intrigues in the newspaper which employs him, as well as the sexual liaisons and personal relationships of those around him. The unseen third-person narrator (presumably the author) relates the progress of the canal and the lives of the workers, engineers and work bosses from an objective standpoint, although at times the two voices merge and are often indistinguishable. The canal was built in the late 1950s, after several stops and restarts, and in all 1,300 kilometres were built. It is obviously a major construction project, requiring substantial financial investment and human effort, and Trifonov seeks to provide a cross-section of those involved in it, from the managers deciding policy, to the workers shifting great volumes of earth on the bulldozers and excavators. But here Trifonov is as interested in the private, emotional sphere as in industrial matters.

Most of the workers, such as Brin'ko, Egers, Mariutin, Esenov, Muradov and Mamedov are enthusiastic and committed to the construction project. For these men, as for the students in Trifonov's first novel, personal motivation is inseparable from political commitment. However, as in *Studenty*, the 'positive' characters are virtually indistinguishable from each other, except that here they belong to different national groups. The exception is Semen Nagaev, a rough and irascible man, older than most of the others, whose only interest is making money. At one point the heat is unbearably intense and he is the only one to go out working, as a result of which he collapses at the controls of his excavator and has to take time off work to recover, thus losing valuable income. Nagaev is not a likeable man: he is reluctant to take on an apprentice as he will be slowed down, and so his wages reduced.[13]

This all-male society is made the more volatile at an early stage in the narrative with the arrival of Marina, Mariutin's twenty-year-old daughter, who comes to live with her father and, of course, turns the heads of more than a few of the young men. They fight and brawl as they vie for her attention, but it is the older Nagaev who eventually wins her heart: she gets lost in a sandstorm and it is he, risking his own life, who brings her back to safety. Shortly after this incident they set up house (or rather, barrack hut) together, although they do not register the marriage. Marina later gets pregnant by him.

Here it is not out of place to reflect on the shift in sexual mores in the few years since *Studenty*. In the earlier novel Palavin's relationship with Valia Gruzinova highlights his own exploitative nature, and nowhere else in the novel is sex outside marriage even hinted at. By the late 1950s, though, the repressive moral maximalism (largely hypocritical as it was) of the Stalin years is gone and now we recognize the more free-and-easy sexual relationships of the modern age. Personal morality is now beyond the purview of the Party, and this novel celebrates the new-found sexual licence: Koryshev's friend Zurabov has several casual affairs, Koryshev himself has a sexual relationship with the girl Katia, Zurabov's wife Lera has an affair with Karabash, one of the chief engineers on the canal project for whom she finally leaves her husband. Such relationships break up families; indeed, the novel seems to contain only one happy marriage, that of Gokhberg, Karabash's colleague, although we never see his wife. Otherwise there is nothing but broken families, separations, divorces, symbolizing the break-up of Stalin's 'great Soviet family'.

Koryshev, like Vadim Belov, fought in the War, he is approximately the same age as Trifonov was then, and shares many other personal details with the author. Koryshev tells us about his father, an Old Bolshevik, a Party member since 1907, who was arrested in 1937 as an 'enemy of the people', never to be seen again, rehabilitated and restored to posthumous Party membership in 1955. Koryshev recalls episodes from his childhood, such as the rainy summer of 1938, as a twelve-year-old boy standing in line with his mother outside the Matrosskaia Tishina prison in Moscow, waiting to hear news of his father and submit food parcels for delivery. He recalls also his subsequent difficulties in completing his studies and getting a job, and both the wider political significance as well as the mundane reality are here often combined: he was fortunate not only to get a job at all, as a tour guide, but doubly so in that his place of work was conveniently only five suburban train stops down the line. Memory brings together two different time planes, the personal drama of Koryshev and the momentous historical and political contexts, so that the passage of time is given a more personal, immediate context.

Past and present are not always easily separable. To Koryshev Moscow is part of his past; his present is taken up with his work as a reporter in Turkmenia. He has been in Turkmenia now for seven years. Time and place correlate, past and present relate to the respective 'homes' for the hero. The geographical distance between Moscow and Turkmenia serves to highlight the absence of any constants in Koryshev's life, although there is considerable overlapping between the two places. The past, though, intrudes, as characters with Moscow connections come in and out of Koryshev's life, such as the film director Khmyrov, who is in Turkmenia to shoot a film, and Aina, a botanist who had studied in Moscow University. She was in Moscow after Stalin's death, and the Moscow she knew was therefore completely different from the one Koryhsev had lived in. Even these minor characters are important for making up the diversity of life, as Koryshev reflects on meeting Aina after so many years: 'There are faces that come into our lives just as butterflies fly through a window on a summer's night, just for a second, and leave a strange, momentary trace, a hieroglyph at the bottom of the soul' (I, 633).

Trifonov is careful also to set the novel not only in a concrete and real place, but also in a specific time. One evening Katia's friend Raia questions Koryshev about the major cultural events of the 1950s: Dudintsev, the first volume of *Literaturnaia Moskva* ('Literary Moscow'), the Picasso exhibition in Moscow, Erenburg's novel *Ottepel'* ('The Thaw'). He, meanwhile, is only interested in comparing the buffets and toilet facilities in the Luzhniki sports stadium with those in the Dinamo stadium: the historic, the cultural and the mundane combine to shape the life of the individual and his interaction with time. The present is also firmly fixed within a historical dimension as the author-narrator gives an account of the first Russian expeditions under Peter the Great, aimed at finding gold and a trade route to

India, and discusses the evolution of the philosophical idea of 'turning the desert into a garden', with examples including the Panama and Suez canals. The Soviet construction engineers working in Turkmenia are the last in a long line of men who wanted to turn the dream into reality. People change in the mean time, as Koryshev reflects on how the revolutionary generation, the people of the 1920s and 1930s, would find the mundane and seemingly trivial interests of the current generation, such as the visit of the Vienna Ice Dance Troupe, 'strange and suspicious'. The continuity of one generation to the next, as affirmed in *Studenty*, is absent in this work, replaced by estrangement and alienation.

The links between past and present are evident in *Studenty* only to the extent that they affirm the Stalinist myth, but in this novel they are more extensive, used not only to highlight personal details of various characters, but also to indicate a greater historical and political awareness. Koryshev's friend and colleague is Sasha Zurabov, with whom he was a student in Moscow. Koryshev fails to remember whether Zurabov spoke up for him at a meeting of the faculty at which they both studied, when he was threatened with expulsion for concealing the fact that his father was an 'enemy of the people'. (Trifonov is here again using his own subjective experience as the basis for his fictional plot: he recounts an identical incident from his own days in 'Nedolgoe prebyvanie v kamere pytok' ('A Short Stay in the Torture Chamber', 1986). See the discussion of this story in the Conclusion.) Similarly, Zurabov fails to remember the expulsion of a fellow student Mit'ka Tsipurskii, or the dismissal of the literature teacher Nikolai L'vovich, who had shown his students some of his articles published in the 1920s. (Nikolai L'vovich, whom we never see in this work, is an interesting mirror image here of Kozel'skii in *Studenty* and Ganchuk in *Dom na naberezhnoi*.) Subjective memory, then, is unreliable, individuals are unable to recall certain events, usually connected with uncomfortable periods in their lives.

For Zurabov Moscow represents the best time of his life, happy and carefree, because his material position has not noticeably improved since then. To Koryshev Moscow was the time of the break-up of his family, a time subsequently of fear of denunciation. Different characters have different attitudes towards the same time and place. Unlike *Studenty*, this novel offers a rich and multi-dimensional sense of time and place.

The occasion of his thirty-second birthday causes Koryshev to go over his past and try to make sense of the present in view of it:

Nobody knew that today, the last Sunday of the summer, I was thirty-two years old. Half my life over. It was strange, here half of it had gone by, and yet I had the feeling that I hadn't really lived yet, that the most important part of my life was still ahead. What had I done with all those years? No, there had been a real life, but only up to about the age of eleven my childhood was real, and then everything was turned upside down: not much of an adolescence, a youth crippled by war, and then a continuous struggle to become a person, no matter what. All my life I had been trying to put right what couldn't be put right. And thousands of others had tried to do the same. Until suddenly time snapped, unexpectedly, like the snapping of a knife. That's where those years had gone – into an unreal life. But there would be a real life, there must be! It would probably emerge unheard, just like young blades of grass, and we won't realize at once that it's here. But it will be here. And it will only seem insufficiently real to someone else, someone who is younger than us. (I, 516)

There is much play in this passage on the Russian word *nastoiashchee*, which means both 'present' and 'real', a double meaning which is impossible to render in English. Trifonov is equating a 'real' life with the notion of being aware of the past in order to give the complex present meaning.

There is much in the relationship between Koryshev and Zurabov that is reminiscent of that between Belov and Palavin in the earlier novel. The links between Belov, Koryshev and the author have already been touched on; Zurabov, like Palavin, was a budding writer in his student days, sharp and humorous, and has the same moral vacuity. Zurabov refuses to commit himself on any matter of principle, will not help colleagues if this help may threaten his own interests, and is careful to sail close to the prevailing political wind. Eventually he writes an article critical of the management of the canal project, with the chief engineer Ermasov as the chief target, and the editor Diomidov asks Koryshev to visit the canal and write a long piece in order to undo the damage his friend and colleague has done. The two characters thus become set against each other. In the style of socialist realism, Trifonov again builds his novel on a basis of the opposition and conflict of two opposing world views, one basically honest, the other self-seeking.

In an interview with Lev Anninskii shortly after the novel was published, Trifonov said that he would return to Zurabov's character in future works, probably putting him in a research institute as perhaps a philologist or historian. To be sure, Zurabov has many features in common with characters such as Klimuk in *Drugaia zhizn'* and Gartvig in *Predvaritel'nye itogi*, both historians and both cynical opportunists.[14]

Another character worthy of discussion is the photographer Denis Kuznetsov. He returns to Turkmenia after sixteen years to look for his former wife and son: his son was a mere eighteen months old when he left for the front in 1941, and since then he has spent time in a German prison-of-war camp, then lived abroad for several years. He is able to return to his native parts only after being amnestied by Khrushchev. Kuznetsov bears the scars of his times more obviously than others in the novel. He is a lonely and isolated man, but he tries to rediscover his family (his wife has since remarried) in order to give his present empty existence some meaning. His past, though, cannot be recaptured, as Koryshev makes clear in the following passage:

Generally Denis Kuznetsov's life seemed to be getting better. Although ... What kind of life was it? He wasn't a happy man. I could see it. He came to this town not to work as a photographer for a newspaper but to find what he had lost here: his home, his son, the woman he had once loved. And he found nothing.

Everything was still there, and even the house, surprisingly, had survived – one of the few houses in the town to do so – but it was all so alien to him now. In all of this what had once been a part of him, Denis Kuznetsov, was now dead, and its place was now taken up by something alien, heartless. And he couldn't demand anything back – what could you demand of time?

His son still thought that his father was called Mikhail Ivanovich. And the woman was concerned with one thing: that the invasion of the 'then' did not destroy her 'now'. (I, 555)

Again, the use of language is here important: the use of military vocabulary in the last sentence reminds the reader of the Nazi invasion of Russia in 1941, the event that is responsible for the 'destruction' of Kuznetsov's life. Kuznetsov is a sad victim of his time: he has lost everything, through no real fault of his own. More than anyone else in the novel he suffers through no real fault of his own. In the end he dies a lonely death as he attempts single-handedly to seal a breach that appears in the canal wall, but in so doing draws attention to it and helps avert a disaster. In death he achieves the heroism and nobility in the eyes of others he never achieved in life.

Past and present also come together in the central political conflict of the novel, in which the role of the journalist assumes considerable importance. This conflict involves an article written by the conservative Khorev, one of the chief engineers of the canal project, attacking and denouncing Ermasov, who is in overall command. The article is printed in Koryshev's newspaper on the initiative of the Stalinist deputy-editor Luzgin, and the attack is all the more acute as Khorev is a Stalinist and has powerful political friends, whereas Ermasov is a former political prisoner. So in the clash of these two is the essential conflict of the age, that of the old with the new, the (Stalinist) world of demagogic repression with the (Khrushchevian) world of progress and greater freedom. Ermasov and his young engineers (Karabash, Niiazov, Smirnov, and Gokhberg) are eventually triumphant, and Khorev and Luzgin are forced into retirement.

The fact that Koryshev is a journalist is important for the novel's extra-textual significance, for in the relationship between the press and political authority Trifonov is begging questions about the literary depiction of reality, questions broadly hinted at in *Studenty*. The appearance or non-appearance in print of an article is dependent on the outcome of the power tussle between liberal and conservative camps, both in the regional newspaper Koryshev works on and in the wider sphere of literary politics in the USSR of the late 1950s. In this novel the newspaper thus serves the function of a synecdoche, it is a microcosm of the broader reality beyond it, just as the institute in *Studenty* is a metonymic representation of the greater concerns of the world outside.

Literary references within the novel from Plutarch to *The Odyssey*, Fadeev's *Razgrom* ('The Rout') to Aleksei Tolstoi's *Bespridanitsa* ('The Girl with no Dowry'), *War and Peace* to the poetry of Akhmatova, remove the work from its immediate social context and place it within the continuum of literary tradition. The place of literature in the post-Stalin age is discussed with reference to a local poet, Maksumov, who spent seventeeen years in Kolyma, and has now been rehabilitated and republished. However, Turkmenian republican newspapers are loth to publish reviews of his book. In their turn local editors are also fearful of doing so. Finally, the journalist Kritskii makes an impassioned plea for democracy and an end to the 'old ways':

'I don't want to be a cog!', he yelled. 'I'm fed up with it! I've had enough! How much more can we take? Nobody takes any account of cogs! You don't have to explain anything to them, be accountable to them – they don't have a voice! But I demand an explanation: why is Ataniaz Durdiev's review of Maksumov's book still lying around, like a pack of cards? We all know that Maksumov spent seventeen years in camps and returned a sick old man. He has been completely rehabilitated, he recently gave an interview on the radio. So what's the matter, comrade editors? Who is putting the brakes on?' (I, 577)

Conversely, in a sign of 1950s *glasnost'* the journalist Tumanian writes and publishes an article on the housing situation in the town following the earthquake of nine years before, attacking the principle that grandiose administrative buildings have been given priority over housing. It is now possible to publish such criticisms, unlike five years ago, although Zurabov ironically comments: 'These days we're all brave in print' (I, 435). He also caustically points out that the article was only published on the sanction of someone whose office is in just one of those buildings attacked in the article. We can assume that Trifonov is poking fun at the inanities of censorship, albeit cautiously, and the dependence of the writer and the journalist on his political overseers.

Koryshev is the first of Trifonov's morally neutral heroes. He passes no moral judgment on the indiscretions of those around him, and despite his difficulties as the son of someone formerly in political disgrace, he bears no grudges. His failure to remember Zurabov's supposed defence of him at the faculty meeting is to him of no significance now: 'Anyway, it's not important. It was all a long time ago' (I, 434). Nor does he moralize on the sexual betrayals he witnesses, whether they be Zurabov's casual affairs (for which Koryshev lends him his hotel room for some privacy, so bad is the housing crisis in the town), or Lera's affair with Karabash. Indeed, in one scene he idly chats with her at the same time as her husband is using his hotel room for just such an extra-marital appointment. Moreover, Koryshev represents the burgeoning literary consciousness of the thaw, a period above all of social change and psychological readjustment. As such he passes contemporary judgment on literary works of the recent past (by implication, including Trifonov's own), when he demolishes the 'conflictless' screenplay Khmyrov wants to publish in the newspaper: 'Your screenplay is five years too late. It's now quite impossible, comrade Khmyrov, to return again to the false and varnished works that stand condemned by our party. Or do you think that here on the periphery it's still acceptable. That here in the provinces we'll take anything?' (I, 583–4).

As a journalist in the forefront of change and progress, and as the author's mouthpiece, Koryshev is perfectly placed to observe the passing of time, as it affects his own mortality:

It seemed to me that I was losing time, lagging behind, I was dying. Dead! If I don't start something very soon and do some serious work – write about something I at least know, my life, Turkmenia, about how time can break in two, how some people come and others go and how I turn round and round in this current as it rushes along amid the noise and the din – if I don't simply start taking down notes, taking down notes every day, I am dead, dead!' (I, 585)

This is the first reference in Trifonov's work to what he later calls the concept of 'living death', that is, being isolated from time, torn from all the links and relationships of human society. Also notable are the early references to water as a symbol of passing time and the individual carried along within it. In this work 'life' and 'death' are also metaphorical: the desert symbolizes the oblivion of the Stalin years, from which the country 'thirsts' to return to its history and to life. The novel's title, therefore refers not only to supplying the Turkmenian desert with irrigation, but also with quenching the post-Stalin age's thirst for truth and justice. This theme is explicit in a conversation at the wedding of the newspaper's literary editor Boris Litovko. Litovko asserts that 'there is a thirst much stronger than the thirst for water – and that is the thirst for justice!'. This theme is then taken up by the veteran literary editor Platon Kir'ianovich and Koryshev's colleague Tamara Gzhel'skaia:

'Bah, what are you shouting for?' said the director of the 'Goroformleniia' firm. 'Do you know how the Turkmenians quench their thirst? Just listen: to begin with they quench "the little thirst", two or three small glasses, and then, after eating supper, the "large thirst", when they'll finish off a whole teapot. And a man coming back out of the desert is never given a lot of water. Just a little bit at a time.'

'Otherwise it will make him sick,' said Platon Kir'ianovich.

'It will make no-one sick! That's rubbish! I don't believe it!' said Tamara excitedly. 'How can there be too much truth? Or too much justice?' (I, 662)

Just like the urban landscape of *Studenty* and of the later 'Moscow stories', the desert is here also a psychological landscape, an externalization of an inner state. It is blisteringly hot and parched, and Koryshev tells us that since childhood, that is, since the arrest of his father, he has 'been attracted by deserts' (I, 432). In one scene Karabash and Lera drive all night through the desert and make love on the sand, thus reclaiming the desert for human life through love:

The sand had gone hard for the night. It was cold and rough. At first it was cool, and they tried to keep each other warm, and then it grew hot, very hot, just as it was during the day, and the sand became soft and pleasant to lie on as they relaxed and breathed in its pure and silicon smell, gazing up at the sky. The stars shone brightly. There was an awful lot of them. (I, 546)

In his subsequent fiction, Trifonov uses the expanse of desert, outwardly hostile and inhospitable, as a means of escape, for both Gennadii Sergeevich in *Predvaritel'nye itogi* and Sasha Antipov in *Vremia i mesto*, from the oppressive pressures of Moscow city life.

The recent earthquake in the area is also a symbolic reference to the ravages of Stalinism. This is Koryshev's account of what the town was like before the earthquake, significantly, nine years before (i.e. 1948):

People say that once it was a pretty town. People say that it was exceptionally green and homely. The greenery is still there. The trees stand much more securely than the houses. Magnificent poplars, acacias with mighty boughs and auburn-coloured *karagachi* arrayed in a dull layer of dust still stand in the places where they were planted half a century before. The horror of that night passed them by. The life that had buzzed beneath them had disappeared or changed forever, all that remained of it was an ossified hallucination, a mirage: piles of bricks that used to be houses, now covered in grass and dust, and broken pieces of what was once pavement. How good it is to be a tree! How good it is not to remember anything! Here they are, new houses, strong and with thick walls, standing evenly, like soldiers – no points on the Richter scale frighten them, all painted the same bright, sandy colour, with identical balconies and terraces, where people sleep on summer nights. (I, 433)

While the rebuilding is also a sign of regeneration and recovery, it is worth remembering that Party and administrative buildings are given priority. In other words, Trifonov is hinting that the relatively liberal atmosphere inspired by the Party since the death of Stalin, be it in the social or cultural fields, is designed first and foremost to restore the prestige and self-esteem of the Party; the needs of the people, as under Stalin, come second. Kritskii's calls for democracy and greater freedom are therefore also a warning about the dangers of 'the desert' regaining its territory from 'the water of life'.

Trifonov makes Koryshev's environment the more immediate by concentrating on the phenomenon of *byt*, everyday routine and concerns. Koryshev's day is made up of chance meetings, insubstantial conversations, exchanges of news or gossip, meals and beers in a local restaurant, offers to help Kuznetsov get work, feelings, emotions, attitudes. In Koryshev's everyday life we have a distillation of the *slitnost'* that is the main feature of Trifonov's world. Koryshev's consciousness links past and present in the novel, as the writer-symbol he stands in the centre of the work's discussion on the relationship of literature to politics, and it is also he who feels most keenly the passage of time. Trifonov's method is to show how Koryshev is connected with other people, with the life of society, and how other characters are linked with each other, so that we have a dense and intricate picture of human society as a vital, thriving whole. Koryshev, Zurabov, Kuznetsov, Katia, Ermasov, Karabash, Lera, Gokhberg, Nagaev, Marina, Brin'ko, Khmyrov, Khorev, Luzgin, Kritskii, Litovko, secondary characters – all are linked, even if they do not know one another. People provide the link between places and time (Koryshev and Zurabov recall Moscow, Kuznetsov has lived in Germany, Ermasov attends a conference in Los Angeles), and between historical ages.

As in *Studenty* everything comes together in the final denouement, which provides a suitable socialist realist climax to the 'production novel' plot. Kuznetsov's death and the discovery of a breach in a dam wall leads to a huge effort to seal it on the part of the workers, management, local population, and even Koryshev ends up driving a bulldozer. Everyone works for two days and nights without rest or sleep, and the communal effort is at last triumphant. The breach is dammed. All petty intrigues and jealousies are forgotten. Only Nagaev refuses to work without extra pay, he leaves the site, ostracized by his former colleagues and by Marina, who is by now carrying his child. She also works herself to a state of exhaustion, to the extent that she miscarries. The common future, though, is made secure as the canal is saved.

Further evidence of the socialist realist positivism of the novel is in the treatment of the nationalities' question. There are Ukrainians, Latvians, Turkmenians, Russians and Azerbaidjanis working together on the canal in a spirit of proletarian fellowship. This is brought into symbolic focus when the Turkmenian Esenov throws himself into icy water to save the Ukrainian Brin'ko from drowning; it is not only heroic in personal terms, but also in the metonymic context of the Soviet 'family of peoples'. The 'small' reality here corresponds to the ideal picture of the 'large'.

The setting of Moslem Turkmenia is also significant for the conflict of past and present, the old and new values. The young Biashim Muradov is working on the canal to earn money for *kalym*, money in order to 'buy' his prospective bride, Ogul'd-zhan, from her family, but as time goes on he rebels against this patriarchal and outmoded system. His throat is cut by the male members of her family when he refuses to pay the money. His death is also symbolic, the lethal consequence of the clash of past and present and impressing upon others in the village the backwardness and barbarity of old traditional ways. As a result, many younger people join the canal project, inspired by Biashim's example. The journalist Ataniiaz is aware of the greater significance of Biashim's murder:

> The war these shop-traders waged with Biashim Muradov was a war between the desert and the canal. They hated Biashim. They hate the canal, which brings not only water into the desert, but another life... They'll start saying that he didn't submit to the Turkmenian tradition, and for that they killed him. But that's a lie! He didn't submit to their tyranny, that's why they killed him. He didn't submit to their greed, that's why they killed him. But there isn't a knife that can cut the throat of a river! (I, 702–3)

A major feature of the novel, one which separates it from the writer's earlier fiction and which brings it close to his mature work, is the fluctuation of narrative point of view and perspective. The use of third- and first-person narrative enables the author to manipulate objective and subjective viewpoints to provide startling and illuminating shifts of emphasis. We can assume that Koryshev, because he shares many features of the author, is the author's voice, especially given that his thoughts on the passage of time and the recent Stalinist past are a constant point of reference for the author. Trifonov's use of this twin narrative stance is frequent, as a seemingly objective account is filtered through Koryshev's consciousness, and, indeed, often the voice of the author and the 'I' blend together. We also see the brewing conflict between Khorev and Ermasov from the point of view of Karabash, and we see Karabash in a wrestling bout with Brin'ko through Lera's eyes. Furthermore, we see several characters from different or unusual angles, such as watching Nagaev approach a shop through the eyes of a dog. Important statements are not confined to a handful of characters, and even casual and incidental meetings have important consequences. Trifonov shows how everything and everyone in society are interdependent, connected by the web of links that comprise the complexity of life. In the main, the author tries to view time from within its flow, and only at the end of the novel does he look down on events from above. Koryshev looks on the desert from the window of an aeroplane flying overhead, and sees from his Olympian viewpoint the defeat of the desert and the life-affirming triumph of water:

From a height of five hundred metres, from the window of a small, delapidated mail and passenger plane that stank of spent fuel I saw the desert pumping out its huge, greyish-yellow body below. I saw the bare and boundless expanse of sand, as old as the earth itself, its death-like pallor of a thousand years hence, when we and our descendants, and everything that has lived on the earth and that has yet to live on it, will become part of this light and wispy greyish-yellow sand. Billions and billions of grains of sand will cover the land surfaces, will swallow up forests, towns, atomic power stations, will cover the whole of our small globe of earth, and each of these tiny grains will contain an extinguished life. That is what will happen if man gives in. If he doesn't have the strength to defeat the desert ... And below the endless sandy steppe stretched out in waves and crescents, interrupted only by a strange, narrow strip. I didn't realise at first that this was the canal. This was the canal! I saw for the first time what it actually looked like. It was remarkably straight and shone under the sun like a thin steel rail. (I, 747–8)

In real and symbolic terms, then, the past can be defeated and a safe future free from apocalyptic visions of destruction can be guaranteed. In the final sentence of the novel the author-narrator wonders what the 'other life' of the future holds, as he stands in the present, on the threshold of the past and the future:

'This happens when you part with someone for a long time, forever, where before you a new life beckons and the old one is seemingly left behind a glass door: people move, converse, but you can hardly hear them' (I, 750).

In conclusion, *Utolenie zhazhdy* has the hallmarks of a typical socialist realist novel about the construction of a major industrial project, with production-method conflicts and the confrontation of 'old' and 'new' ways of thinking, the contrast and opposition of 'good' and 'bad' characters, albeit with certain ambiguities, as in *Studenty*. Again, doubtful characters mouth convincing statements: Nagaev may be unattractive and exaggerated in his drive for more and more money, but his venal motivation is more convincing than the political zeal of others. Zurabov, of all people, recognizes this, and accuses those who think money unimportant to be 'lying' (I, 604).

The climax of the novel is predictably upbeat, with everyone working together to defeat the desert, the natural enemy. Water, like time, leads to the future, just as images of water in Trifonov's later works symbolize the 'current' of time connecting past, present and future. The defeat of 'backward-looking' elements like Luzgin and Khorev represents hope for the future, but this is far from final. Koryshev captures the existential nature of Trifonov's world when he asserts that 'it's not us bringing down Luzgin, but the times, the times! We're only helping the times' (I, 578). Such statements resound in Trifonov's later fiction, such as *Dom na naberezhnoi*, where 'the times' are also held to blame for betrayals and compromises. Neither Trifonov nor Koryshev have yet grasped the fact that it is actual people and the truth they represent who create 'the times', and not vice versa. Nothing essentially has changed in Soviet life, it is still dominated by politics: the very fact of struggles between die-hards and 'progressives' shows that the past is not yet totally overcome.

Trifonov is careful to set his plot in a carefully fixed local environment, with specific locations and period detail, and he is at pains to establish a temporal and historical context where past, present and future are all perceived by the author as part of a continuing process and within which his characters live out their daily lives. In this work, too, the phenomenon of *byt* looms large, with chapters and pages packed with seemingly minor or irrelevant details and snippets of conversation, but which all go to make up the fabric and texture of life. This novel shows clearly how far the author had come since his *Studenty* days, and equally clearly marks the platform from which his controversial works of the 1960s and 1970s were to be launched.

CHAPTER 2

Moscow life, 1966–1975
(Obmen; Predvaritel'nye itogi; Beskonechnye igry; Dolgoe proshchanie; Drugaia zhizn')

At the end of 1966 Trifonov published two short stories in *Novyi mir*, his first publication in that journal since *Studenty*. Trifonov's return to *Novyi mir*, the flagship of the liberal intelligentsia, coincided with the onset of the conservative backlash against Khrushchev's de-Stalinization of the 1950s and early 1960s. Also in 1966, the trial of Siniavskii and Daniel' for publishing supposedly 'anti-Soviet' works in the West under pseudonyms was, notwithstanding Stalin's terror, the first trial against Soviet writers in which 'the principal evidence against them was their literary work'.[1] Once more Trifonov bore witness to a change in the political and cultural climate: as the Brezhnev regime was consolidated, so there was a return to 'old' ways of thinking, and liberalism and democratic tendencies in the arts were actively discouraged. The decade had begun as a time of hope and increased freedom with the Twentieth Party Congress and the publication of *One Day in the Life of Ivan Denisovich*; it was to end with the jailing of more dissidents, the dismissal of Tvardovskii as editor of *Novyi mir* and the expulsion of Solzhenitsyn from the Writers' Union.

Nevertheless, there were publications that reflected the struggle of 'old' and 'new' ways of thinking. 1966 opened with Solzhenitsyn's last Soviet publication until 1989, his short story 'Zakhar-kalita' ('Zakhar Moneybags') in *Novyi mir*. At the same time the provincial journal *Sever* printed Vasilii Belov's short novel *Privychnoe delo* ('That's the Way It Is'), which established the aesthetic criteria, along with Solzhenitsyn's *Matrenin dvor* ('Matrena's House', 1963), of *derevenskaia proza*, and shortly afterwards Tvardovskii published Boris Mozhaev's controversial *Iz zhizni Fedora Kuz'kina* ('From the Life of Fedor Kuz'kin'). If Belov's work concentrates on the lyricism of the Russian peasant's relationship with the land, Mozhaev's is a brutally honest account of the Party's mishandling of agriculture under Stalin, and the constant battle of the peasant to be able to feed his family and survive. Both of these works are important in themselves, but also as signs of social criticism and resistance to the return to the past.[2]

Trifonov's second *Novyi mir* period is thus set against a background of a right-wing backlash and the destruction of the hopes of the thaw and of the generation brought up on those hopes. It is therefore no accident that his writings from the mid-1960s bear traces of Aesopian language, hints and allusions to guide the reader towards a truth that could not be stated openly. Moreover, it is in these years that his concept of *slitnost'* – the unity of past and present, man and the collective, *byt* and history – becomes the dominant aesthetic feature of his writing. Trifonov is ostensibly describing contemporary Moscow *byt*, the everyday life of people faced with an ethical dilemma: to compromise their principles and gain material benefit, or remain loyal to them and continue to live in straitened circumstances. But throughout this cycle there is a subtext tracing the evolution of the post-Stalin intelligentsia, the rise and fall of their hopes over one and a half decades, set within a clearly delineated historical context.

Trifonov's two 1966 stories passed innocuously, and neither explicitly reflected the struggle of the 'liberal' cause against the now sustained assault of the 'die-hards'. But here we see historical truth buried beneath layers of stylized motifs and theme. 'Vera i Zoika' ('Vera and Zoika') concentrates on the two women of the title: Vera, a laundry worker and Zoika, a school cleaner, both deserted by their men. (Vera has a son in a boarding school, Zoika has to feed two children and her own ageing grandmother.) Both of them agree to travel to the *dacha* of the seemingly well-to-do Lidiia Aleksandrovna, to help springclean it over a Saturday and Sunday, and so earn some much-needed extra cash. This hardly dramatic episode in their otherwise humdrum lives is played out against a background of the changing topography of Moscow as old regions with soul and character are pulled down and impersonal multi-storey new buildings put up in their place. The author's attitude here is ambivalent: on the one hand the history of Moscow is being physically removed; on the other it is replaced by accommodation where people will be able to lead normal lives, with heating, plumbing and electricity. This dilemma, historical heritage or material comfort, is at its most banal in an exchange between Lidiia Aleksandrovna, and her taxi driver; as they drive through Moscow on their way to the *dacha*:

'I feel sorry for these little houses. After all, this is the Moscow of old, our history. Krasnaia Presnia ... And here they are being mercilessly burnt down...'
'And a good thing, too! You shouldn't feel sorry for them, they're only good for breeding bedbugs!' said the driver with unexpected spite. 'People used to live on top of each other there, ten people for every seven metres. They don't need your history! Now at least they'll have somewhere to live that is fit for humans.' (IV, 153)

All three women are unhappy, even the seemingly affluent Lidiia Aleksandrovna: they are unloved and lonely. Lidiia Aleksandrovna's first husband died, and her second for some reason (Lidiia Aleksandrovna shows no surprise at this) fails to come and pick them up in his car at the end of the weekend. Zoika's husband left her some years ago, and Vera has a history of being used and abused by various men. Lidiia Aleksandrovna is in her early forties, Vera and Zoika in their mid-forties. The story is about the lack of ideals in the family, the lack of happiness or love in urban society. For these women, socialism has failed to deliver, and men are to blame. The theme of time here is crucial: Vera and Zoika live in the prefabricated houses whose destruction is so heartily endorsed by the only adult male in the story, the taxi driver (not counting Lidiia Aleksandrovna's eighteen-year-old son Kirill). Vera is happy there, Lidiia Aleksandrovna expresses regard for the history these homes represent. Stability and disruption, as with the 'village writers', are represented respectively by women and men. The lack of any happiness or ideal in any of their lives only becomes apparent when they are out of the morass of Moscow and in the relative tranquility of the countryside. Throughout the story motifs of betrayal, both by Vera's colleagues at work and by men in their private lives, the constant lack of money, the poverty of life, all combine with a picture of a changing Moscow. The story also anticipates much of modern Soviet writing on the 'woman question' with its assertion, spoken by Lidiia Aleksandrovna, that 'a woman must not love her hopes' (IV, 159).

'Byl letnii polden'' ('It was a Midday in Summer') is more directly about the course of history. Ol'ga Robertnova returns to the Baltic town where she spent her youth, to help a researcher writing a book about her husband. She is the widow of an Old Bolshevik, an executed 'enemy of the people', and she herself, like Trifonov's own mother, spent years doing hard labour in Siberia. Significantly, her husband, Sergei Ivanovich, went to St Petersburg university, and was active in both the Revolution and Civil War – just like the fathers of Trifonov and his fictional hero Koryshev. She returns to Moscow from her trip home, having found only one woman who remembers the old places from her youth. Time has moved on, but she has rediscovered, however fleetingly, her past life and love. The passage of historical time is thus interwoven with the character's personal time. The warmth of her memories is contrasted to the coldness of the present, for she returns to Moscow to face misunderstanding and alienation from her children. These motifs are to recur: the search for the past, the absence of any 'home', and the betrayal of the revolutionary generation, both by Stalin and the children of those who made the Revolution.[3] In both of these stories Trifonov depicts the passage of time both externally, as places change and develop new contours, but more importantly internally, within the minds and lives of the characters. This is the key shift in Trifonov's writing as a whole.

There are other important motifs expressed in Trifonov's other short fiction of the 1960s. For example, in 'Ispanskaia Odisseia' ('A Spanish Odyssey', 1962) the narrator meets an exiled Spaniard in a football stadium, and learns his life story. He is a committed Communist who was wounded several times while fighting against Franco in the Civil War, who then went to the USSR and fought against the Germans, before going back to Spain and spending thirteen years in Franco's jails. He gives detailed accounts of torture and wholesale executions. No one can doubt the ideological correctness of this story, detailing the horrors of Fascism, but the subject-matter can also be seen as an allegory of Stalinism: Soviet Communists have also done their fair share of torturing and executing so-called opponents. The nature of the allegory suggests the *slitnost'* of the twentieth-century experience, that both Russia and the West share a tragic history, one where human and social values are easily betrayed in the name of politics and ideology. This story is similar to 'Odnazhdy dushnoi noch'iu' ('One Close Night', 1960), where the narrator and two friends meet a Spaniard working in Ashkhabad, of all places. The unnamed Spaniard is married to a Ukrainian. How he came to work in Ashkhabad, while his wife has remained in Kherson, is a mystery the text does not resolve, and the reader, like the narrator, is left merely to ponder the cross-links between individuals and peoples in the modern age.

In the story 'V gribnuiu osen'' (1968) Nadia's mother, Antonina Vasil'evna, dies at her *dacha*, and the narrative deals with Nadia's efforts to come to terms with the fact of death. Nadia is also a lonely and unhappy woman, with a troubled but basically decent relationship with the hard-drinking Volodia. When she finds her mother's body, she tries to lift it on to the divan and then comes to her own realization of life and death: 'Nadia's hands and all her being shook from the power of this superhuman force with which she had never had any contact before, and suddenly she realized that this force was time, transformed into something absolutely real, something like a hurricane which had swept her up and was carrying her along' (IV, 177).

Wind symbolizes the passage of time, and the 'hurricane' Nadia feels sweeping her along corresponds to the actual wind blowing outside: as in *Utolenie zhazhdy*, external and internal landscapes correlate. For Nadia death is suddenly no longer an impersonal and abstract concept, but very real and immediate.

The story's significance lies in its convincing depiction of the shock, confusion, fear, bewilderment of the bereaved Nadia. Trifonov had recent personal experience of the sudden death of a loved one: Nina Nelina had died in 1966. Also of note is that the death of Nadia's mother takes place at the *dacha*, and accusations that are made at the wake to the effect that Nadia has betrayed her mother by working her into an early grave anticipate the central drama of *Obmen*. Nadia has to cope with the feelings of relatives and colleagues at work when she returns: life goes on. Death in Trifonov's works is not only an end, but also offers a new beginning, a threshold towards another life. Amid the grief and the sense of loss there is also continuity and renewal.

Trifonov's most significant piece of short fiction from the 1960s is the short story 'Golubinaia gibel'' ('The Death of the Doves', 1968). Old Sergei Ivanovich is prevailed upon to get rid of the doves that have adopted his balcony as their home. At first there is only one dove, a male, but he then brings along his mate, and before long they have offspring. At first he and his wife, Klavdiia Nikiforovna, feed them and treat them as their own pets. Brykin, a former colonel who has not forgotten his military ways, and now a member of the house committee, orders them to get rid of the birds as the neighbours are complaining. The complaints come from the mother of a boy living in a flat whose balcony is directly opposite. She is worried that her son is so distracted by the doves that he is neglecting his homework. Moreover, he fires at them with his catapult. The birds and Sergei Ivanovich are to blame, and there is no question that the boy may, indeed, study better were he to work indoors, or even choose not to use them as target practice. The boy's treatment of the birds is sharply contrasted with that of Marishka, the girl next door to Sergei Ivanovich who loves them dearly. Having received his warning, Sergei Ivanovich gives the birds to another resident, but they fly back to his balcony. Thereafter, whatever he does – he even takes all three birds in a box on a train to his sister's, 105 kilometres outside Moscow, and puts up a wire mesh fence so that they cannot return to his balcony – they still fly back, hanging upside down on the outside of the wire fence, looking in at him lovingly. Finally threatened with a fine, he despairs and kills the birds. The story is an unsettling one of how a law-abiding and gentle man can be prevailed upon by authority to perform an act of violence. The doves symbolize peace, innocence, hope, and the death of the doves has allegorical implications for Soviet society at the onset of the 'stagnation' years.[4]

There is, though, more to this story. It is the first of Trifonov's stories where the author dissects a community and reveals two categories of citizens: the oppressors and the oppressed. Brykin represents the former, an unthinking automaton who carries out the will of his faceless (and unseen) superiors. He speaks in impersonal, bureaucratic phrases, as when he categorizes the doves as follows: 'Doves are considered a suspicious bird, not needed in the modern age' (IV, 172). The birds are thus characterized in the same terms as 'enemies of the people'. Brykin is a soulless executor of official policy who does not question or qualify what he is asked to do, and whose only touch of humanity is when a smile passes across his face as he looks upon Marishka. Also, the parents of the catapult boy are the recognizably smug and nasty urbanites of Trifonov's later prose who 'know how to live' and can impose their will on others. Marishka's father Boris Evgen'evich is suddenly one night arrested and taken away, for no apparent reason, and Sergei Ivanovich's very willingness to accept that he may be fined for something he has done nothing to encourage testifies to the power of an omnipotent, oppressive regime. We therefore have a ready contrast of characters and types: Brykin and Boris Evgen'evich; Marishka and the catapult boy; this boy's mother and the meek Klavdiia Nikiforovna.

The final paragraph of the story provides a fitting end, not only for its bitter irony, but in order to fix the plot within its time:

There was the summer, long and dry, there was the autumn with its rains, and there was the cold weather, the central heating broke down in entrance hall no. 3, Brykin came and filled in the relevant form, for two nights they slept in their overcoats, Klavdiia Nikiforovna fell ill with toothache, Agniia Nikolaevna and her daughter and old Sof'ia

Leopol'dovna were resettled somewhere on the outskirts of Moscow, and their two rooms were taken over by new residents, seven of them from Tula, then winter ended, another summer went by, they announced the amnesty, Sergei Ivanovich was given a pension, he retired and took to playing dominoes in the mornings. Then an order was issued authorizing the breeding of as many doves as possible for the festival, for the benefit of the foreign guests – and not only were you not fined, but you were even thanked for doing so. (IV, 174)

Trifonov's style has been preserved in the translation to convey the compression of details and the passage of time. Whole months and seasons come and go within a single sentence. The change of weather coincides with the change of the political climate, for the 'amnesty' refers to the post-Stalin release of political prisoners, and the 'festival' is the International Youth Festival held in Moscow in 1957. The decision to encourage the breeding of doves can also be seen as a sign of the new humanism, and the greater respect for life, human or otherwise.

In Trifonov's fiction we often find that animals and pets are treated harshly, and it is tempting to see this treatment as primarily an allegory for the fate of people. The story, indeed, stands comparison with Turgenev's *Mumu* (1852), the story of a deaf-mute serf forced to drown his pet dog. In Trifonov's stories of the 1960s there is a codified language of allusions and metonymy, linked by his perception of the workings of time.

These stories lead us to *Obmen*, which heralded Trifonov's move from short prose forms in the 1960s to the *povest'*. It is, of course, no accident that his use of short forms in the 1950s also helped him to find new themes and techniques.[5] In *Obmen* he achieves a synthesis of themes and motifs that are contained in his short stories of the early-to-mid-1960s. In *Obmen* we also see further developed the structural basis of contrast and use of multiple narrative viewpoints that are to feature in future works. This work is also the first major work in which urban *byt* is in the foreground and dominates the lives of his characters, as he defined it in the *Voprosy literatury* discussion of his 'Moscow works':

Byt is the great test. We shouldn't speak of it contemptuously, as of a base aspect of human life, unworthy of literature. For *byt* is ordinary life, the test of ordinary life, where today's morality manifests itself and is put to the test.

The relationships between people are also *byt*. We live in the muddled and complex structure of *byt*, at the intersection of a multitude of links, outlooks, friendships, acquaintanceships, enmities, psychologies, ideologies. Each city dweller feels every day, every hour the persistent, magnetic rhythms of this structure which sometimes tear him apart. All the time you have to make a choice, decide things, overcome things, sacrifice things. And if you get tired? Never mind, you'll get your rest somewhere else. Here *byt* is a war which knows no truce.[6]

What is this *byt*? It comprises the details of getting out of bed, getting washed, having breakfast, seeing off the daughter to school, the arrival of the mother-in-law to help around the flat, snatches of dialogue with the neighbours, going to work, relationships and meetings with colleagues and higher-ups. Such is the first day of Dmitriev's narrative, the main character of the *povest'*. This attention to detail offers us a picture of modern society and a particular situation where Dmitriev increasingly feels himself 'torn apart', and finds he has to make his choice and take sides in the 'war' of everyday existence.

Obmen, like 'V gribnuiu osen'' and 'Golubinaia gibel'', is about death, and the author's preoccupation with death and its effects on the family unit continues in subsequent works of his Moscow cycle, such as *Predvaritel'nye itogi* and *Drugaia zhizn'*.

The plot is straightforward: Dmitriev, his wife Lena and their daughter Natasha live in one room of a communal flat, which means that they have to share toilet and washing facilities with other families. Dmitriev's mother, Kseniia Fedorovna, lives alone in another flat, also in one room. At the beginning of the story Kseniia Fedorovna is diagnosed as having terminal cancer, and Lena revives a scheme which Dmitriev himself had been suggesting continually in the course of their fourteen-year marriage: to move in with his mother, and arrange an exchange of apartments so that they will be entitled to more living space, preferably a two-bedroom flat of their own, with no sharing facilities. There is no love lost between Lena and Kseniia

Fedorovna, and Lena's plan is not designed to ease the latter's life in any way; she merely wants to inherit the extra living-space when the cancer eventually takes its full course. After much bickering and soul-searching by Dmitriev, the deal is finally agreed, and at the end of the narrative it goes through, almost a year after Lena had mooted it.

Over the years the work has been treated positively by Soviet critics because, they say, it exposes Soviet *meshchantsvo* and the blinkered and uncaring drive for material prosperity. Lena in particular is the object of much comment in this respect. Yet she is not necessarily a 'negative' character. Trifonov is at pains to stress that she is highly intelligent, a gifted translator of English scientific texts (she has even contributed to the compiling of a dictionary), she loves her husband and, as she herself maintains, her ambitions and the methods she uses to achieve them are designed not for her own well-being but for that of the family. It is due to her efforts that at the beginning of the narrative the Dmitrievs are living in a communal flat, and at the end they have a comfortable flat of their own. She fights to have Natasha accepted into a very prestigious English-language 'special school', and makes the right approaches to get herself a good job. Ethics are irrelevant; the final goal is what is important, achieved by whatever means are appropriate. Lena's characteristic feature, as her husband observes to us early in the narrative, is 'the ability to get her own way' (II, 9).

Moreover, in his response to critical reactions in *Voprosy literatury* in 1972, Trifonov stated that his theme was not *meshchanstvo* nor the intelligentsia as a collective mass, but simple, ordinary people, city-dwellers. Also, he asserted that 'the author condemns not Lena, but certain character traits Lena has, he hates these traits, which are common not only to Lena ...'[7] In other words, Trifonov is attacking a caste of mind which subordinates all considerations of scruple to the pursuit of material well-being.

It is also important to recognize that the picture we get of Lena is coloured by Dmitriev's perception of her, for the story is to all intents and purposes his narrative. We learn this in the final paragraph of the *povest'*, when the author-narrator explains that he heard the story he has just related from Dmitriev himself. Thus it is within the context of Dmitriev's spiritual agonizing that we see Lena's seemingly underhand dealings, and therefore it is not surprising that we are encouraged to view them in a negative light. After all, we are only getting one side of the story.

Trifonov's refusal to condemn Lena outright can also be understood, given that the story is not only about this very banal and unsavoury exchange of living space. It is more fundamentally about betrayal, in particular Viktor Dmitriev's failure to stand up for the values of his family. The real theme of the story is the betrayal of the values of the Revolution, and society's shift to a materialistic and self-centred lifestyle. A son's betrayal of his mother, and of his own family's heritage, is also society's betrayal of its past.

Dmitriev muses that life consists of 'happiness', and death is the 'destruction of happiness' (II,31). This is homespun philosophy at its most banal, and suggests the reasoning of a man who has never before had to agonize over spiritual or moral questions. He is unable to oppose resolutely Lena's suggestion, although he does at first resist it. He condemns her blatant opportunism, but then slowly accepts it, just as he had accepted the animosity between her and his mother years ago: 'He agonized, he was amazed, he racked his brains, but then he got used to it. He got used to it because he saw that it was the same with everyone else, and everyone else got used to it. And he was calmed by the simple truth that in life there was nothing wiser and more valuable than peace, and it took all your strength, but you had to guard it' (II, 8). Dmitriev is a man who refuses to make a decision, and who has always opted for the quiet life, free of doubts.

This is not merely a struggle of two women for Dmitriev's soul. The theme of 'exchanging' spiritual and moral values for the sake of material benefit and improved status becomes constant in Trifonov's subsequent work. Indeed, it can be said to have its place, if not a central one, in Trifonov's earlier fiction. Moreover, the tension between the two families represents a microcosm of another area of conflict in Soviet society.

Dmitriev comes from a family with a formidable revolutionary heritage: his seventy-nine-year-old grandfather on his mother's side studied law at St Petersburg university, suffered Tsarist imprisonment as a result of his revolutionary activities, and knew Vera Zasulich when in Swiss exile; he has also spent much time in Stalin's Gulag. His two uncles, Vasilii and Nikolai, fought with the Reds during the Civil War and later worked for the OGPU, Stalin's secret police (it is also hinted that they were purged in the 1930s). His forebears represent the two extremes in the Bolshevik make-up: the self-sacrificing radicalism of the intelligentsia, and the Terror.

On the other hand the Luk'ianov family, Lena's parents, have no interest in the past, their prime motivation is for material well-being in the present. The mother, Vera Lazarevna, is the daughter of a furrier, while her father, Ivan Vasil'evich, is above all a fixer, by trade a leather tanner but since the 1920s an administrator, getting along by means of acquaintances and connections. He manages to hire workers and get hold of bricks and cement in order to repair the cess pit in the *dacha* community where the Dmitrievs spend their summers, and which has remained out of order for so long that the residents have long grown used to the stench. The Luk'ianovs are 'another breed', and belong to those, as Kseniia Fedorovna condescendingly observes, 'who know how to live' (II, 39). Nevertheless, people like Ivan Vasil'evich are necessary in order to get things done in the modern world, they have the know-how to deal with the practicalities of life with which families like the Dmitrievs, with their air of superiority, cannot cope.

This mundane episode of the cess pit is the very essence of *byt*. But it conceals an allegorical working-out of the macro-plot, a heightened metaphor for the real nature of the conflict in the story. Dmitriev's family and their pretensions belong to the past, yet the morality of the revolutionary generation is no longer relevant to the modern world. After all, they, like the others in the *dacha* village, have for years been unable to clear away their own waste, while old Luk'ianov shifts it in a matter of hours. There could hardly be a more vivid metaphor for the stagnation of a community and a society that prides itself on its glorious past, but which is unable to progress or effect even cosmetic improvements to their lot.

Dmitriev's sister Lora looks down on the Luk'ianovs and suspects that the cleaning of the cesspit has been carried out 'by not very noble means' (II, 38). Such indignation is both churlish and hypocritical. The 'means' by which to clean a cesspit should not be the subject of an ethical dilemma. Equally misplaced is her disapproval of Lena's rearrangement of furniture and crockery in the *dacha*, in particular moving the portrait of Dmitriev's father from a room to the hallway, as if this was a symbolic demotion of the Dmitriev family head from centre-stage in the *dacha* to the periphery. Again, banality only half-conceals a battle of forces representing opposing philosophies of life.

But does this mean that Trifonov is explicitly attacking the *meshchanstvo* of Lena's family? There are thousands, maybe millions of them. Lena is hardly exceptional, nor is her father. Such people, we see, are necessary in modern society, they get things done, they know how to get the best out of a rigid and bureaucratic system. Lena's family, rather, is representative of modern consumer-minded city-dwellers, if somewhat exaggerated in their acquisitive urges. Indeed, the author admits that Lena's criticism of her husband's family as 'hypocritical' is largely correct.[8] There is no clear-cut distinction between the two families, one is neither 'good' nor the other 'bad'. The author's subtext is the working-out of historical forces. His characters represent different value systems belonging to different times, and Dmitriev's eventual moral capitulation is not only the final erosion of the revolutionary values of his family, but also an acceptance that he has to adapt to the modern world. The author therefore is justified when he says that he does not need to give any explicit guidance to the reader. But he can be accused of ambivalence: is the author simply showing how time moves on and how values change? Or is he passing a qualitative judgment on the moral and ethical deterioration of modern Soviet society? Such ambivalence remains at the heart of his later fiction, and is aesthetically unsatisfying. But undoubtedly it helped him to remain one step ahead of an ever-vigilant censorship.

The *dacha* is where the decisive confrontations between the two families take place.[9] The grandfather is instrumental here, for as both families go for a stroll around the area, he observes to Dmitriev how places change over the years and decades:

'Imagine, dear Vitia, what your mother-in-law's uncle would have said had he been around when people in goatee beards and pince-nez were taking the air here? Probably something like "Just look at the kind of people in Pavlinovo these days! Riff-raff in loose-fitting jackets and pince-nez ... " Eh? Don't you think so? After all, there used to be an estate here, the owner went bankrupt, sold his house and his land, and then half a century later when his heir was passing by he looked in out of morbid curiosity, to have a look at the wives of the various merchants and civil servants, and the gentlemen in their top-hats, like your uncle,' – here the grandfather bowed to Vera Lazarevna – 'who had just driven up in a hansom cab, and might think: "Ugh! Disgusting! What horrid people!"' (II, 46)

Fedor Nikolaevich is blissfully unaware that such a remark does not fail to cause offence to Vera Lazarevna.

Fedor Nikolaevich is unable to understand how Lena and her mother can address a workman who has come to rewire the lounge in the familiar *ty* form, or how Dmitriev and Lena can boast about giving a shop assistant fifty roubles to lay aside a radio receiver for them. His values are from a different age, and Lena calls him 'a well-preserved monster' (II, 44). Still, he has enough awareness of time, in particular about changing values, to remark to Dmitriev: 'There's nothing more stupid than seeking ideals in the past' (II, 47). It is following this and other observations that the two families go their separate ways amid much ill-feeling and recrimination.

We are told that Fedor Nikolaevich died four years after this episode. This sudden projection into the future is unsettling, and reminds the reader that the narrative is, after all, Dmitriev's, as told to the author-narrator some years after. We can assume, then, that what Dmitriev tells us took place at least five years previously. The *povest'* reminds us that we are all mortal, and death is a major theme. The grandfather's funeral has a central place in the story. Here Dmitriev manages to have a few moments in thought on his own, and realizes that with the death of his grandfather something else was disappearing, something 'that connected Dmitriev, his sister and his mother' (II, 49). His 'exchange' is further shown in terms of utter banality when on his way to the funeral he buys some tins of salmon (*saira*) that Lena particularly likes, puts it in his briefcase, and forgets his briefcase behind a pillar in the crematorium. He only remembers it outside, and instead of going back with the rest of his family for the wake, traditional on such occasions, he has to rush back to collect his precious tinned fish, and disturbs another ceremony taking place.

The funeral acts as a catalyst for the recounting of another seemingly ignominious episode in Dmitriev's life. Levka Bubrik is also there, and Dmitriev recalls how Levka returned to Moscow from three years in Bashkiria and asked his help to get work in GINEGA, the Institute of Oil and Gas Apparatus. Lena, though, has the idea of getting her own husband into this post, which commands a better salary than Dmitriev's present position. So on the pretence of helping Levka, Ivan Vasil'evich talks to the right people, and it is Dmitriev who gets the job. Although Dmitriev takes much of the blame for at least acquiescing in Lena's manipulation of the situation, it is difficult to condemn outright a wife's desire to get her husband a better job. Dmitriev's family enjoy the benefits of Ivan Vasil'evich's way of doing things when it comes to repairing sewage systems, but are quick to condemn 'Luk'ianovization' when it offends their sense of fair play. One of the artistic successes of this work is that Trifonov enables us to see things from opposing standpoints: we understand, and so we begin to accept. From there it is a short step to forgiving.

Levka and Dmitriev, like Belov and Palavin and Koryshev and Zurabov before them, were once childhood friends, and studied together at the same institute. For Kseniia Fedorovna and her father, Levka acts as the yardstick by which they measure the shortcomings of Dmitriev. His mother wanted him to travel to Turkmenia, where Lora was then working, but Lena objected. It is entirely within the terms of Dmitriev's 'exchange' that he consents to Bubrik's deception: it is another example of Dmitriev rejecting his own, and accepting the values of Lena's family. He rejects the values of a family steeped in history, and embraces a family which prides itself on its ability to 'get its own way' in everyday life.

It is not difficult to see that, just like Trifonov's previous works, *Obmen* is structured around contrasting character types representing fundamentally different philosophies of life: Vera Lazarevna-Kseniia Fedorovna; Fedor Nikolaevich-Ivan Vasil'evich; Dmitriev-Bubrik. The alternative to Lena as wife-material is Tania, a colleague with whom Dmitriev has been romantically involved for three years. He, of course, will never leave his family, but their relationship has destroyed Tania's marriage. She knows that she will never be together with him, but still she loves him and wants to be with him whenever possible. Tania is Dmitriev's selfless and pitiful victim, and it is the destruction of her happiness that stands as the clearest condemnation of his weakness. She does not put the happiness of herself or her own family above moral considerations, and she is aghast at the very idea of the proposed exchange. She is therefore a complete contrast to Lena, and would be the kind of wife of whom Dmitriev's family would have wholeheartedly approved. Dmitriev himself knows this: 'Tania would have probably been a better wife for him', he muses more than once (II, 22, 24, 29 and 62 – the latter times without the 'probably').

As has already been stated, the *povest'* is not explicitly sentimental or moralistic about the 'exchange' or betrayal of moral values. Lena's family is stronger and better equipped to live in the modern world, in which Dmitriev's is hopelessly impractical, and he himself has to adapt. This is Dmitriev's moral imperative. When, at the end of the narrative he puts Lena's suggestion of moving in with them, Kseniia Fedorovna tells him the truth he has tried to hide from himself: '"You've already exchanged, Vitia. The exchange has taken place." Again there was silence. She whispered barely audibly, with her eyes closed. "That was a long time ago. And this happens every day, so don't be surprised, Vitia. And don't get upset. It's just that you don't notice it… "'(II, 62).

It does, indeed, happen every day. The subject-matter thus becomes removed from history, and placed squarely back into the context of the here-and-now, of *byt*. Kseniia Fedorovna has long known that the battle for her son's soul is lost, and it is significant that when he visits her, he sees that she is reading *Doctor Faustus*. Dmitriev has not so much 'exchanged' his values as sold his soul.

Obmen achieves a unity of purpose and narrative technique which is not always present in Trifonov's other work. Trifonov succeeds in conveying both a sense of history and the immediacy of the present-day, his characters are clearly delineated and distinguished, and Dmitriev's dilemma put within a historical context. *Byt* – the everyday, the mundane, the here-and-now – provides for the clash of historical ages, and their corresponding codes of morality. All major characters already mentioned, as well as those who appear briefly or fleetingly, such as Dmitriev's colleagues Neviadomskii, Sotnikova, Zherekhov, and his neighbours in the communal flat the Fandeevs and Iraida Vasil'evna, are part of this world, and have their own place and function within it. *Slitnost'* in Trifonov allows for even minor characters to be interconnected, for past and present to be interwoven.

In *The Master and Margarita* Woland looks out on the Moscow public gathered in the Variety Theatre for his performance of black magic, and observes that although they are basically the same as ever, they have become 'corrupted' by the issue of living space (*kvartirnyi vopros*).[10] Trifonov is putting Woland's words to the test, just as Bulgakov's Professor of Black Magic puts his public to the test with fake money and stylish clothes which then disappear. Trifonov observes that *byt* interests him exactly because it is where the 'the morality of today manifests itself and is put to the test', and the exchange of living space, the moral choice it entails, provides an opportunity not only to explore how the morality of the past is different from that of the present, but also to show the evolution of this change. For the choice he makes reveals an individual's moral essence. Not for nothing does Trifonov say that for him 'morality is a historical concept'.[11]

The theme of place is here not simply one taken from the

modern reality of Soviet urban life, though. It also involves the emotive question of 'home', of roots, and of identity. Dmitriev consciously turns his back on his home. Again, the absence of a father-figure is significant: Dmitriev's father, who was a railway engineer and part-time writer of sorts, and even published some humorous sketches, died in the 1930s (we are not told explicitly whether his was a natural death), when Dmitriev was still a child.

From *Studenty* onwards Trifonov's previous works have tended towards a progressive disintegration of the concept of family and wholeness, and here the collapse of the Dmitriev family is framed historically; significantly, Lena's family is strongly united. So the 'home' of revolutionary values is usurped by the new generation of Soviet urban-dweller, as epitomized by the Luk'ianovs. Turkmenia, where Lora and her husband Feliks have worked, also offers an escape for Dmitriev, an opportunity for self-renewal, as it did for Koryshev, but he allows Lena to turn it down. The *dacha*, where most of the discussions take place about where Kseniia Fedorovna should live, is situated in the area of Pavlinovo, and used to be reserved for the families of Civil War Red partisans. Now it is inhabited by a completely different class of city-dwellers, and it is this change that Dmitriev's grandfather comments on. Time moves on, and even this semi-rural haven has to give way: at the end of the *povest'* we learn that recently the whole area was levelled and a football stadium constructed in its place. Significantly, the last person to leave the *dacha* was Lora, whose maximalism remains steadfast throughout the story. Such is the end of the Red Partisans' country retreat, reduced to dust, just as their idealism and values are trampled underfoot by their descendants.

The theme of ethical compromise is further illustrated in the short piece 'Beskonechnye igry', published in 1970, which addresses itself to questions of censorship and bureaucratic battles in the sports section of the newspaper *Moskovskie novosti*.[12] The picture we get of journalism in the capital is one of scheming and settling scores, and is reminiscent of the power games played in the newspaper offices in *Utolenie zhazhdy*. Here, too, the relationship of political authority and the press is explored as the lone journalist attempts to fight for justice with remarkable civic courage. The truth of the printed word, of course, is what is at stake. The central character is the journalist Serikov, who is trying to support and protect the prominent soccer trainer Kiziaev from the attacks of fellow journalists inspired by unnamed officials from on high, and Serikov it is who asserts the primacy of a simple human truth over that which is the usual preoccupation of newspapers (not only Soviet): '"Here we're chirping on in the newspaper about great deeds. And what is a great deed? Not a swim in record time, or the ascent of some glacial peak, or somebody throwing the shot farther than anyone else... A great deed is to understand. Understand somebody else."'[13] Sports journalism serves here as the everyday milieu of *byt*, in which the central character finds his personal morality tested, and is the synecdoche for the working out of larger issues..

Serikov is unusual among Trifonov's heroes in his dogged rectitude in trying to combat injustice, but he pays a high price: in confronting dishonesty in the editorial office, his marriage collapses. Kiziaev, on the other hand, throws in the towel at the last moment, and, although defeated, he saves his marriage. Serikov, unlike Dmitriev, does not seek the quiet life, but maintains his self-respect and integrity despite the pressures exerted on him. In personal terms, though, he loses, and he gets no reward or gratitude from those he has helped.

Turkmenia is the setting for the narration of *Predvaritel'nye itogi*. Trifonov admits that at first he had the idea of writing about a Turkmenian village where he himself spent some time, and another story about Moscow, but then decided to combine them both.[14] As in the later *Starik* and *Ischeznovenie*, we have two motifs united within a structural whole. Trifonov, of course, already knew Turkmenia well as a result of the visits there in the 1950s, and it was in 1966, when he attended the Turkmenian Writers' Congress, that he began work on this story by noting down descriptions of local fauna, birds, trees, and conversations with locals.[15]

The *povest'* resembles *Obmen* in its 'confessional' form. However, whereas Dmitriev's tale is narrated to the author-narrator retrospectively, here we have a first-person narrator who gives the reader a direct and depressing account of the disharmony of his family life, and his own failure to put it right. Gennadii Sergeevich, a Moscow-based translator, surveys the twenty years of his marriage to Rita not only from a temporal distance, as did Dmitriev, but also from a geographical distance, from Turkmenia. More significantly, though, the voice of the author does not intrude into the text, but blends with that of the narrator, and the reader has to work out the author's stance from subtextual inferences. Gennadii Sergeevich's story, however, is bleaker than Dmitriev's, the relationships he describes much more flagrantly exploitative, and the picture of urban *byt* more threatening and hopeless. Furthermore, although again we see them from only one point of view, contrasts are starker, and the cast of characters is more clearly divided into 'positive' and 'negative', however much the author may formally reject such classifications.

Gennadii Sergeevich has been in Turkmenia for two months, and in his narrative focuses on several episodes from his family life, none of them very commendable. Rita is his second wife, and the reason why he left his first wife, with whom he had lived for two years and by whom he has a son. When he first met Rita she was, he insists, very pretty, charming and intelligent ('Scheherezade', he would call her), but whereas she is still at the age of forty very attractive, her mental and spiritual development has taken second place to the quest of blatant and superficial materialism. Moreover, she has the single-minded determination of Dmitriev's Lena to get what she wants, at whatever cost, and enjoys the prestigious company of educated but vacuous individuals such as Gartvig. She prides herself on getting hold of books on mysticism and religion, such as rare (i.e pre-revolutionary) editions of Berdiaev and Leont'ev, although her husband muses that this is obviously done via the black market, and hangs the apartment walls with Picasso prints. Like Dmitriev, Gennadii Sergeevich is powerless to resist his wife's acquisitive urge.

From the sanctuary of Turkmenia, where he is translating into Russian the work of Mansur, a local popular but mediocre poet, he relates the strained relations within his family. He does not shy from his weakness, and his constant capitulation. Whereas Dmitriev's 'exchange' is of the revolutionary idealism and traditions of his family, Gennadii Sergeevich trades in the supposed moral absolutism of a man close to the hub of literary creativity; indeed, the behaviour of this family threatens to destroy any faith in human decency (significantly, his first wife, whom he abandoned, was called Vera: faith).

The style of the *povest'* also suggests the dislocation felt by the hero, both geographical and moral. The narrative is recounted in Trifonov's typically breathless style, with long sentences, endless relative and subordinate clauses separated by commas, semi-colons, or caesurae. English words and phrases crop up on almost every page of the text, upsetting the rhythm and balance of the Russian, as does Nietzsche's phrase *Also sprach Zarathustra*, which occurs several times in the narrative. The Western European cultural link is extended when Gennadii Sergeevich likens himself to 'an insect' and 'a beetle', thus likening himself to Kafka's Gregor Samsa.[16]

Gennadii Sergeevich is nearer the author than Dmitriev in his appreciation of time moving on, and how it changes life, as he looks back on the desolate years of his marriage:

We shouldn't have lived together for twenty years. *Also sprach Zarathustra*: it's too long. Twenty years is no joke. In twenty years forests thin out and soil loses its richness. The best of houses needs repair work. Turbines become inoperable. And just think of the fantastic achievements in science over twenty years! There are revolutions in all spheres of research. Cities are rebuilt. Oktiabr'skaia Square, beside which we used to live, is no longer recognizable. And this is without even mentioning the new states that have emerged in Africa. Twenty years! A period which leaves no hope. (II, 81)

Here the personal and the historical come together as Gennadii Sergeevich reflects on the rapid technological and scientific advances, urban development and new geo-political realities that have framed the latter half of his life.

Gennadii Sergeevich has a son from his first marriage now working as a geologist in Turkmenia. This detail is reminiscent of Dmitriev's sister Lora who, with her husband Feliks (and

Trifonov's own sister Tania), worked in Turkmenia as a geologist. Gennadii Sergeevich does not give us any further details of his first family, but we do learn a lot about Kirill, his son by Rita. Kirill serves as a crystallization of the moral and ethical corruption of his parents. A recurring need in the family, as with the Dmitrievs, is one of money: they are always short, the son asks the father for some, and when he does not receive any, earns it himself on the side in a rock group, or with black marketeers. The family crisis which precipitates Gennadii Sergeevich's departure to Turkmenia is brought about by Kirill's hapless devotion to money and recourse to speculation.

The family has a housekeeper, Niura, a meek, unassuming woman from the countryside. About the same age as Rita, she is a complete contrast, semi-literate, abused since childhood, but never complaining about her lot. The family has had a string of housekeepers in the past, and none of them has been able to work with Rita for very long. Niura, though, has been with them for ten years. She has had a hard life, alone since the death of her parents in the 1930s, and then thrown out of her own house at the age of eleven by her predatory aunt Varvara. Now half-deaf and in poor health, she eventually has a nervous breakdown and has to be taken to hospital, and while she is there asks for an icon entrusted to her by her equally downtrodden and unhappy aunt Glasha to be brought to comfort her. Rita entrusts the icon to Kirill, who, instead of taking it to Niura, sells it to a black-marketeer. In so doing, he is caught by the police. The reactions of his parents are significant: Rita subordinates the question of ethics and moral accountability to the task of activating her connections to prevent him from being expelled from the institute in which he is studying.

Gennadii Sergeevich, on the other hand, accepts that he is himself to blame for this development. The story is not just a misogynistic picture of a materialistic and utterly unscrupulous woman, but of a weak father and husband who has failed to provide any moral guidance or leadership in the family, and is now unable to do anything constructive when a crisis occurs. He leaves the practical business of getting Kirill out of trouble to his wife. Like Trifonov's heroes before him, he lost his father at an early age, in this case in the war against the Finns in 1939. Having been deprived of fatherly guidance at an early age, he is himself unable to instil in his own son any sense of duty or responsibility. As he reflects early in the narrative: 'How should I know if the lad needs a father, when he is one metre eighty, has a Canadian hair-cut, deep voice, can dance for three hours without getting tired, read in a day a whole English detective novel and go up to any girl on the street and get her telephone number' (II, 77–8).

As with Dmitriev's pathetic attempts at self-justification, Gennadii Sergeevich is prepared to blame circumstances for his own weakness and inability to make decisions. The lack of any absolute or even relative moral standards in this family is the real focus of the story, and the inevitable outcome is moral betrayal. Niura is not only the housekeeper, she keeps the home and family together, it is she who embodies the warmth and selflessness of what should be a normal, caring home, as Gennadii Sergeevich is aware. She has been exploited by her own family, and now, when she comes out of hospital and has nowhere to go, Rita and her husband decide that they are not morally bound to provide her with a roof over her head, nor can they look after her. This despite the ten years of service she has given the family. As Gennadii Sergeevich reflects: 'And so this creature, who had so curiously cemented the home together, left us. We, after all, had all been creeping off in our different directions, each to our own room, affairs and secrets, to our own silence, and only she was the real home, the custodian of the stove and the hearth' (II, 103).

The family is surrounded by characters who are mirror images of their own egotism and corruption. Rita's friend Larisa is particularly unpleasant: she is often unfaithful to her husband, despises her mother-in-law despite a superficial air of respect and tolerance, does nothing at work, but has the right connections to obtain tickets for performances of the popular entertainer Arkadii Raikin, and get to prestigious holiday resorts. She also has a similar passion for icons, which she plunders from rural relations. Rafik, through whom Gennadii

Sergeevich receives commissioned translations, is able to ease Kirill's passage through entrance examinations because he is on friendly terms with one of the examiners. The most extreme example of a cynical opportunist is Gartvig, thirty-seven years old, highly intelligent and a keen sportsman. He is an academic, knows four languages as well as Latin, and his particular area of interest lies in the religions of the Middle Ages. His chosen topic of specialization is obviously an ironic comment on his own lack of inner substance. Indeed, the moral wasteland of his inner world can be seen as a correlation of the actual desert Gennadii is currently inhabiting.

In this world even family ties are used for self-indulgence and ultimately profit. At one stage Gennadii Sergeevich and Rita are invited by his cousin Volodia, and his wife Lialia, for a meal, but this is not meant as a purely social or family gathering: Volodia and Lialia are using them to get closer to Gartvig in order to help their daughter through her entrance exams.

Gartvig has been married twice, the first time to an actress, the second to a gypsy dancer, and is currently living with a doctor who does not seem to mind his frequent departures and liaisons. Gennadii Sergeevich is unconcerned about the trips Gartvig and Rita make to various treasure-troves of the Russian past such as Suzdal', Zagorsk and Sviatye Gory. He is equally unconcerned by the prospect that Gartvig may be sleeping with his wife. He merely gives his would-be rival the following telling character sketch: 'Gartvig's main characteristic was his cynical urge to acquire and to consume without giving anything himself. He had no desire or capacity to share his ideas and knowledge with people he considered below him and of no use to him, he wanted only to enrich himself (II, 93).'[17]

The same, of course, could be said of Rita, as her husband sees her. Gennadii Sergeevich later exacts a sweet revenge on Gartvig's aloof self-assurance when he elicits from him the response that Grushnitskii and Pechorin must be characters from Turgenev! This may be far-fetched, for every Russian, and especially one with higher education, knows his or her own classics, but the episode serves to illustrate the momentary though meaningful victory of culture over *meshchanstvo*.

For Gennadii Sergeevich the *byt* of family life is a true hell, for it is a life without standards, love or kindness. Little wonder that he keeps returning to biblical references for a context in which to put the barrenness of his own life. Love and closeness to a loved one are, he asserts, 'biblical gossipology (*bibleiskaia boltologiia*)' (II, 73), seemingly unattainable in Moscow life. Elsewhere Gennadii Sergeevich tries to disabuse his wife of her hypocritical 'pseudoreligiosity' by assuring her that 'the first precept of any religion – especially the Christian faith – is love for those close to you' (II, 89). Gennadii Sergeevich's frame of reference is consistently either a literary or biblical one.

Gennadii Sergeevich's recurring dream is of climbing a staircase but running out of breath, and choking from a lack of oxygen: an obvious metaphor for the stifling environment in which he passes his days. He reflects that in all the years of his marriage to Rita, not a day has gone by without him thinking of leaving her. He reinterprets Tolstoi's famous lines from *Anna Karenina* on families to suit his own situation: 'Tolstoi was only half right, all happy families are alike, it's true, but all unhappy families are also, goodness knows, somehow unhappy in the same way. And it was, after all, he who told the standard story concerning a husband, his wife's lover, and her mother-in-law ... Selfishness is a shortage of love. Unhappiness stems from this same reason' (II, 119).

Rita observes at one stage that 'when three egotists live together, nothing good can come of it' (II, 115). In Turkmenia Gennadii Sergeevich meets a family whose lifestyle and principles offer a complete contrast to those of his own family. He is impressed by Atabaly, the director of the home and general caretaker, who has eleven children.

Gennadii Sergeevich asks himself rhetorically 'But can a man with eleven children be an egotist?' The answer: 'Just unthinkable!' (II, 119–20). To be sure, his experiences in Turkmenia provide a counterpoint to his Moscow life from which he can seek spiritual and moral rebirth. The vitalization of the desert in Turkmenia symbolizes political regeneration in *Utolenie zhazhdy*, and in this story the water of the Kara-Kum irrigation canal, which Gennadii Sergeevich can hear not far from the writers' rest home in which he is staying, infuses him with creative energy with which to work, and, through his contact with other people, helps to revive the barrenness of his spirit. Indeed, the desert is also a symbolic purgatory, from which Gennadii Sergeevich is to emerge cleansed and strengthened.

Atabaly is a jovial character, and alongside his eleven children he has an adopted Ukrainian daughter, Valia, whom he and his wife took in from an orphanage during the War. She has stayed with them, even though her real parents later found her and asked her to go back to the Ukraine with them. Atabaly is always prepared to give an hour or two of his time to have a chat and a smoke, and his wife Iazgul' never takes any money from Gennadii Sergeevich for doing odd jobs – a stark contrast to the mercenary relationships of Moscow. The happiness and sheer vitality of Atabaly's family is a sharp contrast to the dead weight of Gennadii Sergeevich's family life in the capital. As the latter observes: 'Family (*rodnye liudi*) are those who do good' (II, 126).[18]

Contrast and juxtaposition are again the structural pivots of Trifonov's narrative. Atabaly, Iazgul' and Valia stand at opposite ends of the moral spectrum from Gennadii Sergeevich, Rita, and Kirill, just as Glasha and Varvara are respectively Niura's kind and evil aunts.

Valia looks after him in the rest home, and as they meet and talk both become aware of a developing sexual attraction. Valia is the object of amorous intentions on the part of several locals: in one grotesque scene, a parody of a similar episode in *Utolenie zhazhdy*, a dwarf fights with a hunchback to claim the right to court her. Valia refuses to become romantically involved with any of the locals. She is twenty-six years old and, despite having been beaten and maltreated by her husband, is still legally married, though separated. One night she steals into Gennadii Sergeevich's hut, on the pretext of escaping from the drunken and lecherous attentions of Mansur. Somewhat to his surprise, Gennadii Sergeevich finds himself capable of offering comfort, and being comforted in return. They hold hands, embrace, she kicks off her shoes, and they lie together. Any sexual contact is left in the subtext, for Gennadii Sergeevich then returns in his mind to Rita, and the carefree days of long ago, when they would swim together in a rivulet outside Moscow. The experience with Valia is his cartharsis, he sheds tears that symbolize the purging of his conscience and the release of energy, and these tears are clearly linked with the water imagery of his memory and the flowing water of the canal he can hear outside. The last lines of the *povest'* see Gennadii Sergeevich back in Moscow, and then going off to the Baltic with Rita for a holiday, significantly, to a place by the sea. Life goes on, the barrenness of Moscow city life is overcome, and the family unit drinks in new sustenance and is revitalized. So Atabaly, Niura and Valia serve as contrasting figures to the self-seeking Gartvig, Rita, Larisa and Kirill.

Moreover, Atabaly serves to show Gennadii Sergeevich his own inadequacy as a father and as a human being. Separation from Moscow and distance from his family aid above all Gennadii Sergeevich's self-understanding, and, as if taking a lesson from the journalist Serikov in 'Beskonechnye igry', in understanding another human being. Through comparison, juxtaposition and antithesis, of Moscow and Turkmenia, of culture and cynicism, love and egotism, generosity and selfishness, vibrant life and the metaphorical desert of non-being (equivalent to the 'living death' of Trifonov's future works), Gennadii Sergeevich gains strength to face up to and cope with Moscow *byt*, to reconcile his Moscow and Turkmenian experiences, and to comprehend his own life and its allotted place within the passage of impersonal time. There is, though, a deeper level of understanding.

Christian and biblical motifs in the work serve to highlight the lack of spiritual values in Moscow, but are also an important element of the story in themselves. The drama that unfolds around Niura's icon, the allusions to the religious philosophy of Berdiaev and Leont'ev, and the important religious centres of Zagorsk and Suzdal', are all features that provide a framework for this picture of spiritual barrenness. These, the biblical allusions, Gartvig's interest in religious history and the Russian

Orthodox motif of rebirth through purgatory provide a subtext which, along with the literary allusions to Chekhov, Nietzsche and Kafka reinforce the theme of the work: contemporary man may think that he is rationally all-powerful, but in a world without spiritual or moral absolutes he is little more than an insect.

In this work Trifonov has drawn a rich and detailed picture of the modern Soviet condition, complete with concrete social background and a literary and biblical subtext. The story differs from *Obmen* in that it relies more on the use of metaphor, irony and allusion than metonymy. It is interesting to note that Trifonov's original intention was for Gennadii Sergeevich to die.[19] The eventual outcome of the plot suggests that Trifonov himself seems surprised that his hero, or rather anti-hero, is able to achieve his catharsis through human warmth and understanding.

Dolgoe proshchanie more precisely links culture, literature, the past and the *byt* of modern life than any of Trifonov's works studied hitherto, and marks the beginning of a stage in his writing career where a sense of history becomes explicitly intertwined with the present-day existence of his major characters. It too contains important literary and cultural motifs. Moreover, in this work Trifonov's use of character contrast extends to two professional writers, Rebrov and Smolianov, their chosen themes and their approach to their art.

This is also the author's first work in which one of the narrators is a woman. Other women such as Lena and Rita are strong, if unprincipled, characters, and are driven by an unreflecting and single-minded materialism which drags their husbands down to a level of sordid banality. Alternatively, women like Katia and Lera in *Utolenie zhazhdy*, are merely decorative additions to the plot, and serve only to provide the love/sex interest. Liudmila Telepneva, referred to as Lialia in the text, is at the beginning of the *povest'* a career woman, a talented and ambitious actress in the Moscow Academy Theatre. In the narrative she recalls her theatrical past of eighteen years ago, when she was in her mid-twenties, and in particular her emotional relationship with the struggling playwright Grisha Rebrov, whom she had known since schooldays.

It is worth recalling here Trifonov's own knowledge of the theatrical milieu based on his unhappy experience as a would-be playwright in the early 1950s. He had two plays produced in the Moscow Ermolova theatre, and he admits that the figure of Sergei Leonidovich, the director in *Dolgoe proshchanie* , is based on Andrei Lobanov, the Ermolova theatre director who produced Trifonov's plays, and for whom Trifonov had considerable respect and admiration.[20]

However, as the narrative progresses through the years, viewpoints switch, so that at times we see characters and plot developments through Rebrov's eyes or through Smolianov's. We see the *goremyka* (luckless) Rebrov as described by Lialia's father, Petr Aleksandrovich, while elsewhere an all-seeing but unseen narrator relates events beyond the ken of the characters. Thus, for instance, the first twenty pages cover Lialia's acting career, some of her previous emotional entanglements and adventures, as well as the milieu of the theatre, then we learn a little about Rebrov, and then her father. Petr Aleksandrovich Telepnev, originally a metalworker from Ekaterinburg but a now self-taught gardener, is a veteran of the Revolution and Civil War, who since 1922 has been devoted to growing dahlias, and now has forty-eight sorts, the pride of all Moscow.

We are told that his *dacha* used to belong to either a minor civil servant or factory official before the Revolution, but the city has gradually been encroaching, claiming more and more land nearby, and Petr Aleksandrovich now spends his time writing petitions, visiting important people and agitating to preserve his tiny patch of rural splendour as the houses and urban areas close in. For three years this struggle goes on, but for both Petr Aleksandrovich, having suffered his third heart attack, and his precious dahlias, time is running out. The whole area is eventually levelled by bulldozers to make way for a new suburb, and becomes, like Dmitriev's *dacha*, another victim of social progress. The demise of the *dacha*, and in particular its collection of prize flora, representing freshness and vitality, can be seen here once more as a metaphor for the destruction of the idealism of the revolutionary generation, of which Petr Aleksandrovich is part. It is a latterday example of the conflict of the 'machine' and the 'garden', as Katerina Clark characterizes the literature of the early Plan years.[21] Here the 'machine' of history bulldozes into the dust the 'garden' of purity and wholeness. Furthermore, Petr Aleksandrovich and Dmitriev's grandfather are similar types: once committed radicals, they now view with apprehension the changes in the modern world. Trifonov at no stage criticizes them or their values. The *dacha* motif and what it symbolizes is also a clear indication of Trifonov's own disillusionment with the modern world.

The Rebrov of eighteen years previously is close to the author of 1971. Indeed, it is probable that Trifonov is basing Rebrov's own lack of success in the theatre on his own experience in the early 1950s. Having unsuccessfully written pot-boilers about the Korean War and the construction of the University on Lenin Hills, Rebrov now devotes himself to themes that interest him deeply. He is above all a historian who works all hours in the Lenin Library researching characters from Russian nineteenth-century history, be it the little-known dramatist Ivan Pryzhov, the life and ideas of the nineteenth-century nihilist Nechaev, or the actions of the police 'mole' Kletochnikov, with the intention of writing a play about the 'People's Will' terrorist organization. His studies, rummaging in archives, old journals and manuscripts, become more like an addiction, 'like a passion for cards or smoking narcotics' (II, 154). Rebrov's interest in the figure of Kletochnikov is illuminating, as it reflects that of the author working on his historical novel about the 'People's Will' at this time. Rebrov is primarily interested in his hero's personality and the forces that motivated him, and feels drawn to him because of a feature they have in common: the desire to rise above the pressures and temptations of everyday life, of *byt*:

The story of Nikolai Vasil'evich was an example of how one should live, with no concern for the great trivialities of life, with no thought of death or immortality ... It was not even clear whether he was a true revolutionary, that is, whether he was fully conscious of the tasks and aims. He appeared out of the blue, sickly and not in good health, an unknown quantity to all, a lowly provincial civil servant with round spectacles, and offered his services to the revolution. There were doubts, uncertainty – nothing much heroic here, after all! None of the steel-hard muscles of Aleksandr [Mikhailov], the daggers and pistols of Sergei [Nechaev], the erudition of Lev [Tikhomirov], the Carbonari romanticism of Nikolai [Morozov]. Still, never mind. He was a man of action. He carried out the will of others that some called 'the people's'. He infiltrated the police force, got right under its shell, and penetrated its very heart and guts, the Third Department, where he saved, rescued, killed people. He carried out the will of his own conscience. That was all there was to it. (II, 194–5)

Trifonov, of course, was working on *Neterpenie* at precisely this time, and Rebrov's interest offers a neat synopsis of the novel Trifonov was to publish two years later. Rebrov had already written, but failed to complete, plays about the Decembrists, the revolt of exiled Poles in Siberia, and the writers Ivan Pryzhov and Aleksandr Mikhailov. As he exclaims in an animated conversation with Smolianov: 'The soil I work from is the experience of history, all that Russia has suffered !' (II, 172). He despises the idea that popular success based on adherence to topical issues is a measure of literary achievement, and holds in contempt Lialia's theatrical colleagues for their hypocrisy and malice.

Rebrov's 'soil' is his own ancestry, the 'experience' of his own family history: his great grandfather was a serf, one of his grandmothers was an exiled Pole and the other was a music teacher in St Petersburg whose father was a Kantonist,[22] while his grandfather was exiled to Siberia for taking part in student riots. His own father fought in the First World War and the Civil War. All of Rebrov's immediate family – mother, father, brother – all died during the last War. Petr Aleksandrovich observes of him that he is a talented writer, but, unfortunately, without the right connections to get ahead. Rebrov despises those, who like Smolianov, have achieved popular success because they have the right connections and write to order. As with Gennadii Sergeevich's exposure of Gartvig's ignorance, Rebrov's contempt for his rival – both in the literary and emotional stakes, for Smolianov has his eye on Lialia – is justified in literary terms: he suspects that Smolianov has not read Dostoevskii (and his Tolstoi may not be up to standard, either)!

Given Rebrov's interest in the terrorist and revolutionary movements of a hundred years ago, it is not surprising that he uses an idea from Dostoevskii's *The Possessed* as a frame of reference for his own distinctly unmaterialistic lifestyle: 'for a person to be happy he needs just as much happiness as unhappiness' (II, 167). It is, of course, galling for him that as Lialia's career profile begins to rise, his remains on the lowest level. He is without a regular income, effectively a drop-out and a dependent. Smolianov, to add insult to injury, offers to get him a secure and well-paid job in the theatre, but in an administrative role; that is, with the plain intention of stifling Rebrov's creative energy. Rebrov declines the offer.

Rebrov's understanding of life reaches its subliminal heights through the warmth of human contact, as with Gennadii Sergeevich. His realization comes as he lies in bed with Lialia one night, in the knowledge that she is pregnant by him:

His heart began beating, his strength was coming back. Joy, fear – everything together, united [*slitno*]. Just as much happiness as unhappiness: that's all that is needed. And this close, warm feeling is the only proof: I exist!

Here, just as happens in a dream, he became aware of a truth which seemed obvious and ages old: not *cogito ergo sum*, but I love *ergo sum*, and that was all. How was it that people did not guess? Couldn't understand? It was so strikingly obvious. (II, 201)

In this work more than any other previously Trifonov strives to bring together in the lives of his central characters past and present, history and personal happiness, truth and moral integrity: everything that makes up the life of the individual and the dynamics of society. When Rebrov tells him of his interest in the 'People's Will', Sergei Leonidovich, the ageing director of Lialia's theatre, expresses Trifonov's own understanding of the historical process, which is not merely made up of events, dates and names, but is a continuum, with culture, music, the theatre, as well as key historical events:

'Just think of this: for you the year 1880 means Kletochnikov, the Third Department, bombs, hunting down the Tsar, while for me it is Ostrovskii, "Women Slaves" in the Maly with Ermolova in the role of Evlaliia, Sadovskii, and Musil...Yes, yes, yes! Good God, how everything is so cruelly intertwined! Can you see that the history of a country is like a wire with many strands, and when we pull out one strand – no, that's no good! The truth in a time is in its unity [*slitnost'*], everything together: Kletochnikov, Musil...Ah, if only we could depict on stage this passage of time as it carries along everyone and everything!' (II, 195–6)

Smolianov, on the other hand, is a man devoted to the present. He writes mediocre plays on topical themes that reflect the issues of the day, such as the planting of rows of trees to act as wind-breaks (*lesopolosy*). Furthermore, because they are the stuff of socialist realism, and approved from on high, his plays are produced on the Moscow stage. He is, unlike Rebrov, successful in material terms. And he has connections that give him access to closed stores, sell-out concerts, powerful figures. But his life is rooted in the here-and-now, he has little talent and his success is only transitory. Unlike Rebrov, he is not interested in deeper questions of historical continuity or the relationship of past and present. Lialia has a platonic relationship with him, more out of pity – he has a sick mother, a mentally ill wife, and is the butt of the actors' barbs. Until, that is, he attempts to use her to further his career when he acquaints her with the powerful but mysterious Agabekov, with the aim of prostituting her. However, as in melodrama, it is precisely now that she realizes that it is really Rebrov she loves, and she breaks with Smolianov. The well of emotion is not yet exhausted, however, for Rebrov finds out about the 'affair', and discovers that, on the advice of her mother, Irina Ignat'evna, Lialia has had an abortion. Outraged and demoralized, he leaves Lialia and Moscow and travels to Siberia with a party of geologists, which will coincidentally be passing through the place where Pryzhov spent his exile – a parallel action to that of Gennadii Sergeevich leaving the capital for Turkmenia. For Rebrov too his journey from Moscow is a kind of rebirth, a new life beckons. As he travels to the East a fellow passenger dies on the train, and then he witnesses a bizarre incident where a would-be murderer is attacked and apparently killed by a crowd on a station platform, only to jump up as if unharmed when the police arrive. This latter incident serves as a metaphor for Rebrov's own condition, as he begins 'another life'. In short, life goes on, what seems like death is really a resurrection, a new beginning: 'One life had ended, another was beginning. To be sure ... a person lives not one, but several lives. He dies and is born again, attends his own funeral and observes his own birth: again the same sluggishness of movement, the same hopes. And after he has died he can look back over the life he has lived' (II, 214).

There is a clear link between Rebrov and Gennadii Sergeevich: both die metaphorically, and, in a parody of the Christ motif, are reborn. Here too Trifonov is at pains to populate the world he creates with secondary characters, all of whom have a particular function in the world he creates. Smurnyi is an aspiring director who has recently come into the theatre, and has an eye on Sergei Leonidovich's post of director-in-chief. Smurnyi, with Smolianov's connivance, begins a series of intrigues against Sergei Leonidovich and his allies, culminating in the old man suffering a heart attack. Also of note in this respect is Shakhov, a fixer whom Rebrov meets several times in his favourite cafe, the 'Natsional'', and who is able to get him work. This work involves Rebrov writing a historical play, but agreeing to have Smolianov as co-author, thus devaluing the integrity of the work and betraying his own artistic ethos. A mirror image of Rebrov is his friend Shchekov, a war invalid who, unlike Rebrov, has no ambition to enrich himself or gain status. Shchekov's friends include dish-washers, waiters, shop workers – all people on the bottom rung of society's ladder. Shchekov is content with his lot, and has qualities of unselfishness and honesty not immediately evident in Rebrov. Finally, there is Lialia's aunt Tamara, her mother's sister, who is reminiscent of Niura in *Predvaritel'nye itogi*: long-suffering (she has lost her husband and her son), constantly exploited and verbally abused by Irina Ignat'evna, but never complaining about her lot.

Imagery and symbolism in the story are similar to that

encountered in previous works. Water imagery is once again introduced: Rebrov believes he has a surfeit of love and emotion inside him, and like a boat on the sea is about to overturn (II, 186). The malevolent and insidious power of the State is also ever-present. Rebrov's neighbour Kanunov denounces him to the police for living in Moscow without permanent work, and later joins forces with Kurtov, Lialia's policeman neighbour who is vociferous in his aim to destroy her father's garden. Clearly, there are hints of larger things here: the writing community, as represented by Rebrov, under constant fear of denunciation and arrest; the *dacha*, a metaphor for revolutionary values, being attacked and destroyed by the police state.

To Trifonov's credit, few characters emerge in purely black-and-white colours. Smolianov makes up in *bonhomie* what he lacks in talent, and Irina Ignat'evna, implacably opposed to Rebrov as an under-achieving son-in-law, wants only the best for her family, and she does look after the increasingly sick Petr Aleksandrovich with selfless devotion; Bob Marevin, head of the literature section of the theatre and responsible for rejecting or accepting manuscripts, is held in awe and fear by writers and playwrights, but turns out to be a lonely and vulnerable man when his wife dies and he himself is forced into retirement.

Stylistically *Dolgoe proshchanie* shows a certain progression from the clear-cut contrasts and juxtapositions of Trifonov's previous works. Whereas again we have contrasting types – Smolianov and Rebrov; Smurnyi and Sergei Leonidovich; Irina Ignat'evna and her sister Tamara – we are also presented with pairings who complement each other: Shchekov and Rebrov; Kurtov and Kanunov; Sergei Leonidovich and Petr Aleksandrovich; Shakhov and Smolianov; and finally Rebrov and Trifonov the author. Mirror images and contrasts not only represent differing psychological types and philosophies, but also point to the spiritual evolution of the hero, from a refusal to compromise to an accommodation with exigency. The work provides a framework of human relationships, and of values and moral choices within a specific milieu, and at the same time touches on more fundamental questions of the passage of time and the individual life, history as existential experience, and the relationship of literature, the writer and society, across the centuries.

Dolgoe proshchanie, however, offers a more pessimistic vision of the hero's spiritual and moral searching, for whereas the central character of *Predvaritel'nye itogi* returns to Moscow spiritually revitalized, Rebrov's new life constitutes an abandonment of his previously held principles. We learn through Lialia that he is at the end a successful film-writer, twice married, and affluent: he has his own flat and car. In other words, he enjoys the material benefits of life that he once scorned. Success would preclude the possibility that he still writes on the themes he once held so dear. Rebrov's career is itself a synecdoche for the abandonment of idealism and the embrace of a mercenary attitude that characterized so much of the intelligentsia in the 1950s and 1960s. Like Dmitriev, Rebrov cannot ignore the desire to 'know how to live'. Rebrov's 'other life' is double-edged, for it is not only one of release and initial freedom but capitulation. On the other hand, the hacks are also well served; Smolianov is now no longer a writer, but earns his income solely by renting out his *dacha* during the summer months.

The author-narrator then goes beyond Lialia's purview to add that Rebrov often thinks back to the times when he was poor and struggling to make a living as 'the happiest years of his life' (II, 216). Not only was he poor, but he was honest and therefore free. The engineer Dmitriev, the translator Gennadii Sergeevich and the writer Rebrov are all linked in that they are unable ultimately to rise above 'the great trivialities of life', they all 'exchange' a personal idealism for the temptation of material success. By showing how his characters progress through the years, and by focusing on them at the particular moment when they face their choice, Trifonov captures the essential features of his time and his society. In a society where material affluence is the privilege of the very few, to attain any measure of well-being involves sacrificing principles once held sacred.

The work is almost a synthesis of the concerns of *Obmen* and

Predvaritel'nye itogi: it achieves an integration (*slitnost'*) of history, and in particular revolutionary history, cultural values, personal integrity and the relationships between people that change, develop, or are broken off with the passage of time. At the very end of the story the narrator gives us a characteristically compressed, almost breathless account of how the past eighteen years have affected Lialia, now in middle age and married to a military man whose hobby is motor sport, and with a teenage son:

Mother, father, Aunt Toma, Uncle Kolia and even the unlucky Maika, who was five years younger than Lialia, died in these years; her old friends from the theatre disappeared, and she didn't want to see any of them anyway (Lialia spent a long time challenging her dismissal, she fought desperately and developed asthma as a result, but she had to give in), and now Lialia had a new circle made up of military men, engineers and motor enthusiasts. (II, 215)

Perhaps the most interesting feature of Trifonov's works from 1966–71 is that no explicit reference is made to the social and political environment of the day. This is in contrast to his earlier works, where Stalinism or the thaw period feature very largely in plot development and the differing attitudes of the characters. In the Brezhnev era no-one has any clear-cut political conviction or commitment, people strive for purely material gain by whatever means come at hand, or, if they live not by utilitarian values, ultimately give in to those who do. He offers us a historical dimension to modern city life, where the dominant morality is traced from its heady revolutionary idealism, only to be betrayed and degraded by succeeding generations. We see this process in the everyday material and choices of *byt*, in the destruction of garden and *dacha* motifs, in the alienation of man from his fellow men. In the end, the real hero, and the only true constant, in these stories is Moscow itself, ever changing and developing, an embodiment of impersonal time and history, as in the lines that bring *Dolgoe proshchanie* to an end:

And Moscow rolls on and on, over the line of the outer ring road, over gullies and fields, piling up tower upon tower and mountains of stone on to millions of shining windows, turning up ancient clay and hammering into it gigantic cement pipes, filling in construction pits, pulling down, putting up, pouring in asphalt, destroying things without trace, and in the mornings on underground platforms and at bus stops there are masses of people, with each year more and more. Lialia was amazed. 'Where do all these people come from? Either there are a lot of visitors, or else the kids have all grown up.' (II, 216)

In conversation with the East German scholar Ralf Schröder, Trifonov agreed that *Drugaia zhizn'* was a 'turning point' in his writing, where the 'phenomenon of life' was first conveyed.[23] It combines both the *byt* of the present with historical investigation, and much more fundamentally than *Dolgoe proshchanie*. It therefore stands between the *byt* of Moscow and the preoccupation with historicity of the 1970s.

The style of the narration is somewhat more complex than in Trifonov's earlier stories. For example, it opens with a third-person account of the heroine waking up again in the middle of the night as the voice of her conscience calls on her to 'try to understand'. Her reaction is to wonder if she is guilty of something, and then we delve deeper into her consciousness and her memories. These memories are haphazard, but introduce us to several important circumstances in her life. She remembers *him* coming home from a cafe, though we do not yet know *his* name. Similarly, a certain Fedorov is mentioned, though we do not know who he is. In other words, from the outset Trifonov relates the heroine's world in her terms, through her eyes. Unlike the previous Moscow stories, this is not only memory, but consciousness, bringing to life a whole subjective world. It is the author's first deliberate attempt at 'stream of consciousness' writing.

Still within the first two pages, further details emerge. We learn of her sixteen-year-old daughter Irishka, of the troubled nature of her marriage (for example, the clink of the metal alarm clock on the linen drawer as *he* would switch it off would annoy her and was the cause of much distress), problems at his place of work. We also learn that *his* mother, Aleksandra Prokof'evna, now lives with her and blames her for her son's death from a heart attack last November at the age of forty-two.

So there are three generations of women sharing the same flat. Only at the end of the second page do we learn that the heroine is called Ol'ga Vasil'evna and her late husband Sergei.

Minor, seemingly banal details from everyday life, such as the recollection of the alarm clock, assume a greater, almost symbolic significance, in the overall structure of life together in a house that resembles I. Grekova's 'ship of widows'. Aleksandra Prokof'evna reproaches Ol'ga for buying pretzels now, as she never used to buy them. She also wants to buy a new, larger TV – she and Sergei had long been saving up for one. Aleksandra Prokof'evna's caustic comment is like a slap in the face: 'Why should you go on denying yourself such a luxury?' (II, 223).

Through Ol'ga Vasil'evna's memories we are introduced to other characters, such as Sergei's aunt Vera Prokof'evna (i.e. his mother's sister) and her daughter, his cousin, Tamara. We learn that before marrying her Sergei had relationships with other women; and that she had earlier consorted with Vlad and Gendlin. In other words, as in *Dolgoe proshchanie*, we are introduced to the past of the major characters, and the circumstances that have made them what they are in the present. Her mother very much wanted her to marry Vlad, and likened him to Pierre Bezukhov. In a startling switch to the present, we learn that this Vlad is now a university teacher, head of his section, with three children. Yet all those years ago Vlad and Sergei went with Ol'ga and her friend Rita to Gagry on the Black Sea for their summer holiday, young people just out of university and full of verve and energy. Vlad was devastated when Ol'ga fell for Sergei. Rita, likewise, was not too happy, with her eye on Sergei, and accused her friend of 'being selfish'. (In this story the word 'egoism' is consistently used as a euphemism for people's failure to attempt to understand one another.) These recollections are related in rapid-fire succession, suggesting Ol'ga's own thought processes, without chronology or logical succession, but with juxtaposition of past and present, and incidental characters, such as the tennis coach Otto Ivanovich. In an amusing digression he takes a fancy to Ol'ga in Gagry and offers her lessons free of charge (although we are led to believe that he would have expected payment in kind). Such characters appear and then disappear, as her memories move on.

Ol'ga's father died when she was six, and her mother then married Georgii Maksimovich, an artist seventeen years her senior (when Sergei appeared on the scene she was forty-three and he sixty). If Sergei and Vlad are compared in terms of their material success (or, in Sergei's case, lack of it), the contrast between Sergei and Georgii Maksimovich is an internal one. Georgii Maksimovich was trained before the Revolution, studied in Paris and personally knew Chagall and Modigliani. In his youth he was known as the 'Russian Van Gogh', but on his return to the USSR he was 're-educated', and was forced to earn a living sketching slogans and posters. After the War he was recognized once more, but now he is a sad, pathetic figure who is often ill: a broken man, who survived only through compromise and betraying his art. (At his funeral near the end of the work we are told that he destroyed his best work in the 1930s.)[24] A contrast to him is Vasin, another artist who lives with his wife Zika in the same artists' house as Ol'ga's mother and Georgii Maksimovich. Vasin earns his living by painting official portraits, and destroys himself at the same time through drinking. Nevertheless he is a real artist who only comes alive when he paints, he gives it all his energy, but he also has an elemental joy of life similar to Sergei. The picture Ol'ga Vasil'evna gives of her husband is equivocal: he is a drunkard and womanizer, infuriatingly selfish (*egoist*) and totally self-centred. But he is immersed in his studies, which he pursues with great personal integrity and self-belief. It is as if Ol'ga is herself trying to weigh up the good and bad points about her husband, to arrive at a complete picture of the man she has lost.

Ol'ga's narrative, then, is so far about their married life. We do not yet know much about Sergei, except of the coldness between him and Georgii Maksimovich when they first meet. We know in passing that Sergei's mother was a political commissar during the Civil War, and that his father died in the early months of the Second World War. With time Irishka is born (Ol'ga has had several abortions since then), the couple move out of her mother's flat and on to Shabolovka, where his mother lives. Sergei works for seven years in a museum, then enrols in an institute. The names of Klimuk and Kislovskii crop up, but at the moment for the reader are just names without faces or significance. The passage of time affects the careers of both Ol'ga and Sergei: Ol'ga begins her professional life as a schoolteacher, then she becomes a senior researcher at a research institute, and then head of a laboratory; Sergei (by now we know he is a historian) gets nowhere with his proposed book on Moscow in 1918, despite numerous phone calls, meetings and establishing acquaintances. Other colleagues, such as Klimuk, rise up the career ladder and are successful, while Sergei changes the subject of his thesis to the 1917 February Revolution and the Tsarist secret police.

Let us return though, to *byt*. On the nature of marriage Ol'ga Vasil'evna serves as a mouthpiece for the author's own experience: 'Each marriage is not a union of two people, as is commonly thought, but the union or fusion of two clans, two worlds. Each marriage consists of two worlds. Two systems meet in the cosmos, and they fuse together, for good, till death' (II, 246). Such a statement is based on Trifonov's own profound and mixed experience of married life. Indeed, Oklianskii considers Lena and Rita in *Obmen* and *Predvaritel'nye itogi* to be images of women based on his first wife.[25] Ol'ga in *Drugaia zhizn'* is based on Trifonov's second wife, Alla Pastukhova, to whom the work is dedicated. Ol'ga and Sergei Troitskii were married for seventeen years, and Sergei's recent premature death, at the age of forty-two, gives her an opportunity to survey the years of their life together, a difficult and often acrimonious life.

The temptation to compromise is aptly illustrated at a meeting Sergei attends at his *dacha* in Vasil'kovo. The purpose of this meeting is ostensibly to discuss Sergei's proposed trip to Paris to consult materials associated with the Tsarist secret police and the Russian emigration. Sergei and Ol'ga are there, as are Klimuk and his wife Mara, as well as Klimuk's superior Kislovskii with a young girl dripping in silver jewelry who is obviously his mistress. It becomes clear, though, that Klimuk is using Sergei and Ol'ga Vasil'evna to provide a bed for Kislovskii and his girl (neither of whom were invited), and is furious when Sergei refuses. Needless to say, the Paris trip later falls through. Sergei also later refuses to help Kislovskii by handing over materials the latter needs for his doctoral dissertation.

The *dacha*, as we have seen, is in Trifonov a metaphor for purity and integrity. It is against this background that Sergei refuses to compromise, both his views on history, but also his personal values. As he says later: 'I suddenly realized that I was faced with a trade-off. Our little *dacha* was something to be used in the deals he was arranging ... I suddenly felt that I was one of the traders, and was taking part in some long and tedious sell-off. I felt sick, and turned them down' (II, 288–9). It is here also that much fun is poked at Klimuk's pomposity. He and Sergei studied together, and Klimuk is still remembered as a poor, underfed student addressed by his friends as 'Gesha'. Subsequently Klimuk is further humbled by Ol'ga Vasil'evna's play on his Christian name and patronymic: Gennadii Vital'evich becomes reduced to its bare essentials: Genital'ich.

Klimuk is the 'academic secretary' of the faculty. He succeeded Fedia Praskukhin, a friend from his and Sergei's student days who was a much more affable personality and more sympathetic to Sergei than Klimuk. Fedia had been of assistance to Sergei in changing the topic of his thesis, but was killed in a car crash seven years previously. Klimuk was travelling with him, but he survived. Klimuk had asked Sergei to break the news to Luiza, Fedia's widow, and this he did. This act of courage, and friendship, by Sergei serves to intensify Klimuk's subsequent betrayal, for Klimuk occupies Fedia's post almost immediately, and it is with his appointment that Sergei's troubles begin. But Klimuk is not all bad: he arranges money to be sent to Luiza, as well as flowers and presents for New Year and birthdays.

Troitskii rejects money for his Paris trip offered by Georgii Maksimovich. He is a maximalist who refuses to destroy his work, unlike Georgii Maksimovich, or even to start again. His interest in history is not just professional, it is a passion which consumes him, at times almost drives him mad. He is forever searching out details, no matter how minor or seemingly irrelevant, in order to obtain as full a picture of the time as possible. He works in archives from morning till night, has filled thirty-six notebooks with facts about the Moscow *okhrana*, the pre-revolutionary secret police, but, like Rebrov in his early days, he is unable to finish anything, and his thesis is rejected at the discussion stage. However, he refuses to compromise by handing over valuable material to the careerist Kislovskii. Troitskii seeks historical truth, and his honest approach to history is diametrically opposed to the Party-minded hack Klimuk, who insists that 'historical expediency' is 'the only strong thread worth holding on to'. To Troitskii this 'expediency' is 'diffuse, crafty, like a bog', and he retorts: 'I wonder who will determine what is expedient and what isn't? The academic council perhaps, by a majority of votes' (II, 287). Troitskii's caustic remark is an undisguised attack on the Marxist – Leninist view that history can be tailored to suit the prevailing ideology. Troitskii can have no future in resisting and criticizing the official ethos so brazenly.

Troitskii also researches his own past, in particular his father's family, when he discovers that his father was active during the Revolution in examining the files of the Tsarist police to uncover informers and spies, and then worked in the Commissariat of Enlightenment under Lunacharskii. Trifonov invests Troitskii with his own passion for studying his father's career. Significantly, both of them lost their fathers at an early age. Furthermore, Troitskii knows that further back in the past his ancestors included runaway serfs and schismatics. Revolt, indeed, seems to be in his blood. Troitskii determinedly integrates his own personal life, his own lineage with his professional life. Troitskii is the latest in a line of major characters stretching from Belov and Koryshev through to Rebrov who serve as the author's *alter ego*.

Beneath the surface of intrigue and betrayal, the work is about history, and the various interpretations and meanings that can be put on it. Ol'ga Vasil'evna has a rather simplistic view of history:

What could be simpler than what has already gone before? Every branch of science is concerned with movement forward, building the new, creating something that has no precedent, and only Serezha's interest – history – reconstructs the old, recreates the past. History was to Ol'ga Vasil'evna a long, endless queue in which epochs, states, great men, kings, military leaders and revolutionaries stood in line one after another, and the task of the historian was something akin to that of the policeman who, on première days, comes to the box-office of the Progress cinema and keeps order: to make sure that epochs and states did not get mixed up and change places, that great men did not rush to the front, did not get into arguments and did not try to get their tickets to immortality out of turn... (II, 297)

Hers is the positivist, Marxist-Leninist approach which deems all questions of history solvable by rational means, and only the future worthy of discussion.

Sergei's view was different. He, like his creator, saw the individual as the centre of history, his personality and his relationships with others as the most important element in historical progress. Sergei looked for 'threads, connecting the past with the even remoter past and the future', which his widow goes on to elucidate:

Man is the thread stretching through time, that most sensitive nerve of history, which you can tease out and separate and use to ascertain a great deal. Man, he would say, will never be reconciled with death because he has within him a sense that the thread of which he is a part is endless. It wasn't God who rewarded man with immortality and not religion which instilled in him the idea, but this encoded sense passed on through genes that he is a part of infinity... (II, 300)

Eremina and Piskunov note that 'Sergei cannot be satisfied with indifferent abstractions, he yearns for a personal attachment to history... All of Sergei's efforts are concentrated on debunking the fatalist acceptance of the historical process and overcoming history's estrangement from people.' Geoffrey Hosking is more forthright when he says that Sergei 'implicitly rejected the simplified notions of progress, causality, historical expediency and class struggle obligatory in his Institute'.[26]

Troitskii goes on to explain to his wife in more detail his theory of history, as they lie in bed in the *dacha*, one night:

'After all, nothing is broken off and then disappears ... There is no such thing as a complete break! Do you see? There has to be something afterwards, it can't be otherwise, that much is clear ... You probably think I've gone off my head, don't you? But you know my idea: the thread, passing through generations ... If it is possible to dig down and go back, then it is possible to find the thread that leads into the future ... ' (II, 313–14)

Troitskii sees history as a vital and continuing process, a sense of simultaneity beyond rational categories of time. Such a view is irreconcilable with Soviet notions of teleology. For Troitskii, as for Trifonov, the boundaries between past, present and future are not as clear-cut as they are for Ol'ga Vasil'evna, or for Klimuk. History – the measurement of human time – cannot be rationalized to serve as the basis for political legitimacy. To Troitskii political events such as wars, revolutions, uprisings, are not important, they are the mere surface details of man's spiritual and moral development through the centuries. To him each individual carries within himself the 'threads' of history, and is therefore linked in time to those who have gone before him and those who will come after him. The *slitnost'* of urban life that is emphasized in the other Moscow stories is here expanded in temporal terms: not only does everyone in Trifonov's world have his or her own place and role in a specific community, but everyone also has his or her own meaning within the flow of history. But to find out truth and meaning in the past it is necessary 'to dig down and go back'; the task in the conditions of Soviet Russia is too daunting, and Sergei is physically unable to do it.

From such an overview of human progress Trifonov returns us to the human mind, its powers and its weaknesses. Sergei and Ol'ga are at Luiza's six years after Fedia's death (one year before Sergei's death), along with the Klimuks and other friends of Fedia. A relatively mild discussion of the powers of the academic secretary results in a furious row in which Sergei accuses Klimuk of being a mediocrity and Klimuk accuses Sergei of being envious of the success of others. Then the Klimuks leave, as do most of the other guests from the institute, and the conversation turns to parapsychology and Dar'ia Marmedovna, a gifted medium.

Ol'ga Vasil'evna suspects a threat from Dar'ia Marmedovna, and although there is no direct evidence of an affair with Sergei, it is this character who introduces him to parapsychology. Parapsychology provides a link with the past, and at a seance the voice of Pobedonostsev, the Procurator of the Holy Synod during the reign of Tsar Aleksandr III, is heard to speak. A link is also established with the sixteenth-century Swiss Franciscan monk Arnulf, the Spanish Inquisitor Torquemada and Aleksandr Herzen. Sergei becomes increasingly fascinated by the seeming ability to enter into direct contact with the past, which offers him the perfect opportunity to put his theory of history as beyond reason into practice. Parapsychology can not only unite personalities from different historical epochs on a non-material level of existence, but also allows people to understand themselves in the here-and-now as the author, in a rare textual intrusion, himself declares:

We are surprised because we don't know why we don't understand each other, or why others don't understand us. That's where all the trouble comes from, we think. Oh, if only others understood us! There wouldn't be any quarrels or wars... Parapsychology is a dreamy attempt to get inside someone else, to give oneself to another, to cure oneself through understanding, it's a song that goes absurdly on and on... But where do we poor people run to, trying to understand others, when we don't even understand ourselves? Good God, we have to be able to understand ourselves to start with! But no, we haven't the strength, we haven't the time, or maybe we haven't enough intelligence or courage... (II, 356).

This is Trifonov's final statement on the potential for good inside man, given the peculiar circumstances of everyday life and the historical experience of the Soviet Union. Truth and responsibility are attained by Ol'ga, as with Gennadii Sergeevich, through human contact and emotion; that is, by confronting her pain and feeling of guilt, she can, like him, pass through her own purgatory and look forward to a better life in the future. Sergei, on the other hand, strives toward his concept of truth in his own way, by searching through the past, looking for truth in historical documents, and for 'links' and 'threads' through the centuries to make the present explicable.

Wisely, if one considers the vigilance of the censorship apparatus in the mid-1970s, the author resorts to several caveats. We must not forget that the whole of the narrative in which Troitskii features is recounted by his widow, and is therefore coloured by her views and prejudices. She speaks in comfortingly orthodox terms. For her 'everything begins and ends with chemistry. The universe and beyond contains nothing but formulae' (II, 300). Troitskii and Trifonov, however, assert that nothing disappears without trace, implying that there is a level of existence beyond the material.[27]

At the heart of all the intrigues and relationships Ol'ga Vasil'evna resurrects in her memory is the very stuff of *byt*: queuing in a shop, observing the surliness of the staff and which goods are and are not available. There are also the arguments that are part and parcel of domestic life in a shared flat, resulting in a poisoned atmosphere at home, reconciliation, tears and headaches. *Byt* is not mere background or setting, but the very fabric of life which has to be faced and overcome every hour and every day.

A contrast to the unhappy or grasping urban couples is the couple who own Sergei's *dacha*, Aunt Pasha and Ivan Panteleimonovich, simple and unassuming rural types. The generation gap, though, is even more pronounced in the countryside than in the towns: their long-haired motor-cycling son Kol'ka is happy only when drunk, and soon lands in prison. Pasha and Ivan Panteleimonovich are reminiscent of Atabaly and Iazgul' in *Predvaritel'nye itogi* in their contentment and innate goodness. There is more town – village contrast when Sergei and Ol'ga Vasil'evna travel to the village of Gorodets to seek out old Koshel'kov, a former Tsarist agent. The village in places still resembles a pre-revolutionary place of poverty and backwardness, but it has urban-like shops and houses, something neither totally urban nor recognizably rural. Koshel'kov's family, however, are recognizably rural, especially the surly grandson Pantiusha, but they are not the types usually found on the idealized pages of 'village prose'.

Pantiusha is fascinated by the clothes these townspeople wear: Sergei's trousers, shoes, watch and sweater, and Ol'ga Vasil'evna's shoes and suede jacket. There is much pent-up frustration here, and after inquiring about their clothes he then threatens Sergei with violence for bothering the old man with questions relating to more than half a century ago. We are left with a picture of a poor, demoralized, drunken, aggressive rural population, envious and suspicious of their urban neighbours, who may as well be from another planet. The rural temperament is indeed unpredictable, for Pantiusha, though drunk, then drives them seven kilometres to the nearest railway stop.

Their conversation on history is worth noting: Pantiusha mocks Sergei's eagerness for the past: 'History, history ... Enough of it. There is one kind of history, we don't need any other.' Sergei responds: 'History is not just mine, it is yours, too, and your grandfather's. It belongs to everyone. For example, your village of Gorodets here is a very old one ... ' (II, 325, 326). Pantiusha's outburst expresses not only resentment, but also the alienation from history felt in the countryside. The 'history' that Sergei speaks of and which he tries to relate to these poor and unresponsive peasants has no relevance for them. They have already suffered enough through 'historical expediency'.

In the end old Koshel'kov can remember very little, certainly not about the February Revolution. All that remain are a few scattered memories about the tailor's shop in which he worked on Petrovka Street, and other shops in the neighbourhood. That is, he can recall details from his immediate everyday environment, but the larger, historically momentous events are of no importance to him. To Sergei the meeting is a success because Koshel'kov is living history, a living link with the past.[28]

Ol'ga Vasil'evna's memories end with Sergei's resignation from the institute to start 'another life'. Klimuk is now deputy director of the institute, and his place as academic secretary has been taken by the rising star Sharipov, only twenty-eight years old but already the author of several books and a candidate of sciences.

Ol'ga's sudden and decisive realization of the truth of her life is in a dream. This is the last time we enter her mind. She, Sergei and Irishka, here twelve years old, are in a forest collecting mushrooms. They get lost and are unable to find the road where the bus stops. Trifonov has described his city as 'a forest', and his city is itself a synecdoche for the interconnectedness of modern life as a whole. Ol'ga muses: 'How can I live in this forest alone?' (II, 358). They stop at a fence where there are four men, one of them suffering from Down's Syndrome, and a woman. They assert that there is no road, that this is a forest. The woman leads them a little way through the forest, up and down some slopes, and then stops before a small bog, which she says is the road. Let us remember that Sergei had earlier said that the 'historical expediency' Klimuk professed was 'a bog'. Here the road through life is also as treacherous as a bog. Ol'ga experiences a 'numb, cold torpor' (II, 359) as she realizes that she had lived by false, treacherous values of 'expediency', and she at last comes to an understanding of her husband. She realizes that the values of the 'bog' had destroyed him.[29] The dream expresses in symbolic and metaphorical terms the deadness of the life she had led with Sergei, and for her 'another life' is about to begin. The dream of the forest is for her a therapy, rather like the desert for Gennadii Sergeevich and Siberia for Rebrov, and offers a way forward. It stands as a crossroads between the unhappiness of the present and the uncertainty of the past, a landmark pointing the way to the future.

The new life she makes for herself brings the work to an end. We are several years on, Irishka is preparing to get married, and Ol'ga herself is involved in what appears to be a platonic relationship with an unnamed married man. They are outside Moscow, at a place called Spasskoe-Lykovo. They climb to the top of a church bell-tower, on top of a hill, where they get a panoramic view of Moscow receding into the distance as evening sets in. Ol'ga is finally out of the forest, she feels no more guilt for the death of Sergei because all around her is 'another life ... as inexhaustible as this cold expanse, as this boundless city fading away in expectation of evening' (II, 360).

On one level this is Trifonov's most pessimistic work, in terms of character typology, and in terms of how a free-thinking individual is defeated by a self-serving and vindictive bureaucracy. Ol'ga recalls her husband dividing people into three categories: the scoundrels, the moderates and the irreproachable. This categorization corresponds well with Trifonov's own depiction of people as either tyrants or victims, or as *neudachniki*, those who fall in the middle ground.[30] Klimuk and Kislovskii undoubtedly belong to the former category, and Sergei and Fedia demonstrate that it is impossible to remain long in the latter. Most other characters go into the middle category, such as Georgii Maksimovich, who survives physically by selling his soul. Furthermore, as in *Studenty* and *Dom na naberezhnoi*, the mediocrities triumph over men of talent and ideas. The tyrant, Klimuk, rises to eminence literally over the dead bodies of his friends.

On the other hand, Ol'ga's final triumph over loss and her feelings of guilt shows an optimistic strain in the novella. She overcomes her past, she assesses and understands the truth of her husband's life, and his passion for historical inquiry, and she is able once more to live a normal life.

A word should be added about the female characters of the Moscow stories. The wives of Dmitriev and Gennadii Sergeevich, and the women who provide a contrast, have already been discussed. All of these women serve as catalysts for male behaviour, and have little other function. They are heroines, in Barbara Heldt's phrase, 'used lavishly in a discourse of male self-definition'.[31] Lialia, too, vacillates between men, and Ol'ga's 'other life' only has meaning when she has a relationship with another man. Moreover, in *Drugaia zhizn'* females outnumber the male characters, although most are lonely and unhappy, like Luiza, Ol'ga and her best friend Faina. Even the teenage Irishka has boyfriend problems (resolved, we assume, by the end of the narrative when she is about to marry). Old Aunt Pasha is a former 'maker of history', an anachronism now ridiculous in her War Communism tunic and trousers as she goes off hiking alone in the countryside. Mara Klimuk is an outward reflection of her husband's inner rottenness: she is fat, greedy, over-bearing, quick to boast about her foreign holidays in Rome, Paris and Nice and always dressed in the latest Western fashions. In all of these stories we learn nothing about the aspirations or hopes of these women other than their longing to be happy. Moreover, happiness equates with being loved by a man. Even when the narrative is recounted from their viewpoint, as with Lialia and Ol'ga, their careers and spiritual development take second place to those of their respective husbands.

The Moscow stories all have much in common with each other: similar motifs, images and symbols recur, and character typology remains consistent as tyrants and 'scoundrels' oppress their victims, and the 'moderates' (another word might be *neudachniki*) try to hold on to their principles and their integrity. Also, each story has an embedded plot. In *Obmen* it is the erosion of revolutionary idealism and the hopes of the thaw; in *Predvaritel'nye itogi* it is the failure of the intelligentsia and its cultural and spiritual traditions to withstand the consumerism of the modern age; *Dolgoe proshchanie* shows the conscious abandonment of integrity and traditional Russian cultural values by the literary intelligentsia; *Drugaia zhizn'* demonstrates the futility of opposing institutionalized conventions and ideology.[32] Taken as a composite whole, the 'cycle' reflects the oppressive social and cultural ethos of the Brezhnev years.

At the same time, however, Trifonov manages to give expression to and develop his vision of the world and human society. In all of these works Trifonov shows in detail the everyday lives and loves of his characters, and the links that bind them to the community, and to the past. Yet each of these novellas has its own temporal dimension on the level of plot. *Obmen* introduces characters with direct involvement in key historical events to develop a family lineage stretching back to the early years of the century. *Predvaritel'nye itogi* contains allusions and references that link the work with the Russian and European literary and spiritual legacy. In *Dolgoe proshchanie* Rebrov becomes interested in historical figures and writers, and attempts to explore the 'soil' of Russian history. Troitskii continues his search, and becomes a victim of the 'historical expediency' he had sought to refute.

In these stories we see the progressive demoralization and eventual destruction of Trifonov's hero: Dmitriev makes his compromise and survives, while Gennadii Sergeevich may just salvage something from the wreckage of his marriage; Rebrov prospers by espousing values he once spurned, while Troitskii dies trying to maintain his integrity. We can see here Trifonov's own increasing disillusion with his society, and so it is no accident that his later works are more interested in the workings of history, the tracing of the malaise to a specific set of historical circumstances peculiar to Russia.

CHAPTER 3

The house on the embankment
(Dom na naberezhnoi)

Dom na naberezhnoi is in many ways Trifonov's best and most satisfying work. It is a return to the territory of *Studenty*, with the denunciation and dismissal of a respected professor in a higher educational institute the pivotal event of the narrative. But there the resemblance ends. Geoffrey Hosking remarks on the two novels:

> The gentle, plush world of the Stalin Prize novel has become bitter, harsh and violent. There are yawning differences in status, power and privilege between the different characters; and the main plot now hangs on intrigues and denunciations. The only feature that the two novels have in common is the meticulous and detailed description of everyday life, of *byt*, as the Russians call it. Even here, there is a great difference: in the first novel, *byt* is the red carpet that leads into the future, its smoothness and attractiveness a proof that it is indeed the highway to 'magnificent prospects'; whereas in the second, *byt* is a viscous fluid, a sticky, invincibly present here-and-now that overwhelms and drowns nearly all the characters.'[1]

But the two novels are not merely different in their approach to rather similar subject-matter; the later novel is not only darker, but considerably more complex in terms of its narrative technique.

It is safe to assume initially that there are three narrative voices: the author's, the narrator's (the 'I' of the text) and the protagonist's. At times these voices blend and are difficult to distinguish from each other, so that, for example, the opening lines of the novel could be spoken by the author or the narrator:

> None of those boys is alive now. Some died during the War, some from disease and others vanished without trace. And a few of them,

although they are still alive, have become different people. And if these different people through some sort of sorcery were to meet those who were now gone, in their cheap fustian shirts and their linen, rubber-soled slippers, they wouldn't know what to talk about. I fear that they would not even guess that they had met themselves. Well, God be with them, if they're so slow-witted! They don't have the time, they fly, swim, are carried along in the stream, their arms flapping, farther and farther, quicker and quicker, the hills recede, the forests thin out and shed their leaves, the sky darkens and the cold approaches, they have to hurry, but have no strength to look back at everything that has come to a stop and is frozen, like a cloud on the edge of the horizon. (II, 363)

The use of the first-person would suggest that this is the narrator's voice, but the seeming omniscience of this voice would suggest someone above and beyond the narrative; that is, the author.

The plot of the novel opens on a stiflingly hot August day in 1972, when Vadim Glebov, a successful middle-aged academic, goes into a furniture shop on the outskirts of Moscow in search of a particular antique desk with which to decorate the cooperative flat he and his family are shortly moving into. There he stumbles across someone from long ago, Levka Shulepnikov, a school friend and fellow student from his days at the Gor'kii Literary Institute. Levka refuses to recognize him, but later that night rings him up, drunk and barely coherent, and verbally abuses him. Glebov is, not surprisingly, taken aback, and the bulk of the remaining narrative is taken up with his recollections of the past. He is bothered by one question: why did Levka fail to recognize him in public?

As the past comes alive again, the narrator expands the narrative purview, and begs other, more fundamental questions. He informs us of events Glebov conveniently cannot recall, and makes the reader aware of another moral dimension to these events. It is the narrator who leads us back into the past, initially to the student days of Levka and Glebov, and then back to their schooldays. The narration then gradually merges with Glebov's consciousness, and we begin to see things either directly through his eyes, or coloured by his feelings, emotions and perceptions.

The narrator, for example, relates the following events. Levka Shulepnikov and his parents (or, more precisely, his mother and stepfather, whose surname he has adopted), move into the house next to Glebov's, the large, multi-storeyed house on the embankment, when both are in the fifth or sixth classes at school (age eleven or twelve). At school Levka is initially disliked for his affluence (symbolized by the leather trousers he wears) and his arrogance. The other boys make an attempt to shame him in the schoolyard by pushing him to the ground and pulling down those 'amazing squeaky trousers' (II, 374). He reacts, however, by firing his foreign-made toy gun, and creating momentary chaos and confusion. After this episode he is treated with more respect, not to say awe. The headmaster reflects the overriding imperatives of the time when he enters the class accompanied by a policeman, intent on finding out who attacked Levka. Later he calls on the rest of the class to denounce those responsible for the attack: 'Courage is not in hiding, but in telling' (II, 375). No-one does.

Glebov's attitude to Levka can be summed up in one word: envy. Glebov's mother works in a local cinema, and through her he offers to get his friends in to see the action film *Goluboi ekspress* that children would not normally be allowed to see. The source of his power in the class lies in his ability to choose anyone he likes to accompany him, be it friends such as Khimius or Morzh, or girls like Dina Kalmykova, who bribes him with the promise of a kiss. Levka momentarily destroys this sense of omnipotence when he invites class-mates back to his flat, and proceeds to show *Goluboi ekspress* on his own cine-projector. Glebov is crushed. He is, though, very impressed by Levka's life-style, and begins to feel ashamed of his own humble domestic circumstances. Glebov's feelings of envy, and his growing desire to have what Levka has, are to remain with him throughout the narrative: even in 1972 he is still governed by the acquisitive urge, with his desire to buy a particular antique desk. In August, and on such a hot day, most people are resting, but Glebov goes in search of furniture.

Glebov's consciousness again merges with the narrator's voice when we approach Glebov's first act of betrayal. The episode of the attack on Levka in the schoolyard is far from dead. Levka's stepfather enters the fray. We are not told his profession, but it is not hard to deduce from elliptical references that he is a secret police official. He often works all night, and sleeps at his place of work. He, too, wants to find the 'bandits'. Levka himself refuses to tell, and is locked all evening in the dark and cockroach-infested bathroom. But he does not inform on any of his class-mates, and overnight is in the eyes of the rest of the class turned from an enemy into a hero.

The culprits are eventually named – by Glebov, several months later. Glebov's uncle, Volodia Burmistrov, is a typesetter, accused of 'wrecking' (although whatever mishap has been caused is probably the result of his drunkenness). Glebov's mother has the idea to ask Shulepnikov senior to intercede on Burmistrov's behalf. Levka's stepfather (whose first names we are not told) uses this pretext to persuade the twelve-year-old Glebov to name the boys who attacked his stepson. What follows is a masterly picture: Glebov's stomach starts to rumble, and he blurts out the names of Medved' and Maniunia as a means of ending his embarrassment. Glebov then tries to justify himself: 'Basically, he acted correctly, and only bad people would be punished. But an unpleasant feeling remained, as if he had betrayed someone, although he had told the honest truth about bad people – and this feeling did not leave Glebov for a long time, probably several days' (II, 398). He fails to mention himself as one of the instigators, and it is left to the narrator to inform us that it was Glebov who came up with the idea in the first place. This is the first example of Glebov's inability, or unwillingness, to remember his own role in unsavoury past events.

Shulepnikov's stepfather indeed seems an omnipotent figure: people who come into his orbit tend to disappear. We learn that Levka's actual father, the one before Shulepnikov, 'died or mysteriously disappeared out of Levka's life' (II, 396). We later discover that he was purged as an Old Bolshevik, but posthumously rehabilitated after Stalin's death. The Bychkov family, especially the fifteen-year-old Min'ka and his younger brother Taran'ka, with whom the Glebovs share their communal flat and who tyrannize not only them but the whole neighbourhood, make the mistake of beating up Levka. The next day they are visited by a man 'dressed in a long leather overcoat' who shoots the dog Abdul, and terrifies the whole of the hitherto mighty Bychkov clan. Then: 'After the death of Abdul the Bychkovs' affairs became shaky and then crashed all at once. Min'ka was arrested for thieving, old Semen Gervasievich collapsed in the middle of the yard and was rushed to hospital, and before long all the other Bychkovs vanished into thin air, as if they had been carried off by the wind' (II, 390). The families of the unfortunate Medved' and Maniunia also disappear: 'Medved''s parents were transferred to another place of work and left Moscow, and Medved' went with them, Maniunia did badly at school, was expelled, ended up in the 'forest school', ran away, got involved with undesirables and sat out the War in a camp as a criminal' (II, 398). The language of Shulepnikov's questions to Vadim are straight from the interrogation room: 'Tell me, Vadim, who was the instigator of the bandits' attack on my son Lev?'; 'This is a group affair, but there must be instigators, organizers. Who are they?' (II, 397).

Shulepnikov senior is not only the representative of a system which encourages twelve-year-old boys to inform on their school-mates, he is its apotheosis. This is Stalin in all but name, the supreme arbiter in a society which divides its citizens into oppressors and victims. This is the physical description of him:

Shulepnikov himself, Levka's step-father, was a somewhat plain, cross-eyed and short man, who spoke quietly and whose face struck Glebov because of its total lack of colour. Such faded, expressionless faces Glebov had never before seen on people. Levka's stepfather walked around in a grey tunic fastened with a thin Caucasian belt embroidered with silver, grey breeches and boots. (II, 396)

The reference to the Caucasian belt reinforces the allusion to Stalin, himself from the Caucasus, and who is in Stalinist fiction depicted wearing a military tunic and boots. Furthermore, the *liftery*, the curt and brazen individuals who guard the lift of the Shulepnikovs' house, are reminiscent of the secret police, determined to know the business of anyone who wants to visit.

They embody perfectly the secretive and self-protective nature of the regime, as well as its insidiousness. There are no secrets they do not know about.

The unnamed *liftery* of the house on the embankment watch people entering 'suspiciously', 'with a vigilant and incorruptible eye' (II, 379), and subject visitors to 'interrogations and re-interrogations ('*doprosy i pereprosy*') (II, 380) – all words and phrases not out of place in the lexicon of the NKVD, Stalin's feared secret police. All the children living in the house, and Glebov who visits them, are afraid of the various *liftery*, with the exception of Levka. Levka alone does not feel threatened.

In the text the house on the embankment is continually referred to as '*Bol'shoi dom*': the large house. The same term is used in everyday Russian to designate the KGB building in Soviet cities, and its use here is hardly coincidental. The house, its guardians and its inhabitants become a metaphor for the Kremlin itself, tightly guarded and whose main inhabitant, like Shulepnikov, works at night and dreams up plots and conspiracies at every turn.

Trifonov is describing the house on Bersenevskaia Embankment that his family lived in before the arrest of Valentin Trifonov, a house reserved for high-ranking government and Party officials. Glebov's home is a communal apartment in a two-storey building where he has lived since birth, 'beside a huge, grey house with a thousand windows that was like a whole city or even country... The grey colossus loomed over the narrow lane, in the mornings blocked out the sun and in the evenings voices from the radio and music from gramophones drifted down from above' (II, 373). This house represents to Glebov the world of the élite, the well-to-do, which he is determined to enter. It is the 'other life', access to which is restricted to a few and guarded jealously, but which promises social success and material riches. Even as a child Glebov feels himself drawn to this world.

Before leaving Glebov's childhood years, though, another character should be mentioned: Anton Ovchinnikov. Anton is the same age as Glebov, and a complete contrast to him. The young Glebov regards him as 'a genius':

Anton was a musician, an admirer of Verdi – he could sing the whole of 'Aida' from memory, from beginning to end – and besides that an artist, the best in the school, particularly noted for drawing historical buildings in water colours and profiles of composers in Indian ink; he was also the author of fantasy novels about the exploration of caves and ancient archaeological sites, and he was also interested in palaeontology, oceanography, geography and, to a lesser extent, minerology. (II, 379)

Anton is exactly what Glebov is not: a person of intense feeling and genuine talent. He displays courage, loyalty and great power of will – also traits lacking in Glebov. He founds a society 'for testing the will', and is the first to subject himself to ordeals such as walking along the thin balcony wall of Sonia Ganchuk's ninth-floor apartment. We learn that Anton is killed during the War. We can see his death as the symbolic demise of the true intelligentsia, while the hacks such as Glebov, and the reprobates such as Levka, survive and prosper.

It is not dificult to see here Trifonov's use of character contrast and juxtaposition: Anton and Glebov are two different types, and Glebov and Levka represent two opposing poles of social status. In time, Levka will slide down the social scale, whereas Glebov climbs ever higher. Trifonov's purpose in drawing the character of Anton is not simply to resurrect a long-dead childhood friend (Anton is clearly based on Lev Fedotov). Rather, Anton's brilliant mind and striving for physical perfection (he, like Lev, practises ju-jitsu, and wears short trousers in winter) show up in stark relief the mediocrity of others around him. More importantly, his courage in doing battle with the thugs of Deriuginskii Lane, despite the injuries he is bound to suffer, provides a moral ideal, a perspective from which to view and judge the future cowardice and opportunism of others, in particular Glebov.[2] Childhood for Glebov is indeed a hateful time, for the ideals and values Anton embodied are lacking in Glebov, the boy known as Vad'ka Baton.

Throughout the narrative Glebov's memories are related in the third person. The 'I', who is nominally separate from the author, represents another consciousness. At times this narrator sounds like Glebov's *alter ego*. Both the narrator and Glebov have a lot in common: both love Sonia, both play the same childhood games, both have the same friends. Perhaps the narrator is Glebov, but as he would have been had he made different moral choices, had he been more like Anton. Anton's ghost is the voice of his conscience. Thus there are two Glebovs in the text: the one who is, and the one who might have been. Indeed, both are present at and witness the same events, including childhood pranks such as the balcony-walking incident, or later, at the Ganchuks' *dacha*, the blossoming romance between Glebov and Sonia. The narrative 'I' seems to be party to Glebov's innermost thoughts, knows intimately Glebov's childhood friends and acquaintances, was involved in all their games and adventures, but clearly disapproves of Glebov and is quick to judge him. The Glebov depicted in the third-person narrative may hate his childhood, but the narrator does not: 'All of childhood was wrapped in a purple cloud of vanity... The soft, juicy, crimson flesh of childhood. You could not compare it with anything else' (II, 390–1). Whatever Glebov thinks, feels or does, the narrator asserts the opposite. It is a dual consciousness, by means of which Trifonov the author can reveal Glebov's soul more clearly, to juxtapose pragmatism with morality, 'expediency' with integrity. By dissecting his main character in this way, Trifonov is able to get to the very core of his main character, to explore the motivation of millions like Glebov who built their careers on Stalinism, regardless of the cost to their moral integrity.

The plot's structure resembles that of *Obmen* and *Predvaritel'nye itogi* in that in all three works the central character recounts events that happened some time ago. In the case of Dmitriev and Gennadii Sergeevich, the only other consciousness in the narrative to provide comment and perspective is that of the author-narrator (who represents the same moral consciousness). The same is true here, except that the narrator, the 'I', actually takes part in the narrative. The 'I' has features common to the author: in particular, he recalls moving out of the house on the embankment following the arrest of his father, and moving with his grandmother into one room in a communal apartment on the outskirts of Moscow. This is in 1938 (seven months after the fall of Madrid). He later tells us that he worked as a fireman in Moscow in the early months of the War, and we later discover that he is a writer working on a book about the 1920s.

We are never in any doubt that the views of the narrator are also those of the author. The narrator, moreover, helps to distance the author from Glebov, to remind the reader of another set of moral imperatives, different from Glebov's. The use of the 'I', of course, is also designed to protect the author from accusations of undue bleakness, for, as with the narrative structure of *Obmen*, the author can reasonably claim that he is recreating reality as his characters perceive it, a valid viewpoint that he as the creator of the work does not necessarily have to share. Furthermore, the author's attitude toward Glebov is clearly reflected in the narrator's judgment. However, as we see from Markov's comments this balancing act did not convince the hawks of the literary establishment.[3]

The story moves on to the autumn of 1947, when Glebov next meets Levka after a break of seven years. Both are now studying at the Gor'kii Literary Institute. Glebov is immediately struck by Levka's American leather jacket: it reminds him of the lifestyle and affluence to which he aspires: 'It was just what he needed: manliness, elegance, a flash of style and practicality. The devil only knows what he wouldn't give for such a thing!' (II, 399). Levka's leather jacket, with its suggestion of the good life, is another indication of Glebov's infatuation with the pursuit of status and rank. It is clearly linked in Glebov's mind with the leather trousers Levka first wore in school, all those years before. Glebov, just as he was when he first made Levka's acquaintance, is fascinated by him. Levka is surrounded by girls, is the owner of a German-made BMW motorcar presented to him by his stepfather, a trophy from the War, and later becomes one of the first people in Moscow to own a TV set. He is fond of telling people of his exploits during the War, which, if he is to be believed, included working undercover in the enemy's rear and training as a secret agent, and of his travels to Istanbul and Vienna. The exotic mystique around him intensifies as he tells of his failed marriage to Maria, an Italian beauty seven years his senior. Levka has not changed since childhood: he is a cheerfully cynical egotist whose main motivation is his own material enrichment. He is the sort of person others of more humble means yearn to get to know.

The house on the embankment has by now lost most of its former inhabitants, and its aura of other-worldly impregnability. Levka's mother has remarried, his new 'father' carries the surname Flavitskii or Fiveiskii. Shulepnikov, Levka's stepfather, is dead, found asphyxiated in his car in a locked garage. Flavitskii-Fiveiskii is from the same organization, however, for he was in charge of the investigation into Shulepnikov's suicide, and this is how he became acquainted with Levka's mother, Alina Fedorovna. Significantly, the house no longer has any lift guardians, the inhabitants now being 'plainer and the conversation not the same' (II, 405).

Glebov can now enter the house more or less at will. However, he does not yet belong, as he realizes when he tries to stroke the dog of a resident of the house. The dog growls and bares its teeth, as if telling him: 'The fact that you are allowed into this house and go up and down in the lift doesn't yet mean that you're one of us' (II, 406). Glebov yearns to be 'one of us', and this ambition determines all his actions. Glebov is now visiting the Ganchuks. Sonia was in the same class at school, and now studies with Glebov at the Literary Institute, where her father is professor of literature. Glebov begins to visit the Ganchuks after six months of study, not to see Sonia, whom he barely has time for, but to ingratiate himself with her father, whose acquaintance he regards as 'extremely valuable' (II, 403). The reader may rail against Glebov's blatant opportunism here, but it would be a mistake to feel excessive sympathy for Ganchuk, for he exploits Glebov in his own way: asking him either to compile a bibliography or move the rubbish across the yard outside. The same calculation applies when, a good two years later, Glebov decides to become Sonia's lover. Glebov, after all, does nothing out of feeling or genuine interest, but merely out of expediency, in order to advance his career.

Professor Nikolai Vasil'evich Ganchuk and his books, the walls lined with bookshelves and the busts of ancient Greek and radical philosophers in his study (compare Kozel'skii's bust of

Schiller), all represent to Glebov the kind of life-style to which he now aspires. Much is made in the text of Glebov's poverty and humble background: he has only one pair of shoes, one shirt, one tie, he is constantly undernourished, his mother is dead and his father is becoming a depressive alcoholic. His ambition to climb out of the gutter and begin 'another life' is justifiable; the means he uses towards his end are not. Ganchuk is a legend, a former Civil War Red Cavalry and Cheka officer, merciless and feared by the enemy, later a political poet and inspired orator. He was personally acquainted with the writers Aleksei Tolstoi and Maksim Gor'kii, the historian Mikhail Pokrovskii, and the Commissar for Enlightenment Anatolii Lunacharskii. He later became celebrated as a committed and furious participant in literary debates:

He could remember in particularly sharp relief all the shifts and upheavals in the literary battles of the 1920s and 1930s. His speech was precise and resolute. 'Here we dealt a blow to the Bespalov group... They were throwbacks and had to be hit hard... We gave them battle ...' Yes, they were really battles, and not disputes. True understanding was worked out in the bloody battle. (II, 404)

Ganchuk has 180 academic publications to his name, his work has been translated into eight European languages, and he is a corresponding member of the Academy of Sciences. Glebov reasons that if some of the greatness of Ganchuk is reflected on him, then he, too, will have eminence thrust upon him.

Nikolai Vasil'evich and Sonia are blind to his opportunism, but Iuliia Mikhailovna, Ganchuk's wife and Sonia's mother, is more astute. She accuses Glebov of exhibiting a 'petty bourgeois' interest in the material wealth of their apartment and *dacha*. Iuliia Mikhailovna is insistent on the 'danger of petty bourgeois elements', blissfully unaware of the glaring 'petty bourgeois' affluence of her own life-style. She more than anyone else is offended by Glebov's inability to commit a personal judgment, and is always trying to pin him down for an opinion, be it on an article recently published, or the dismissal of a colleague and friend. Iuliia Mikhailovna and her sister Ella are of German descent, daughters of a Vienna banker. Kuno

Ivanovich has a similar opinion of Glebov. Kunik, as the Ganchuks affectionately call him, is a junior scholar in Ganchuk's department who, although he has his own apartment, is accepted by the Ganchuks 'almost as a relation'. The old professor uses him as his secretary. Glebov resents Kuno's presence in the flat, and uses the occasion of an evening meal to criticize an article Kuno has recently published. But he criticizes it not from the point of view of content or ideas, but form: it was obvious 'that Russian was not the author's native language' (II, 415).

Glebov is not only trying to eliminate a possible rival for Sonia's hand; he is aware that there is another, more substantial chasm separating them. The editors of the journal in which Kuno's article had appeared had initially insisted on some changes, but Kuno had resisted and in the end triumphed. Such steadfastness and integrity – Kuno in some ways resembles Anton, with the latter's physical frailty and vulnerability – stand in contrast to Glebov's opportunism.

The contrast becomes starker still when Ganchuk comes under attack at the Institute. Kuno Ivanovich has no hesitation in writing an eight-page letter to the editors of a newspaper which has printed the initial attack on Ganchuk, regardless of the danger that he will himself be open to attack. He acts as Glebov's conscience by reminding him of the ethical priorities involved, and of a greater reality:

'Who are you, one wants to ask? A chance witness or a participant? Well, all right, let's leave that, there are reasons, there is another reality... We'll accept that... But now, now what are you going to do? How are you going to live afterwards? Are you going to carry on waiting your chance, as ever? There's no more time. On Thursday will be your execution, Dima. I can see that you don't have the strength to get up and say: "This is not true!" Execution, in other words... That's the way it will be... Sometimes your own silence is your execution.' (II, 473)

Glebov finds that the pressures to commit himself are irresistible, as Ganchuk is himself threatened with dismissal. Iuliia Mikhailovna has already read the signs before Ganchuk or Glebov, with earlier news of the dismissal of Astrug. Astrug is

Ganchuk's colleague and former pupil, denounced and dismissed when Ganchuk was himself on study leave in Prague. Iuliia Mikhailovna senses that Ganchuk's enemies are really aiming for him, and that this is only the first salvo.

Astrug is responsible for teaching Glebov's special course on Dostoevskii, but, we later learn, he also teaches an option on Gor'kii. Gor'kii is regarded as the founder of socialist realism, the fount from whom all positivism flows. Dostoevskii, on the other hand, denounces the rationalism and Godlessness of materialists, and occupies the opposite pole in Russian aesthetics to Gor'kii. In *Studenty* Kozel'skii's book is on Dostoevskii, and in 1950 this is enough to confirm that the old professor is at best out of touch, at worst an ideological reactionary. In *Dom na naberezhnoi* Astrug's course embraces the two extremes of Russian literary thought: the religious impulse and the rationalist argument. In *The Brothers Karamazov* rationalism ultimately leads to patricide, just as atheism is the murder of God. When God the father is dead, 'everything is permitted'. Gor'kii, on the other hand, insists that man's actions are dictated not from within, but by the exigencies of social conditions. The philosophies of Gor'kii and Dostoevskii cannot be reconciled.

Apart from the narrator, Iuliia Mikhailovna is the only character in the novel to see Glebov for the opportunist that he is. It is, though, the narrator, who is in a better position to provide interpretation and meaning, as well as to provide information from beyond Iuliia Mikhailovna's purview about Glebov's past. The narrator's intrusions into the text are often introduced by the phrase 'I remember'. Thus we learn, for example, that Glebov's nickname at school was 'Baton', because once he brought to school a loaf of bread (*baton*) which he shared out amongst his class-mates during a break between lessons (compare the boy Belov's nickname in *Studenty*: *keks*, 'bun'). More fundamentally, the 'I' can pass a qualitative judgment on Glebov's character:

This Vad'ka Baton interested me for a long time as a somewhat enigmatic personality. For some reason many people wanted to be friends with him. He seemed to suit everyone. With some he was like this, and with others he was like that, neither malicious nor kind, and neither very avaricious nor very generous, not quite an octoped, but not an omnivore either, neither cowardly nor brave, and probably not very cunning, but then again not quite a simpleton. He was able to be friends with Levka and Maniunia, although Levka and Maniunia couldn't stand each other. He was on good terms with Anton, visited Khimius and Levka at home and got along with the ruffians of Deriuginskii Lane, who hated the rest of us. He was friends with both Anton Ovchin and Min'ka Byk at the same time! (II, 432)[4]

Once into adult life, this ability to be anonymous, to hide one's own face behind a show of reticence, reaps considerable rewards:

He was a complete nothing sort of person, Vad'ka Baton. But this, as I realized subsequently, is a rare gift: to be nothing. People who have the brilliant ability to be nothing go far. The main point is that those who have dealings with them have no background to work on, and have to fill in the thinking and the sketching of everything dictated to them by their own fears and desires. These nothing people are always lucky in life. (II, 433)

There can be no doubt that this is the impression of Glebov the author wants the reader to have, for events as they are depicted serve only to confirm the narrator's words.

This narrator is also perfectly placed to contrast Glebov with others from within his family. His cousin Klavdiia, daughter of the aforementioned Burmistrov, condemns her own mother for moving in with Vadim's father after the death of his wife, whereas Vadim himself refuses to pass a moral judgment. Vadim senses 'a different structure, something alien to the family' when he talks to her, for she is astonished that he can accept such seeming amorality with such 'indifference' (II, 439). Klavdiia condemns her mother for destroying the family before the War, for it was due to her, she asserts, that Vadim's mother died. Klavdiia's moral maximalism is clearly contrasted with Glebov's absence of any value judgments whatsoever.

Crucially, the narrative 'I' is present at the decisive moment which determines Glebov's betrayal of Ganchuk. Glebov is approaching the end of his undergraduate studies, and is working on his Final Year diploma project when he is suddenly called in to the office of the recently appointed academic dean,

Druziaev. This Druziaev would seem singularly out of place in any normal academic institution: until recently a military prosecutor, he is dressed in an officer's tunic but with civilian trousers half-concealing creaking boots. But for the sadness in his eyes, reflecting some human frailty, he is clearly linked with Shulepnikov's first stepfather, the all-powerful secret policeman. Druziaev's protégé is the postgraduate Shireiko who, significantly, has replaced Astrug as the teacher of the course on Gor'kii (but not Dostoevskii). Shireiko's star is rising fast, and he has prepared an article for publication denouncing Ganchuk's 'unprincipledness'. As Shireiko is himself so vicious and cynical, this accusation is, to say the least, highly ironic. But the 'I' is also present, and it is he who relates the details of the three-cornered conversation. It is also he who gives it a wider temporal perspective. If only, he declares, Glebov knew where this would eventually lead to. If only Druziaev himself knew that within two years he would be seriously ill following a stroke, and in three would be dead: 'Druziaev disappeared as suddenly as he appeared. And he appeared as if merely to fulfil a speedy mission. He came, he fulfilled, he vanished' (II, 445). Such a breadth of vision is obviously not accessible to Glebov, but belongs to the author.[5]

It is the 'I' of the narrative that formulates the nature of Glebov's dilemma. Glebov comes to resemble the hero-knight (*bogatyr'*) in the famous painting by Vaznetsov, astride his horse at the crossroads, wondering which path to take: he is 'one of those who doesn't decide anything himself, but leaves the horse to make the decision' (II, 452).

Druziaev's observation on Ganchuk's nepotism is, however, relevant: both he and his wife work in the same faculty, and Glebov, about to become their son-in-law, is preparing to enter postgraduate research, with Ganchuk the supervisor of his diploma project. Glebov, whose first instinct is self-preservation, heaves a sigh of relief: 'There was even a little bit of defiance in his manner, because he realized that he was not the real target' (II, 445). Druziaev makes it clear to Glebov that he must have someone other than Ganchuk as his supervisor. To Glebov this all seems perfectly straightforward; he appears not to suspect that a student's rejection of a prospective supervisor is merely a pretext, the first stage in the dismissal of an academic. Neither the narrator nor the author indicate that Glebov is aware of the darker reality.

Druziaev is to Glebov as Porfirii Ivanovich is to Raskol'nikov in *Crime and Punishment*: he prods him into doing what his inner self wills. Glebov will betray Ganchuk. Levka also puts into words what Glebov himself inwardly understands: '"You don't need Ganchuk at all!"' (II, 452). Another illustration of how others articulate Glebov's subconscious is at a party Sonia holds. An unnamed guest brings to Glebov's consciousness the fact that he is, to all intents and purposes, courting Sonia. The thought had previously not entered his head.

Druziaev, Shireiko and Dorodnov, the deputy director of the Institute – all are representative of the type who not only prospers under Stalinism, but who is one of its prime movers; just like Shulepnikov, Levka's powerful stepfather, they decide the fate of others. Druziaev is in awe and more than a little afraid of Shireiko, but both are the puppets of Dorodnov (as with Astrug, we never actually meet Dorodnov in the narrative). Levka, too, is part of this scheme: he can accommodate himself to anyone. Cynical and totally self-centred, Levka recognizes these qualities as the dominant feature of the times, the impulses that motivate actions. It is no accident that he gets on well with Shireiko. These are the types who surround Glebov, who prompt him into moral betrayal, working on Glebov's own insecurity, envy and greed. *Dom na naberezhnoi* is therefore not only a dissection of the psychological pressures of Stalinism, but also a picture of personal weakness when faced with implacable, relentless forces.

If the Shulepnikovs, Dorodnovs, Shireikos and Druziaevs of this world are the oppressors, the tyrants who toy with the destinies of others, then the victims are above all the Ganchuks. Iuliia Mikhailovna, we learn, is also under attack, for as a foreigner, she is a clear target for the xenophobic 'anti-cosmopolitan' campaign in Soviet academic life of the late 1940s. The fall of the Ganchuks is an ironic development, because Ganchuk himself was a committed fighter for the new world back in the Civil War and then in the literary and cultural debates of the 1920s. He is fond of relating stories of his own fearsome reputation in the Civil War, of how he never flinched from killing enemies and ridding Russian soil of all 'bourgeois' traces. Ganchuk, once the maker of history, becomes its victim – just like Trifonov's own father. Similarly ironic is the attack on Iuliia Mikhailovna, an ardent advocate of the international socialist brotherhood, now persecuted for her nationality.

Characteristically, Glebov fails to discuss his conversation with Druziaev and Shireiko with Ganchuk, but Sonia is astonished that he did not refuse outright to have anything to do with their scheme; she can see that it is 'an ambush' (II, 447). Glebov says nothing to her parents about what he is asked to do, and it is Sonia who explains it to them, sweetening the pill with news that she and Glebov are to marry. Glebov by his actions betrays not only his professor and would-be supervisor, but Sonia, the girl he thinks he loves and wants to marry. Sonia is ultra-sensitive to the pain of others, even those who commit evil deeds. Glebov reflects that 'the main feature in this character was her pained and undiscriminating pity for others ... Her first reaction to every collision with life and with people was to feel pity' (II, 412). She tells Glebov again and again that he is 'absolutely free' in his actions. Again, it is the Mephisthophelean Levka who tells Glebov his own innermost thoughts: that he will not marry her.[6]

The reference to Mephistopheles is not frivolous, for Trifonov is using literary allusions here, as in previous works, to expand the plot's thematic parameters. Apart from the Dostoevskii – Gor'kii debate, Trifonov also alludes to Bulgakov and Goethe. Bulgakov's *The Master and Margarita* has as its epigraph a quotation from Goethe's *Faust*:

> 'Nun gut, wer bist du denn?
> Ein Teil von jener Kraft,
> Die stets das Böse will und stets das Gute schafft.'[7]

The Master and Margarita combines the story of the Crucifixion of Christ on the Bald Hill with a supernatural tale of witches and devils at work in contemporary Moscow. Here Levka accuses his mother of being a 'witch': 'Why do I need witches? On the Bald Hill? Even if my mother is one of them, I don't want them! I send them all to the devil, enough, I'm leaving!' (II, 467). Furthermore, Bulgakov's novel maintains that the worst sin is that of moral cowardice, and Glebov's moral cowardice is at the heart of Trifonov's work. Furthermore, Glebov, like Faust, feels that he is not in control of his own will. But this is not so: Glebov wills everything that happens to him, he makes his decisions, despite his protestations of being the instrument of impersonal forces. It is not enough to blame 'the times', he must carry moral responsibility for his actions. Trifonov again uses literary allusions to suggest a totality, *slitnost'*, of experience: social, cultural and moral.

Oklianskii juxtaposes Pavel Evgrafovich in *Starik* and Glebov: both ask the eternal Russian question 'who is to blame', and both reply: 'the times'. In other words, *everyone* is to blame, and therefore *no-one*. The abnegation of moral responsibility thus eases the conscience.[8] The generation that lived through Stalinism and its horrors is collectively responsible for the evils, current and subsequent, of this society.

Glebov not only acquiesces in Ganchuk's destruction; he actively provides ammunition for the enemy. He acts as the spy in the household for Druziaev and Shireiko, relating details of the interior of Ganchuk's study to them, right down to the busts of philosophers adorning it. He is required to make a speech denouncing Ganchuk, and is unable to refuse. Ganchuk's supporters also demand that he speak up, but in favour of the old professor. Glebov's appearance at the meeting is 'more than necessary', for both sides. His initial inability to take a stand now has the inevitable consequence: both sides think that he is with them.

The evening before the crucial meeting of the academic council Glebov weighs up the four options available to him: defend Ganchuk, and throw away his chance of the Griboedov fellowship and any possibility of further study, and with it rapid social advancement; attack Ganchuk, lose Sonia, but gain a career; say nothing, and earn the opprobrium of both sides; not turn up, through some accident. He is saved by a morbid piece of luck: his grandmother Nila, who has been living in the Glebovs' flat, and has been ill for some time, dies in the night. Glebov attends the funeral and is unable to get to the meeting on Thursday at which Ganchuk is denounced and dismissed.

The death of Nila is not without some symbolic significance. Nila is a long-suffering and totally selfless old woman who has given the Glebovs years of her life helping out in the household. She resembles Niura in *Predvaritel'nye itogi*. She recalls to Glebov her own childhood seventy years before, how she enjoyed travelling from Moscow into the village during the summer months. She represents a passive innocence whose origins stretch back into the past, into a Russia that disappeared in 1917. She embodies, moreover, a moral consciousness that dies the night before Glebov must decide which road to take. Nila's death foreshadows that of Sonia: such devotion and innocence of spirit have no place in this world.

Ganchuk's dismissal has been engineered by Dorodnov, the deputy director of the Institute. This conflict is a mirror image of that between Kozel'skii and Sizov in Trifonov's earlier novel, just as the relationship between Levka and Glebov corresponds to that between Belov and Palavin. Let us not forget that Kozel'skii wrote a book about Dostoevskii. But Dorodnov is a far cry from the ideologically irreproachable Sizov: he was a fellow-traveller in the 1920s, not a member of the Party, who then, in Ganchuk's phrase 'changed his colours' (II, 460). Ganchuk sees his animosity as personal, a desire to exact revenge. This is exactly the same feeling that Kozel'skii senses is behind Sizov's actions in *Studenty*. Furthermore, we are never actually introduced to Dorodnov, he remains a shadowy figure in the background, orchestrating events. However, the author-narrator informs us of future developments, in particular that Dorodnov was to be dismissed himself a few years later.

Ganchuk, though, is not a figure to be necessarily pitied. He is perceived by others as demagogic and authoritarian in his running of the department, and clinging to the dogma of twenty years ago ('vulgar sociology') in his critical appraisals of writers. Thus, his own persecution and downfall he explains in ideological terms, as he says to Glebov: 'Do you know where the mistake was? In the fact that in 1927 we spared Dorodnov. He should have been finished off.' Glebov is soothed by these words, for they tell him that he is not to blame: 'he realized that the old man was still the same as ever. This meant that everything that had happened was correct' (II, 489). In other words, Ganchuk can only see his downfall within the terms of his own dogma, as the result of a political struggle. This is the only outcome Ganchuk, with his life's experience and ideological fervour, can countenance. Whereas his defeat affects his external status, it does not change his inner convictions, his view of the world.

Yet immediately before this statement he had asserted the opposite to Glebov. There is here an instant of enlightenment, the dawning of an awareness of a deeper struggle:

There was a strange, vague, unstructured conversation. For some reason about Dostoevskii. Ganchuk said that he had underestimated Dostoevskii, that Aleksei Maksimych [Gor'kii] was wrong and a new understanding was needed. Now he had a lot of free time and would work on this. Iuliia Mikhailovna looked at her husband with sad and passionate attention. He said something like this: what tormented Dostoevskii – the theory of 'everything is permitted', if there was nothing but a dark room with spiders – exists to this day in a trivial, everyday form. All problems have become transformed to the most pathetic degree, but they still exist. Today's Raskol'nikovs do not axe old money-lenders to death, but still torment themselves as to whether they should cross the same dividing line. And after all, is there essentially a difference between an axe or something else? Between killing someone and elbowing them aside in order to create some more space? Raskol'nikov, after all, did not kill for the sake of world harmony, but for himself, to save his old mother, rescue his sister and then for himself, for himself, for goodness sake, somehow, somewhere in this world... (II, 488)

The battle of good and evil is referred by Ganchuk in Bulgakovian terms of light and dark. While Glebov is in the professor's flat, waiting to see him, Iuliia Mikhailovna brings a lamp into the room, claiming it is too dark: '"Mehr licht", as Goethe said before his death' (II, 486), she explains. In later life we learn that Sonia, who is mentally ill, cannot stand the light, and wants all the time to be in darkness. It presumably reminds her of the 'dark room with spiders' of Glebov's soul, where 'everything is permitted'.

Ganchuk concludes his momentary insight by further cementing the link between Glebov and Raskol'nikov:

'You, Dima, why should you come here? This is absolutely inexplicable from the point of view of formal logic. But there is, perhaps, another way to explain it... There is here, perhaps, a metaphysical explanation. Do you remember how Raskol'nikov was always drawn back to that house... But no, that's not it!' With a precise professor's gesture he cut short his own presupposition. 'Then everything was much clearer and simpler, for there was an obvious social conflict. But now man does not fully realize what he is creating... Therefore it is an argument with oneself... He convinces himself... The conflict goes into the heart of man, that's what is happening...' (II, 489)

Ganchuk has a brief insight into broader truths, but he cannot accept that the values by which he had lived are inadequate for an understanding of human actions. The Gor'kii-Dostoevskii debate touches on the very foundations of the Soviet state, of Marxist-Leninist philosophy.[9] The Goethe-Bulgakov-Dostoevskii-Gor'kii literary axis of the work is not mere decoration. Trifonov alludes to the darkness of the soul created by the victory of Godlessness, whose rational apotheosis is the Stalinist state.

Glebov in the 1970s blames 'the times', just as Ganchuk before him relies on external criteria for meaning. It is left to the narrator, in the work's final pages, to fill in the gaps in Glebov's memories. Glebov does not remember, for example, the second meeting of the academic council called to discuss the Ganchuk case, where he did make a speech, and where he did denounce the old professor. He does not remember a chance meeting in a snow-bound Moscow street with Kuno Ivanovich in the mid-1950s. We are not told what Kuno said, but Glebov pushed him to the ground and almost throttled him. He tries to forget the ashen face of Iuliia Mikhailovna after her meeting with Druziaev at which she was informed of her dismissal. He tries to forget meeting Ganchuk again some years later, when only he among those present at an editorial conference can detect the venom in the old man's words. And, finally, he tries to forget meeting Sonia, again accidentally, many years later in a cafe in Riga. All of these chance meetings with the people whose faith, trust and even love he had betrayed come back to haunt him, like the prickings of conscience. But, the narrator, armed with the author's breadth of vision, goes on: 'Perhaps all of this was not quite like that, because he tried not to remember. And what he could not remember ceased to exist. This had never taken place' (II, 483). Glebov did not know that 'he was living a life that never happened' (II, 484).

What he does remember from that time are the ridiculous minor details: half an hour after the meeting which had denounced him, Glebov recalls seeing Ganchuk in a confectioner's shop, tucking into a 'Napoleon' cream cake with evident zeal. This episode corresponds to his rumbling stomach at the time of his first denunciation to the older Shulepnikov. In both cases he does not remember his own ignominious behaviour, merely the banal, the trivial.

Glebov cannot escape his past, no matter how he tries. The unexpected meeting with Levka and his phone call later that night is one such example; another is almost two years later, April 1974, when he meets Alina Fedorovna on a train bound for Paris. He is on his way to an international congress, she to visit relatives of her sister, who left Russia half a century before. The last we see of Glebov in the novel, when he is unpacking his suitcase in a poorly lit hotel room off the Place Pigalle, and putting his toiletry items beneath the mirror in the bathroom, is a suitable way to leave him: he is still surrounded by darkness, and still preoccupied with banalities. As Kuno Ivanovich predicted all those years before, Glebov has 'executed' himself, doomed himself to a life without memory, without truth.

The plot ends, as it begins, with Levka Shulepnikov, now calling himself Prokhorov, after his real father, the purged Old Bolshevik. Ganchuk is still alive, living alone in a one-room apartment, with Iuliia Mikhailovna and Sonia both dead. He is now aged eighty-six, concerned only with TV programmes or articles in popular science magazines. The narrator, working on a book about the 1920s, seeks him out in order to record the old man's memories of that time, but finds out very little: 'And the point was not that the old man's memory was weak. He didn't want to remember. It held no interest for him. Everything that had taken place then was much more interesting to me than to him' (II, 492).

Ganchuk and the narrator go to the crematorium where Sonia is buried, on the anniversary of her death. They are at first refused admittance by the sullen watchman, who turns out to be Levka, preparing to close for the night. The narrator recognizes him. As they seek out Sonia's headstone in the darkness, the narrator muses that 'there is nothing more terrible than a dead death' (II, 493). He refers not only to the gloom-shrouded crematorium, but also to a life without memory, like that of Glebov and Ganchuk. Ganchuk rushes home from the crematorium to catch a TV programme: as with Glebov, the banality and relative easy living of the present are preferable to reliving an uncomfortable and confusing past. The author leaves both Ganchuk and the narrator to return briefly to Levka on his way home, still wearing his leather jacket from the late 1940s, staring out of the trolleybus window at his former home, the house on the embankment, and wondering whether life will bring him any further changes in fortune.

The novel thus achieves a symmetry of structure: the plot begins and ends with Levka Shulepnikov-Prokhorov, caught in poses that differ so drastically from each other. The text, though, begins and ends with statements on the nature of time that must belong to the author. We are left with an image of desolation, a crematorium that is no longer open, whose only living inhabitants are the crows, tended by a man who has lost his former power, and visited by two characters who have seen their fair share of change and suffering in the past quarter of a century. Levka soon lost his affluence as a result of the misdemeanours of his second stepfather, became a drunkard and inexorably slid down the social ladder, until he now tends a place of death and sorrow. Ganchuk tries to forget his past life, and lives only for the banalities of the present. The narrator represents the childhood of Glebov and the author, surveying the wreckage of the present from the vantage point of the past.

As Levka drives past his old home, he hopes that maybe there will be another change in his life. The author thus stands above his characters, not explicitly judging them, but not condoning them either: simply he indicates that for them time has not stopped, life goes on, bringing with it the possibility of fresh changes.[10]

In purely literary terms *Dom na naberezhnoi* is Trifonov's most successful work, combining recollections, literary allusions and multiple narrative viewpoints. To compromise is to side with the devils and sell your soul. Moral cowardice leads to a 'living death', where the past is forgotten. In terms of subject-matter, the work has much in common with other works, not least, of course, *Studenty*. It does not have the temporal scope of the historical novels, but it delves deeper into the soul of man, to explore the nature of betrayal and moral capitulation. The novel is an anatomy of Stalinism: a depiction of the time and its atmosphere, and how it affects individuals and their destiny to this day. With its psychological and moral dissection of Glebov, the work attempts to explore the moral essence of the time.

CHAPTER 4

Terrorism, Civil War and the present (Neterpenie; Otblesk kostra; Starik)

Neterpenie was written for the series *Plamennye revoliutsionery* ('Ardent Revolutionaries'), and Trifonov worked on the novel at the same time as he was publishing his Moscow stories of 1969–71. The actual writing of the novel took place in 1972, and it was eventually published in 1973.[1] It is from the outset no run-of-the-mill Soviet historical novel. Just as he is thorough in cataloguing the unremitting pressures of urban *byt* in modern Moscow, so his eye for historical detail and accuracy is likewise impressive.

A journalist who visited Trifonov in 1976 noted the historical books on the writer's bookshelves: all fifty-seven volumes of *Byloe* ('The Past'), the journals *Katorga i ssylka* ('Hard Labour and Exile'), *Golos minuvshego* ('The Voice of the Past'), *Krasnyi arkhiv* ('Red Archive'), editions of *Obshchestvo politicheskikh katorzhan i ssyl'noposelentsev* ('The Society of Political Hard Labour Prisoners and Exiles'), memoirs of 'People's Will' activists Anna Pribyleva-Korba, Vera Figner, Nikolai Morozov, Mikhail Frolenko, Osip Aptekman, Ivan Popov, German Lopatin, and the bibliographical dictionary *Deiateli revoliutsionnogo dvizheniia v Rossii* ('Figures in the Revolutionary Movement in Russia'). He also possessed the 1919 book *Moskovskaia okhrana i ee sekretnye sotrudniki* ('The Moscow Secret Police and its Secret Personnel'), which must have come in useful for Troitskii's researches in *Drugaia zhizn'*, Aleksandr Egorov's *Razgrom Denikina* and the memoirs of Vladimir Antonov-Ovseenko from 1924, both of which are relevant for *Starik*. Also of interest is the volume *Frantsuzskaia revoliutsiia v pokazaniiakh i memuarakh sovremennikov* ('The French Revolution in the Testimony and Memoirs of its Contemporaries'), whose author, the Vicomte H. de Broc, is mentioned in *Starik* alongside Robespierre as among the favourite reading of Shigontsev, a Bolshevik.[2]

Trifonov writes that 'to make sense of the present, one has to understand the past'.[3] This statement should be borne in mind when reading the novel's opening lines. *Neterpenie* opens thus:

> By the end of the 1870s it seemed perfectly clear to people of that time that Russia was ill. They argued only about the nature of the disease and how to cure it. Categorical advice, prophecies and curses resounded inside the country and abroad, at clandestine meetings, in the clamorous newspapers, fashionable journals, in bloodthirsty underground pamphlets. Some found the cause of Russia's dark sickness in the impoverishment of the national spirit, others in the weakening of state power, and others, on the contrary, in its excessive strengthening, some saw the poison come from petty thieves at home, others from the Poles, and still others from Byronism, which Russia had been unable to shake off for a hundred years, and one great writer reckoned that the culprit was the small tarantula, the *piccola bestia*, known as Beaconsfield, who had rushed off to Europe. There were some who demanded the total demolition of this rotten system, and only then would it become clear what it could be replaced with. But what, after all, was going on? Everything seemed to be going its true course: cities grew, railways seemed to be spreading in all directions, entrepreneurs amassed fortunes, peasants revolted, landowners drank tea on their verandahs, writers published novels, and still there was something wrong with the country, an ulcer was eating away at it somewhere. All of Russia languished in disillusion. (III, 7)[4]

There is a clear contemporary perspective from the outset, for Trifonov's eye for historical continuity can surely see that, just as a hundred years before, Russia in the 1970s was certainly 'ill'. He was just as surely acutely aware of 'the nature of the disease'.

The use of historical analogy, the juxtaposition of contemporary mores with those of a past age are not new in Soviet literature, but Trifonov aims not to justify history, as in countless socialist realist novels, but to assert the continuity of the historical process. In an interview published shortly after the novel's appearance, he points to the affinities between this work and the earlier *Otblesk kostra*: 'Twentieth-century revolutionaries are inseparably linked with their predecessors, the representatives of earlier phases in the Russian liberation movement.'[5] Here he is talking about those who fought for the Bolsheviks during the Revolutions of 1917 and the Civil War, but elsewhere he likens the revolutionary terrorism of the *Narodnaia Volia*, the 'People's Will', to that of the terrorists of the modern day, who think nothing of taking innocent lives as part of their struggle.[6] Moreover, one can easily extend the analogy to the dissidents fighting with mere ideas and words for 'liberation' in the Soviet Union of the 1960s and 1970s. Mikhail Agurskii makes the following bold insertion: 'Trifonov in looking for parallels between the *narodniki* and the Soviet dissidents, emphasizing the futility of their struggle ... Is he not trying to find [in this novel] a reply to the question of his own attitude to the Soviet opposition, seeing in them the same people as were in the period of the *narodniki*?'[7]

Trifonov is certainly 'looking for parallels,' but between political groupings and their ideas. Social and political conditions are similar. To this end, *Neterpenie* is written in the same style as Trifonov's 'modern' stories, with the author at pains to create an authentic picture of life in the burgeoning cities of nineteenth-century Russia. The concentration of detail and the attempt to achieve historical verisimilitude are reminiscent of the Moscow stories, and so give a contemporary significance to the events described. Thus the gap between the two centuries is further closed. As he states in his 1974 interview: 'I wanted to write a modern book in the language of a modern writer and therefore I structured the prose in exactly the same way as the prose of my novellas (*povesti*) and stories. Here was not only an aesthetic consideration: I wanted to show the continuity (*slitnost'*) of historical periods'.[8] He goes on to admit that theoretically the novel and his Moscow stories share 'an inner connection' in the 'moral' sphere. For here too, characters fight the evil they see in society.[9]

The plot of *Neterpenie* concentrates on the years 1878–81, with particular focus on Andrei Zheliabov and his revolutionary activities from 1874. Zheliabov was the leader of the *Narodnaia*

Volia from 1879–81. Born in 1850, he was expelled from university in 1871 for protesting at the expulsion of a Jewish student. He married in 1873, and was arrested for the first time in 1874. He was released the following year, and in 1879 accepted into the organization *Zemlia i Volia* ('Land and Liberty'), the precursor of the *Narodnaia Volia*. He is the central figure of the narrative, and it is largely from his point of view that we see the main events of the novel: the first assassinations of policemen and state officials, and the split of the *Zemlia i Volia* party into two independent parties. These parties were the *Narodnaia Volia*, which concentrates on the use of terror to achieve its aims, and the *Chernyi peredel* ('The Black Redivision'), which rejects violence and chooses to conduct agitation among the peasantry. Other events include the Populists' adoption of a political programme; the creation of a conspiratorial party; arrests, imprisonments and executions; successive failed attempts on the Tsar's life; and the increasing repression and the decimation of the party's leading lights, including Zheliabov's own arrest. This latter circumstance is somewhat ironic, for the culmination of the party's activity, and the goal to which all its energies have been devoted – the assassination of Tsar Aleksandr II on 1 March, 1881 – takes place without Zheliabov's participation, as he is in police custody at the time. With the death of the Tsar the remaining members of the *Narodnaia Volia* are swiftly rounded up, and the party ceases to exist. However, as with all of Trifonov's fiction, the chief interest lies not only in the story, but also in the manner of its telling.

The ambivalent nature of the novel's opening paragraph is borne out by further developments in the novel and its plot. On one level *Neterpenie* is a realistic and straightforward chronicle of the birth and blood-stained activities of the *Narodnaia Volia*, and while Trifonov succeeds in conveying the specific atmosphere inside the party at the time, there are also motifs ostensibly rooted in the nineteenth century which have an unmistakable contemporary resonance. These include the illegal nature of any clandestine gathering, and the repressive measures of the police, including imprisonment, hard labour and Siberian exile (many of the *narodovol'tsy* are sentenced to death, a penalty to which the Soviet government never subjected the dissidents, although some died in the camps); the constant danger from spies, informers and *agents provocateurs*; the existence of underground printing-presses and the publication of illegal proclamations, newspapers and news-sheets, akin to *samizdat* publications such as the *Khronika Tekushchikh sobytii* ('The Chronicle of Current Events') of the 1960s and 1970s. Indeed, a faint echo of the *Khronika* is in the name of one of the pamphlets issued by the radicals: *Izvestiia noveishikh vremen* (III, 114). The radicals' formulation and propagation of alternative policies; the struggle within the country's ruling circles of 'liberal' and 'conservative' factions; appeals to Western public opinion – these and other factors serve to draw closer the Soviet Union of the 1970s and Russian society of a century before. There are more substantial parallels, though: the description of conditions in the Tsar's jails, with regular beatings and torture; prisoners' protests about conditions in the jails and their struggle for the few rights they have; the rape of women prisoners; threats from the warders and the pressures to 'confess' to crimes, in order to discredit colleagues and party; the use of informers as cellmates; the prolonged lack of sleep during periods of interrogation. All this, as well as the danger of being re-arrested upon release for some minor offence, the attempts of the police and prosecution to establish the existence of conspiracies and groups, and the staging of large-scale show trials, remind us of the conditions in Stalin's Russia as described in Solzhenitsyn's *Gulag Archipelago*, and suggest, at the very least, that the police mentality and their methods, as well as Russian prison conditions, have not moved on significantly since the nineteenth century. The use of the word *glyba*, 'boulder', to characterize the Tsarist regime (III, 153) is immediately associated with the book *Iz-pod glyb*, the collection of dissident articles published in Paris and edited (with Igor' Shafarevich) by Solzhenitsyn, where the 'boulders' of the title refer to the oppressive weight of the Soviet regime under Brezhnev.[10]

Similarly, Zheliabov's dispute with his father-in-law over the true direction of dissent echoes similar debates of modern times.

The older man insists on the need to extend the powers of the *zemstvo*, in order to improve the life of ordinary people in practical terms by constructing and repairing schools, orphanages and local buildings. Zheliabov, on the other hand, wants to dismantle the system itself. This debate can be seen as a mirror image of the Roy Medvedev–Solzhenitsyn debate in the 1960s and 1970s: the former is a party-minded reformist, whereas Solzhenitsyn sees national rebirth only in the demise of the Soviet state itself. And Zheliabov's reflections on the peasant commune in the 1870s are reminiscent of the arguments about the Russian peasant and his way of life as they resurfaced in Russia in the 1960s:

> The peasant commune, said the historians, is a fragment of that lost paradise, the ages-old Russian sense of freedom (*vol'nost'*). For some reason the people have preserved this memory, as if they want to return to a great time, to their ideal of a life based on law and truth. But just as the people's power of old did not have the muscle to stand up to Ivan the Terrible's iron fist, so the commune was too weak – transparently weak! – to support any hopes of doing battle with autocracy. It was a shadow from the past, a museum containing the relics of forgotten customs and forlorn dreams. (III, 64).

Zheliabov's thoughts here also half-conceal Trifonov's own rejection of the view of *derevenshchiki* of the 1960s that the peasant and the village were a panacea for modern Russia's ills. But concepts of 'truth', 'freedom' (spiritual *volia* and political *svoboda*) and the historical identity of Russia are also important, not only for this work, but for Trifonov's historical vision in general.

Trifonov, with his eye for historical continuity and parallelism, could not ignore the similarities between the backwardness of Russia in the 1870s and what has since been termed the 'stagnation' of Brezhnev's Russia. Trifonov prided himself on being a writer who was able to stand above history and see its true patterns. Also, he was a man of wide reading and cosmopolitan outlook, and so must have been aware, as were many of his contemporaries, of the political and social inertia of the society in which he lived. Thus, in a political conversation at which Zheliabov is present along with his father-in-law, we are made privy to statements such as 'only the joint efforts of the authorities and society can provide salvation' and 'between the government and society a void has developed'. These ideas also reflect attitudes of the liberal intelligentsia during the 1960s and 1970s, just as the idea that 'what you call a void is the absence of strong government! There is from top to bottom overall uncertainty!' (III, 77) undoubtedly holds sway a hundred years on among conservatives and hardliners dismayed at any manifestation of nonconformity or opposition in the modern Russian state. The conditions in the two Russias are therefore similar. Russia is ill, and it is therefore not surprising that dissidents and malcontents want to put it right. The difference between the various groupings is merely whether to use bombs or pens. Here we have the germ of a debate common to Russian intellectual circles: the search for national identity based on historical experience; the search for a middle way between Western liberalism and savage despotism.

Finally, Trifonov occasionally draws together past and present to expand his geographical parameters. Using Zheliabov as his mouthpiece, the author likens the *narodovol'tsy* to the Irish Fenians, who in their turn use terror as a means of achieving their goals: they blow up prisons, attack prison convoys and carry out the assassinations of Lord Cavendish and his secretary Burke, as well as of trial judges. Zheliabov sees himself as a Russian Parnell, and dreams of a Russian Constituent Assembly, where he would command the centre stage as does Parnell in the British Parliament. We could add of course, that even now nothing much has changed and that in the early 1990s the 'Irish question' is far from resolved. In this respect, too, the temporal distance between the 'then' of the narrative and the 'now' of its creation is reduced.

The Irish parallel closes another gap, that of place: it serves to bring Russia and Europe together, to strengthen the idea that Russia and Europe share the same historical destiny. Trifonov distances himself from the Slavophile view that Russia has a destiny separate from the rest of Europe, a view often put forward by neo-Slavophiles of the 'village prose' school in the 1960s–1970s. In *Neterpenie*, Paris and Vienna serve as the centres of the Russian emigration, and Geneva and England also offer sanctuary. European culture influences and interacts with Russian ideas: German philosophers have influenced the nihilists and other radicals, who trace their own lineage to the French Revolution. Zheliabov likens his friend and fellow-revolutionary Ivan Koval'skii to Fra Diavolo, the Neapolitan brigand who fought the French occupying forces at the beginning of the nineteenth century. Early on Zheliabov is himself likened to Saint-Just, the bloodthirsty French revolutionary. Also, in the wider historical arena it is not just the Russian Tsar who is threatened: we learn of attempts on the life of the German Kaiser. Furthermore, after the *Narodnaia Volia* has penetrated the Winter Palace and planted a bomb, the alarm bells start ringing across Europe: 'If palaces in Petersburg are blown up, where is the guarantee that these devils won't get as far as the Elysée Palace in Paris?' (III, 267). Trifonov's view of the wholeness (*slitnost'*) of culture and history brings together ideas, times and places.

The simplistic Western view of Russia as barbarous and primitive, set apart from European civilization by its elemental savagery, is put by a German doctor (unnamed) who is resident in Odessa. At the time of considerable revolutionary activity in 1878 ('Die schrekliche Zeiten' (III, 70)), he is terrified by the violence of what he sees as the 'wild und barbarisch' Russian revolution, and, unable to leave his house for two days, he declares: 'A country which cannot guarantee its citizens peace has no right to rank itself among European countries' (III, 71). The author here has his tongue firmly in his cheek, especially since these words are spoken by a German, and the German state is unable to 'guarantee peace' not only to its ordinary citizens, but even to its Kaiser.

Thematically the European dimension of Russia's political condition is of immense importance, but in terms of style it provides one indication of the scope of Trifonov's narrative. Another is the cast of characters. The dramatis personae of this drama – indeed, tragedy – include many historical figures, beginning with the very top of Russian society, Tsar Aleksandr II and his son and heir, the future Aleksandr III. The liberal

Tsarist minister Valuev, the head of the Holy Synod Pobedonostsev, the chief of police Loris-Melikov, the prosecutors Fuks and Dobrzhinskii all play no small part, and the writers Lev Tolstoi, Vladimir Solov'ev, Aleksei Suvorin and Fedor Dostoevskii make up the cultural and intellectual backdrop. This background is painted in some detail: Dostoevskii's *The Possessed*, a novel about the revolutionary terrorism and nihilism of the day, is discussed by various characters more than once, as is the work of Lev Tolstoi, Afanasii Fet, Aleksei Pisemskii, Nikolai Chernyshevskii and Aleksandr Herzen. Moreover, the terrorist Nechaev, the subject of *The Possessed*, is further likened to the subject of Machiavelli's book *The Prince*, so widening Trifonov's literary and political frames of reference. Portrayals of actual figures from the revolutionary movement include, apart from Zheliabov himself, Plekhanov, Nechaev, Sof'ia Perovskaia, who is to become Zheliabov's accomplice and lover, Vera Figner, Vera Zasulich, Aleksandr Mikhailov, Aleksandr Vasil'ev, Nikolai Kletochnikov, Stepan Khalturin and a gallery of lesser-known figures. In a wide-ranging narrative the author's attention occasionally settles on ordinary citizens and passers-by, soldiers, shop-owners, janitors, sailors, workers, peasants, landowners, policemen, prostitutes, students – a cross-section of society, spread across the length of Russia, from Odessa to Khar'kov, Moscow to St Petersburg. And Siberia, to which many of these revolutionaries will be exiled, is never far from their thoughts. As in his other works, the totality, the *slitnost'*, of Trifonov's vision of the world is the dominant aspect.

Analogy and parallel apart, Trifonov shows himself to be a scrupulous and thorough researcher and compiler of historical detail. Trifonov has been shown to have used about 450 separate historical sources, he was working on the novel throughout the late 1960s and corresponded both with historians such as N. A. Troitskii, professor at Saratov University and author of several books on the *Narodnaia Volia*, and descendants of the terrorists involved, including Zheliabov and Grinevitskii. In short, he left no stone unturned.[11] Actual historical documents are quoted, such as the diaries and private notes of Aleksandr III and Valuev, letters of Lev Tolstoi and

Pobedonostsev to Aleksandr III, trial transcripts and speeches of defendants, extracts from various publications, such as the journal *Narodnaia Volia* and the news-sheet *Listki Zemli i Voli* ('Leaflets of the Land and Liberty'), almost the whole programme of the *narodovol'tsy* and a long letter from Zheliabov to the exiled Ukrainian nationalist leader Dragomanov. The reader is also struck by the author's seeming familiarity with the lay-out of nineteenth-century Odessa and Petersburg, the cities where the bulk of the action takes place, as we are led through streets and squares to safe houses, through shops, stores and taverns, even down the dark corridors, dank cells and interrogation rooms of the capital's prisons.[12] Trifonov describes the *byt* of city-dwellers of a hundred years ago with the same sureness as he does of those in the modern age: the reader feels present as they drink wine or tea and exchange small talk, he is part of a crowd jostling along Nevskii Prospekt in Petersburg, hears snatches of dialogue or news in a restaurant or bar, or he is with the author on a train observing fellow-passengers, their facial expressions and the cut of their clothes. Trifonov makes us feel involved, almost part of the scenes he describes.

These scenes include actual historical events, such as the celebrations for the twenty-fifth anniversary of Aleksandr II's rule in 1880, and the funeral of Dostoevskii in January 1881, when Zheliabov is caught in the procession and carried along by it. Others are alluded to, in order to establish a clear factual background: famine, pestilence and peasant riots in the provinces in 1880, leading to mass migration to the towns, the assassination of policemen, informers and prosecutors, and the increasing regularity of arrests. Together with the multitude of characters, the accumulated impression is one of a sure grasp of detail and an attempt to create a historically authentic picture of a society, and the historical, cultural and political forces working out the destiny of the state and its citizens.[13]

In *Drugaia zhizn'* Sergei Troitskii believes that 'man is the thread, stretching through time, the subtlest nerve of history', and it is man in whom Trifonov is primarily interested. Man links ages, past and present, man passes on legacies from one generation to the next, and it is about a man, his psychological motivation, including his doubts and vacillations, that Trifonov writes in *Neterpenie*. This he states outright in a letter to the historian N. A. Troitskii (is Trifonov's fictional use of the surname a coincidence?) dated 28 February 1973: 'Suddenly a personality forced its way through the fetters of facts, protocols and documents that tie a historical personage down. Do you recall Marx's slogan regarding "doubts". There you are, doubts and hesitations are a purely human characteristic. And long may they prosper, as long as man with his complex and multi-layered soul continues to exist.'[14] Trifonov, consequently, is intent to humanize his other historical personages, such as Migulin in *Starik* and, most successfully of all, his own father in *Ischeznovenie*.

What does separate the terrorists of the *Narodnaia Volia* from their dissident counterparts in the post-war Soviet Union, and which links the former to the ruthless international terrorists of today is, of course, exactly the use of terror, violence and assassination. Andrei Zheliabov is the terrorist *par excellence* here, unrepentent to the end, rationalizing murder, bombing and maiming as part of a struggle, as the means towards an end, and shifting the blame for the suffering of innocent bystanders, as do terrorists and 'freedom fighters' the world over, on to what he characterizes as an oppressive and impersonal state.

Trifonov devotes much space to Zheliabov, dissecting the terrorist mentality in order to show how a perfectly ordinary family man can become a ruthless killer. The longest chapter in the book is the first, which gives an account of Zheliabov's early years, his marriage and the birth of his son, and his eventual separation from his wife, Ol'ga, in order to pursue revolutionary activity and, in all probability, to die for his cause. It is with his break with his loved ones that, like Rebrov in *Dolgoe proschanie*, he begins another life: 'He couldn't go back to Ol'ga, just as he couldn't go back to being himself as he used to be' (III, 21).[15]

Zheliabov's personality is brought to the fore, and we get to see the world through his eyes and memories. He is of peasant stock, appalled at the injustice and arbitrariness of serfdom (when he was eight his aunt Liuba was raped by the landowner Lorentsov, whom he swears to kill in revenge). Expelled from

Odessa university in 1871 for protesting against the arbitrary expulsion of a fellow-student, he becomes involved with radical groups and is first arrested and imprisoned in Odessa in 1874, to be released on probation in 1875. He is involved with 193 others in what became known as the 'Great Trial' (*Bol'shoi protsess*) of revolutionaries in St Petersburg in 1877–8. He is released, while dozens of others are sentenced to exile or hard labour, and then becomes involved with the *Zemlia i Volia* radicals, becoming accepted into the party in 1879. After the split in the party, he is by 1880 the political leader of the *Narodnaia Volia*.

Trifonov not only shows us Zheliabov from inside, but from other viewpoints. To this end the third-person narrative is disrupted by the 'voices' of several people peripheral to the plot but who are either eyewitnesses or indirectly involved, and who have a story to tell. Most of these voices concentrate on the personality of Zheliabov, and relate their stories in the first person.

For example, Pimen Semeniuta was a radical close to Zheliabov in 1878–9, and judges him at that time as 'markedly ambitious', a person who 'could not stand anyone else's superiority' (III, 84). Zheliabov's fellow-terrorist Mikhail Frolenko gives a portrait of him later in 1879: 'When I met him in June in Lipetsk, I didn't recognize him: an out-and-out terrorist! And not simply a terrorist, but a passionate theoretician and architect of terror. It strikes me that his most important strength as a personality was the strength of rationality. He had the iron will to think everything through to its conclusion' (III, 117). Aleksandr Sytsianko recalls Zheliabov in November 1879, and marvels at the man's 'quite frightening strength', which he takes to be 'the deification of his own will' and 'supreme egotism' (III, 200).

Through this use of multiple perspectives, Trifonov is able to juxtapose and contrast him with other revolutionaries, and so to arrive at a composite appraisal of the man, as viewed by others. Semeniuta compares him unfavourably with Valerian Osinskii, a dashing Robin Hood-like figure who rescues comrades from jail and persuades rich men to donate money to the cause. Zheliabov, in Semeniuta's estimation, envies and distrusts

Osinskii, afraid of conceding the limelight to someone else, especially someone from the gentry class. Zheliabov himself vainly regards Aleksandr Mikhailov as his *alter ego*, 'a man of action, while he, Andrei, was perhaps a man of reflection' (III, 124). If anything, the opposite is true. The clearest picture we get of Zheliabov's credo is from Semeniuta, on how he 'changed': 'the man began by wanting to learn from the people, but came to the conclusion that he had to teach history what to do' (III, 83).

It is in the evolution of Zheliabov's ideas about terror and socio-political change that Trifonov epitomizes the dilemma facing the *narodovol'tsy*, or, indeed, any radical or opposition group with serious pretensions to power. It is clear that Zheliabov's hatred of the system stems from his childhood years and his loathing of serfdom, and, following the Peasant Reform of 1861, one of the Populists' demands is the nationalization of all land and its handing over to the peasants. Semeniuta notes that when he went underground, Zheliabov preferred the idea of 'giving history a push' to the peaceful adoption of a constitution (III, 83). Zheliabov comes to believe that the end justifies the means, does not shrink from the use of violence and admires those who carry out murders. The use of violence for political ends is the main issue responsible for the split in the *Zemlia i Volia* party. Plekhanov walks out on the congress in protest against its adoption, so establishing the novel's political orthodoxy in contemporary Soviet eyes, distancing the 'Father of Russian Marxism' from the espousal of terror and violence. It is at this congress in 1879 that the party, now calling itself *Narodnaia Volia*, adopts violence as the primary method of struggle with the Tsarist system. Two years later, in 1881, Zheliabov's final words at his trial for murder could serve as the manifesto of any radical prepared to use violence for 'the common good': 'The aim of my life has been to serve the common good. For a long time I worked towards this aim by peaceful means and only then was forced to turn to violence. I would say as follows: I would have probably rejected terrorist activity if there had been a change in external conditions' (III, 404).

The twin tragedies of the *narodovol'tsy* are that they sacrifice themselves for what they see as the future welfare of society, but they do not flinch from murdering others. Here is a group of young people, most in their twenties and some of them mere adolescents, who honestly believe that they love the people, and that what they do will ultimately benefit society. Zheliabov's heartfelt commitment to this ideal is never open to doubt. That is not to say that Trifonov idealizes them; rather, he shows us their readiness to kill innocent people, and the frame of mind that can rationalize such acts in the name of a greater good. As in his Moscow stories, Trifonov does not moralize or explicitly condemn the actions of his 'heroes'; he merely shows the effects and consequences of those actions. The moral perspective, however, is evident.

The novel also shows the environment in which Zheliabov and his confidants scheme and work. Trifonov shows us life in nineteenth-century Russia through the eyes of several characters: Nikolai Kletochnikov, a former bank clerk who infiltrates the dreaded Third Section, the Tsar's secret police, and becomes the terrorists' 'mole'; Grisha Gol'denberg, terrorist and murderer, as he languishes in prison and prepares to denounce his comrades in the messianic but mistaken belief that he will avert further bloodshed and save Russia; Tsar Aleksandr II, vain and pompous, trying to recapture his youth with elixirs from Sweden, out of touch with events in the country, unable to comprehend the assassination attempts, and recalling with fondness his finest hour, the defeat of the Turks at Plevna. We are touched, however, by his love for the Princess Iur'evskaia, his companion now for fourteen years, a direct descendant of Iurii Dolgorukii, the founder of Moscow. Aleksandr III also bares his soul to us, and is no less uncomprehending than his father, contemptuous of the Emancipation of 1861 as 'some semblance of beneficence from above, and not an action forced from below' (III, 212), and regarding any current concessions to liberal sentiments in the same light. All in all, the impression gained of the Tsar's leadership of the country, and that of his government ministers, is one of hesitation, prevarication and uncertainty; the exact opposite can be said of the actions and aims of the *Narodnaia Volia*.

By structuring his narrative around multiple viewpoints, the author shows us history as it is perceived and experienced by individuals, terrorists and Tsars alike. The reader therefore becomes a witness to events as they unfold, he gets a ground-level view of the movement of history. At the same time the novel has scope, no more so than with the figure of Clio, the Muse of History, who stands above human affairs and enables the historian to relate and interpret events from an impersonal, Olympian viewpoint: 'There is nothing, except events, facts, names, titles, years, minutes, hours, days, decades, centuries, millennia, endlessly disappearing in the flood that I, Clio, oversee, the flood that knows no sorrow, is devoid of passion, that flows neither slowly nor rapidly, not without sense but without any destination, the flood that consumes everything' (III, 88).

The Clio-72 sections represent the author looking at events from the perspective of 1972, when the novel was being written, and so correspond to those 'voices' recalling events from another time, for example Semeniuta in 1906, Sytsianko in 1896, Dragomanov in 1889. Clio-72 concludes several chapters by relating the subsequent fate of Zheliabov's abandoned wife Ol'ga, who changed her name and disowned her husband after the assassination of the Tsar, of the sad end of Kletochnikov and Mikhailov, who both died in prison, and includes details of the trial in 1925 of the bomb-maker turned informer Okladskii. Finally, we learn of the few who survived into the Soviet era, Figner and Frolenko among them. On the significance of the Tsar's murder, Clio disappoints the hopes of the revolutionaries, who supposed that the entire Tsarist edifice would collapse overnight: 'The huge Russian iceberg did not split, it did not crack and did not even tremble. Something did, however, shift inside the iceberg's mass, deep down, but this only revealed itself decades afterwards' (III, 396).

The novel does have its shortcomings: it is uneven in that the first half tends more to authorial reflection and analogy, and is easier to link with the writer's other, 'modern' works, whereas the second half concentrates more on plot development and reads more like a conventional thriller as arrests, conspiracies and bombings escalate. Also, at times the plethora of characters and names is overwhelming, the reader is easily lost as he tries to keep up with and identify various characters and their aliases, and with the exception of well-drawn characters such as Zheliabov, Perovskaia and Kletochnikov, others come across more as types, only thinly sketched and more often than not mere cannon fodder. But the events are real, and well presented. The multiplicity of viewpoints belonging to Zheliabov's contemporaries, and the all-seeing historical perspective from above, reflect the author's painstaking attempt to give as broad and as detailed as possible a picture of history in the making, to bring it to life and at the same time give it meaning. He is certainly successful in conveying the all-pervading atmosphere of fear in the country bred by terrorism, and the ensuing repression that turns Russia into a police state. Furthermore, the portrayal of an underground party, bound by conspiracy and the need for secrecy, where individuals arrive and then disappear – and are interlinked across the land – gives the author the opportunity to express his view of the human community as we see it in the hurly-burly of modern Moscow: individuals connected, however slightly, with others, links stretching across cities, classes, countries, continents. Nothing is seen in isolation, nothing disappears without trace. The main event of the narrative – the assassination – has its ultimate consequence in 1917. The consequences of this revolution are, of course, still with us today. The novel offers a perfect illustration of Trifonov's concept of *slitnost'*.

As has been said, the use of allegory, and the possible parallels between the radicals of a hundred years ago and the dissidents of Brezhnev's Russia, point to an authorial statement on the condition of modern Soviet society. But there is also a deeper historical enquiry. At one stage the terrorists discuss the Zaporozh'e Cossacks. The Cossacks were an independent people descended from Tartars and runaway serfs, and lived in self-governing communities. The Zaporozh'e Cossacks were one of the main Cossack communities in Russia, along with the Don

Cossacks from whom Valentin Trifonov was descended, from the sixteenth to the twentieth centuries. In the nineteenth and twentieth centuries they were increasingly used to suppress demonstrations and civil disorder. For Trifonov's Populists, the Cossacks' love of freedom (*vol'nost'*) was the 'greatest and most blessed treasure' they possessed, and they once rejected the 'chains' of all those who tried to subdue them:

And how did it come about that in the most freedom-loving land the vilest autocracy became established, whose cruelty had no equal in the world and the Cossacks, the first people to rebel and defend their freedom, became the loyalist defenders of this despotism? Not immediately, not immediately, you have to think. Centuries went by, it all happened slowly, so that now it is firmly entrenched, and has chained to the earth the past, the future, men's ambitions and hopes. (III, 172)

Here Trifonov is pinpointing the historical moment when freedom in Russia was usurped, when a freedom-loving people became the agents of repression. The same principle is true of the Populists. In *Neterpenie* the *narodovol'tsy* abandon the principle of personal responsibility for their actions by choosing terror and political assassination as the means towards their end. By renouncing their own inner freedom, that is, moral accountability, they thereby embrace a form of tyranny. They are linked to Glebov and others in Trifonov's fiction in that they too blame 'the times' for their actions. Trifonov thus reveals himself as a writer with historical vision and awareness of the centuries-old dialectic of tyranny and freedom.

The corruption of freedom, the degeneration of a noble idea, is one that is at the root of Trifonov's historical fiction. It is tempting to see in the writer's use of historical and political parallels the creation of a codified language of hints, allusions and half-truths. The 'People's Will' terrorists were the first to threaten seriously the existing order, and the Bolsheviks inherited their aims and completed their work. The ethical values of the 'People's Will' became irrevocably corrupted when they chose to use violence and terror, and the original ideals of the Bolsheviks, too, became seriously impaired in the course of their reign. The theme of ends and means, and its implications, is taken up again in Trifonov's second historical novel *Starik*, which, because it explores the conditions of the Revolution and Civil War, lends political immediacy to such questions of Russian history as the nature of truth and justice, and the price of freedom.

Starik is a fictional continuation of *Otblesk kostra*, a documentary account of the Revolution and Civil War. *Otblesk kostra* was first published as a short essay in two instalments in the journal *Znamia* in 1964, and came out in book form in 1966. This book version is a considerably expanded text of the journal version, containing details, dates, events and in particular personal testimonies of eyewitnesses who contacted the author after the original publication. The bare bones in the *Znamia* publication are fleshed out in the book both by various personal details, memoirs, diaries, and additional factual material. It is written with one aim: 'to write the truth, however brutal and strange it may be. And the truth will surely be of use – some time or other...' (IV, 45). The 'truth' is about Valentin Trifonov and his Revolutionary and Civil War record, and constitutes a son's duty to rehabilitate his father and attack those to blame for his arrest and execution. As such, it is an attack above all on Stalin, and so bears the features of the period of Khrushchev's de-Stalinization, during which it was researched, written and originally published.[16]

Trifonov's aesthetic view of history is stated in the opening pages: 'Every person bears the reflection of history. On some it glows with a hot and fearsome light, on others it is barely visible, barely warm, but it is there on everyone. History blazes like a huge campfire, and each of us throws into it our own brushwood' (IV, 7). The interconnectedness of man and his time, the history of a society and the life of an individual, is an idea with which we are already familiar from the pages of *Drugaia zhizn'*. Trifonov has personal reasons for aligning himself with the historical forces of de-Stalinization, as this book is his attempt to clear his father's name. 'Probably nothing,' he writes towards the end of the book, 'is attained with greater difficulty than historical justice' (IV, 140). Especially, we may add, in a country where political legitimacy is upheld through the falsification of history. Furthermore, he adds, it is attained not so much through sifting through heaps of papers in archives, or debates, as by the passage of time, represented in the case of his father by a change in the political leadership.[17]

Trifonov undoubtedly learned much of the researcher's meticulous craft when he was working on *Otblesk kostra*, and this experience proved invaluable for the writing of *Neterpenie*. In *Otblesk kostra* he is scrupulous in recounting the details of his father's services to the Revolution and to the Party, beginning in 1905 when Valentin was only seventeen years old. Several other newspaper articles Trifonov wrote in the mid to late 1960s about witnesses of the 1917 Revolutions testify to the strength of his researches into this period.[18]

Otblesk kostra is not only Trifonov's personal memoir for a father he hardly got to know, but also a lament for a generation that created the new world. It is above all a personal attack and bitter condemnation of the whole phenomenon of Stalinism, where the blame for the destruction of Lenin's comrades-in-arms, the Old Bolsheviks, is laid squarely at the door of Stalin, Molotov, Voroshilov and their ilk. Moreover, the values and integrity of the Old Bolsheviks are not open to doubt, only those of Trotskii, Stalin and their followers. In this respect, the book follows the official Party view of history, that Lenin represented the 'true' path, and Trotskii and Stalin deviated from that path.

The fundamental flaw of the Leninist path is in sheer human terms. Natal'ia Ivanova points out one extremely relevant detail. Trifonov the author mentions that in 1920 his father saved two technical specialists from summary execution by writing a telegram to the members of the tribunal handling their case in Dagestan, insisting on their usefulness to the Reds. Trifonov the writer is proud of his father's humanity, but, as Ivanova indicates, had these men not been useful to the Bolsheviks, would Trifonov père have interceded on their behalf? To Valentin Trifonov, as to other Reds, the cause was more important than lives.[19] Trifonov the writer does not seem here to have lost his faith in the ideals of the men and women who made the Revolution, but he does not accept the world that emerged.

As the book goes on the author devotes particular space to the time his father spent on the Don, returning to his birthplace and fighting under the charismatic Cossack leader Fillip Mironov, and the last third of the book is as much about Mironov and the Cossacks as about Valentin Trifonov. The Bolshevik leaders doubted Mironov's allegiance to their cause, and suspected him of harbouring separatist notions. Twice during the Civil War he was arrested, charged and sentenced to death. The first time in 1919 he was reprieved and eventually appointed commander of the Second Cavalry Army, the second time, in 1921, he was transferred to Moscow and shot in mysterious circumstances without trial, in the courtyard of the Butyrki prison. Mironov's second arrest and execution were the result of his unauthorized decision to march against Denikin, a decision provoked by increasing frustration at being denied the front line. His advance prompted fears that he and his Cossacks were about to go over to the other side to fight against the Bolsheviks. As the author concludes: 'Mironov, of course, is a complex figure. All the contradictions and complexities of this figure are a kind of reflection of those contradictions and complexities concealed in 'the Cossack question', for the issue of how to deal with the Cossacks was one of the most painful of the Revolution' (IV, 120). The 'Cossack question' is treated in more detail in *Starik*.

Mironov was officially rehabilitated in 1960, despite being regarded as a traitor by Marshal Budennyi up to 1958 (IV, 111). Mironov is treated negatively by Konstantin Fedin in his 1948 novel *Neobyknovennoe leto* ('An Unusual Summer'), and after 1933 all positive references to Mironov in *And Quiet Flows the Don* were omitted.[20] The author's intention in *Otblesk kostra* may well have been to tell the truth about his father, whom he last saw when he was eleven years old, but he has also touched on larger themes: the arbitrary violence and injustice of the Civil War, the questionable methods used by the Bolsheviks, and the subsequent corruption of the ideals of a generation that made the Revolution. On the surface the book is about Valentin Trifonov; the subtext, though, broaches questions of freedom and tyranny: the political legitimacy of the victors, in short. The legacy of the past is at the root of this book, as he reflects in a digression:

Father has been dead a long time now, Litke also disappeared somewhere, and the old field notebooks almost perished, too, which had imprinted in them that distant, feverish life, which some of us find so difficult to comprehend today. So why do I turn its pages now? They excite me. And not only because they are about my father and about people I knew, but also because they are about a time when everything was beginning. When we began. (IV, 97)

In *Otblesk kostra* the writer is playing two games: on the one hand, he is trying to get to the truth; on the other, he is trying to understand the father he lost at an early age, and the uncomfortable details of his father's career are not faced. Valentin Trifonov is made into a hero and a martyr, but such a picture does not tell the full story. The book goes no further than explicitly blaming Trotskii for the arbitrariness of the Red Terror in the Civil War, and Stalin for the injustices that have since scarred Soviet historical development. The book's political orthodoxy is not open to doubt. But greater issues are not far from the surface: the methods used during the Civil War, the genocidal policies of the Bolsheviks towards the Cossacks, and by implication towards other forms of opposition, and philosophical issues of freedom and truth. These questions provide the link between *Neterpenie* and *Starik*. However, the continuation and development in *Starik* of these themes involves a clearer, more objective look at the Civil War, and dark, disturbing allusions to the spiritual and moral condition of modern Soviet society.

The actual writing of *Starik* was obviously complex: Trifonov states that he began writing it in 1967, when he travelled to Rostov to collect historical material about the year 1920.[21] This is shortly after the publication of the expanded book edition of *Otblesk kostra*. His work on the novel continued into the 1970s, and in an interview in 1973 he said that he was still collecting material for a book on the Civil War: meeting veterans and writing down their recollections.[22]

The problems of interpreting Trifonov's historical prose, or finding the author's own attitude to the reality he depicts, are highlighted as never before in *Starik*. Western reactions to this work are indicative. Iurii Mal'tsev's 1978 review was half-hearted in its praise of a work in which 'the truth' is presented in 'scant and measured pinches, with one eye on the leadership'. Although, he went on, 'there are no blatant lies', the 'whole atmosphere is distorted' due to the author's need to 'pass over in silence' the 'main truth'. Similarly, Igor' Efimov in 1983 asserted that the author's battle with 'the all-powerful Lie' had produced 'illusory' victories, repeating the argument of many an *émigré* critic that literature written under the conditions of censorship was bound by the very fact of its publication to be a compromise, a 'deal with Hell'. On the other hand, Herman Ermolaev concludes that, far from providing sops for the censorship, in *Starik* Trifonov had come as close as possible to the bounds of the permissible in expressing his opposition to Bolshevik rule, and that this therefore was his 'boldest and most original work'.[23]

Like *Dom na naberezhnoi*, *Starik* concerns events that took place in the past, but which are recalled in the contemporary present (that is, the early 1970s) by the central character. Also, both works revolve around temporal shifts and flashbacks, where at times both past and present exist side by side within the individual consciousness. Although the theme of memory and the past is common to both works, the nature of the subject matter – the Revolutions of 1917 and the Civil War – has more far-reaching implications.

Pavel Evgrafovich Letunov is the old man of the title, an Old Bolshevik, veteran of the Revolution and Civil War, who suffered imprisonment and exile in the 1930s and who is now living out his last years in lonely retirement. The glory and fervour of his youth is contrasted to the emptiness of the present: he is saddened by the heavy drinking of his son, Ruslan, and his daughter Vera thinks that he is becoming senile. His wife Galia died some years ago, and he still misses her terribly, often imagining that she is beside him and holding conversations with her. To those around him he conveys the impresson of a doddery old man living on his memories, and out of touch with the present. Indeed at one stage he is examined by psychologists who are invited by Vera into the *dacha*, posing as prospective holiday-makers.

It is now 1973, and the factual background to the narrative is provided by the series of fires that destroyed much of Moscow's surrounding woodland that summer. Pavel Evgrafovich's memories are often triggered by the smoke and smell of burning, which he associates with the violence and devastation of the Civil War years. It can be no accident that flames and smoke are chosen as a backdrop to the contemporary scene, as fire is in this work and *Otblesk kostra* a metaphor for war and revolution. This fire presages not glory and a new world, but rather demoralization and tyranny. It leaves in its wake a wasteland. Moreover, Pavel Evgrafovich has devoted his last few years to the noble task of rehabilitating Sergei Migulin, a Cossack leader with whom he fought and who was shot as a counterrevolutionary in 1920. To this end he has written an article, published five years before, designed to clear Migulin's name. But for him the burning question still remains: why did Migulin disobey orders and take his command out to meet the enemy?

Migulin is largely based on the figure of Mironov: they are the same age (about fifty at the time of the Civil War), both with a young wife, both having served with distinction in the Tsar's army, and both having joined the Bolsheviks following the October Revolution. Many of Pavel Evgrafovich's memories concentrate on the suspicion and mistrust of Migulin felt by most of the leading Bolshevik military and political leaders, suspicion fuelled by the official attitude of the Bolsheviks towards the Don Cossacks and the subsequent policy of 'de-Cossackization'. The historians Sergei Starikov and Roy Medvedev in their book on Mironov quote Lenin on the significance of the Don Cossacks to the Bolsheviks:

As for the Cossacks, they represented social strata from a frontier region of Russia of wealthy, small and middle landowners (the average holding was fifty desiatinas of land [about 137 acres]) who had preserved a great many medieval traits in their style of life, economy and everyday existence. Here we can detect the socio-economic foundation for a Russian Vendée.[24]

Given Lenin's ideological hostility to the Cossacks' way of life, Starikov and Medvedev go on to explain why the Cossacks were such a military threat to the Bolsheviks:

> Potentially, the Don Cossacks constituted a huge fighting force. According to data for autumn 1917, the following units stationed in all districts were under arms: sixty cavalry regiments and seventy-two squadrons; dozens of artillery units and Cossack infantry battalions; two Cossack guards regiments and several dozen local units. It was therefore not without reason that the domestic counter-revolution placed its chief hopes in the Don region.[25]

'De-Cossackization' (*raskazachivanie*) was adopted as policy in 1919, to improve grain requisitions. Starikov and Medvedev quote a directive of the Bolsheviks' Central Committee Orgburo which puts the purpose of de-Cossackization in brutally direct terms: it was 'the unique correctness of the most pitiless struggle against all the upper strata of the Cossackry, by means of their extermination to a man'.[26] It is this murderous vision, where people count not as human beings, but as representatives of a social class, that Trifonov lays bare in *Starik*. Furthermore, as we shall see, its devastating effects mould the psychology and the values of subsequent generations.

Lenin's reference to the French Revolution is not fortuitous for Trifonov's novel: historical allusions and parallels are evident throughout. Ruslan and Nikolai Erastovich, Vera's husband, discuss Ivan the Terrible in the context of the times he lived in:

> 'Those were hellish, cruel times, just look at what was happening in Europe and the world at large ... What about the religious wars in France? The massacre of the Huguenots? The exploits of the Spanish in America?'
>
> 'How do you justify a bigot? A sadist, the cruellest of men! And a sex maniac!' yelled Ruslan, jumping up from his chair and waving a thick, powerful hand close to Nikolai Erastovich's face; it was clear he had been drinking since morning. 'The times, the times! What times, for God's sake? It was the Renaissance, Michelangelo, Luther...' (III, 414)

The argument is not only an expression of the *slitnost'* of cultural, philosophical and political factors; there is also a fundamental question being posed, with relevance not only for the conditions of the Civil War: can violence and savagery be justified by the times in which they were committed? Or is there an absolute standard for judging human behaviour, not based on external conditions or concepts of relativity? Again, Trifonov returns to the figure of Ivan the Terrible and his terror, as he looks to the terror and violence in Russia in the more recent past. Ivan is further compared to his contemporary, the French King Charles IX. Nikolai Erastovich juxtaposes Ivan's ruthless suppression of Novgorod in 1570 with the massacre of the Huguenots in 1572: 'Nobody calls Charles IX a villain, although the Massacre of St Bartholemew's day and the suppression of Novgorod took place at about the same time. The Russian Tsar, of course, is made out to be nothing short of a monster' (III, 414).

Nikolai Erastovich sees Ivan as a great Russian leader, and agrees with the positive assessment of him. By analogy this can be equated with the glorification of Stalin, for example in Eisenstein's film *Ivan the Terrible* (1944–5). Such a positive rationalization is the orthodox Soviet approach to Stalin: despite his excesses, he nevertheless made the country a great power and defeated its external enemies. Ruslan, however, challenges this view, condemning Ivan's ruthless imperialism and terror. He blames Ivan for the subsequent destruction of much of the Muscovite state by the Crimean Tartars led by Khan Davlet-Geray in 1571, and the obvious historical parallel here is Stalin's purges and Russia's unpreparedness for war with Nazi Germany in 1941.

Further parallels occur. One of the brutal Bolshevik commanders waging war on the Cossacks is Braslavskii, whose approach to the 'Cossack question' is characterized by executions, hostage-taking, wholesale destruction of Cossack villages and property. He declares his intention of 'going like Carthage' through a village (III, 472), thus leaving no-one in any doubt that this village is about to suffer the same fate as did Carthage at the hands of the Romans.[27] Furthermore, revolutionary events in Russia are not seen in isolation, but as part of a wave spreading across Europe: strikes in England and France, revolution in Germany, peasant uprisings in Rumania and Bessarabia. But it is the French Revolution that provides the most relevant parallel.

During the Civil War the Bolsheviks generally used the terror of the French Revolution as a frame of reference for the activities of the Cheka, the secret police. Shigontsev, another Bolshevik leader in *Starik*, constantly sees parallels between the two Revolutions, and likens the Cossacks' rebellion to the resistance of Lyon to the National Convention in 1793. He is also fond of quoting Danton on the use of terror, and his favourite reading is Robespierre and the Vicomte de Broc. Ianson, member of the Southern Front's Revolutionary Military Council and Migulin's prosecutor at his trial, is also fond of using the French Revolution for ideological analogy:

'Remember the French Revolution and the struggle of the Vendée with the National Convention. You will see that the Convention's troops committed some terrible deeds, terrible from the point of view of the individual. The actions of the Convention's troops can only be understood in the light of a class analysis. They were justified by history because they were committed by the new, progressive class, sweeping away from its path the survivals of feudalism and popular ignorance.' (III, 580)

Revolutionary morality brooks no absolutes, such as the sanctity of life. History is written by the victors, and their moral code becomes the dominant one.

The justification of violence and atrocities brings us back to Ivan the Terrible, and the lessons of Russian history. Trifonov, as we have seen, is profoundly concerned with questions of freedom and state power, the relationship of the individual and political authority, and historical identity. In *Ischeznovenie*, the figure representing Trifonov's father traces the political use of terror back to Ivan; Stalin is merely inheriting an age-old Russian historical tradition.[28] It was with Ivan that the unified Russian state began, but it was Ivan who enshrined the concept of absolute rule at the expense of individual liberty. Consequently, the brutal methods Ivan used to extend and consolidate the borders of Russia have been used by successive rulers since, most notably Peter the Great and Stalin. Such methods serve to separate Russia from the democratic strivings of Western Europe, and Trifonov the historian is obviously fascinated by the coexistence, the *slitnost'*, of violence and state power in Russia through the centuries. Little wonder, then, that Trifonov is so interested in the fate of the individual in history, for it is exactly the so-called great men of Russian history (Ivan, Peter, Stalin) who have been responsible for the violence and tyranny that so mark that history.[29]

In *Neterpenie* the radicals are inspired by the freedom and independence once enjoyed by the Cossacks, but their noble aim of social justice, with an elected parliament and a constitution, becomes perverted into the pursuit of terrorism and the bland acceptance of murder. The past is also part of the present, indeed, as Trifonov says, the present cannot be understood if the past is ignored. Here the Bolsheviks' bloody policies are easily seen as a precursor of Stalin's future purges and terror, which in turn have as their consequence the moral and spiritual desolation of Brezhnev's Russia.

In *Starik* Trifonov's interweaving of historical detail and interpretation is not confined to historical analogies. As in his other historical novel, he introduces into the narrative a host of historical personages. Trotskii, Denikin, Kornilov, Krasnov, Filippov, Krymov and the Cossack hetman Kaledin are all involved, and others, such as Mironov and Smilga, appear under other names. Smilga was Mironov's prosecutor, and was himself fond of comparing the Cossacks with the Vendée, and appears in the text as Ianson, Migulin's accuser.[30] Braslavskii is reminiscent of Syrtsov, the Director of the Donburo in 1919, vigorous in encouraging de-Cossackization. (Also, the two Communists Mironov threatened to shoot, Bukatin and Lisin, appear in the narrative as Logachev and Kharin.) The author occasionally retains the name of an actual figure, but gives it to a fictional character, such as Izvarin, one of the older Pavel Evgrafovich's neighbours in the novel. The real Izvarin was a witness called at Mironov's 1919 trial, was later a member of the Don Cossack Military Assembly and makes an appearance in *And Quiet Flows the Don*, espousing the cause of Cossack self-rule.

Trifonov's meticulousness as a chronicler is also in evidence, as he makes extensive use in the novel of newspaper articles, official communiqués and trial transcripts, pinpointing exact dates, in terms of months, days and even hours.

The most innovative use of an actual historical personage in the novel is Trifonov's introduction of his own father, under the name of Shura Danilov. Danilov shares many biographical details with Valentin Trifonov: both are of the same age, both share involvement in the 1905 Revolution, and subsequent imprisonment and hard labour. Also, Danilov, like Valentin Trifonov, was active organizing workers on Vasil'evskii Island in Petrograd in March 1917. More importantly, Danilov refuses to judge people according to ideological criteria or prejudice, but tries to see the cost of the struggle in more human terms. In this crucial respect Danilov differs from the picture we get of Valentin Trifonov in *Otblesk kostra*. Danilov tries to prevent the sons of the schoolteacher Slaboserdov from being shot as counter-revolutionaries by the hetman Bychin, a Bolshevik who has lived for many years among the Cossacks but who nevertheless hates them. Bychin's grudge against the Slaboserdovs is rooted in a personal grievance in the past, of which Danilov is aware. Bychin thus reduces political conflict to the levelling of personal scores. And, unlike Valentin Trifonov's similar representations as reported in *Otblesk kostra*, although Danilov is widely respected, he is unable to stop the execution.

Danilov alone is prepared publicly to defend Migulin's unauthorized advance, he alone among the leading Bolsheviks tries to understand the differing social and economic strata of Cossack society, and deplores the use of terror. Trifonov the author invests Danilov with Clio's ability to discern the patterns of history:

Grim was the year, grim was the hour hanging over Russia... Like volcanic lava this grim time flowed on, swallowing and burying everything with fire. And against this background of fire something new, unprecedented was born... When you're flowing in the lava-stream you don't notice its heat. And how can you see time if you're in the middle of it? Years have gone by, a life has passed, and you begin to get to grips with the how and the what, why this happened and why that... It was a rare man who could see and understand all this from a distance, with the mind and the eyes of another time. Shura was such a man.[31]

But this vision is ambivalent, for while he refuses to compromise his own integrity by being included in the tribunal at Migulin's trial, the verdict of which he sees as pre-ordained 'political theatre', he thereby abandons Migulin, leaving him completely at the mercy of his enemies. It is hardly an act of courage, more one of petulance and, ultimately, cowardice: he fears either being proved wrong, or even being tainted with Migulin's guilt. The author's representation of his father is therefore ambivalent: he is far-sighted, humane, but powerless to stop unjust executions, and at the last minute he deserts Migulin.

Danilov is easily contrasted with the other Bolshevik figures in the novel. Danilov knows Shigontsev, for instance, from their days together doing hard labour in Tobol'sk, but the latter's philosophy is more akin to that of Nechaev: he believes that 'mankind will perish unless it changes its psychological make-up, unless it rejects feelings and emotions' (III, 454). Shigontsev is, indeed, likened to Nechaev by Pavel Evgrafovich's mother, Nechaev 'as described by Zasulich' (III, 456).[32] Shigontsev embraces Nechaev's credo of self-abnegation, of disregarding the means or the cost in pursuit of the main goal. It is this type of dehumanizing rationale that brings the Bolsheviks of *Starik* close to the terrorists of *Neterpenie*. Whereas Danilov seeks laws and patterns in order to establish truth and justice, Shigontsev relies on historical parallel, in particular the French Revolution. Jokingly Danilov refers to him as the 'Count of Monte Cristo'. Braslavskii is a Jew whose hatred of all Cossacks goes back to the pogroms of 1905, and he, like Shigontsev, is intent on creating widespread terror through mass killings. Naum Orlik is the same age as Danilov, he is more widely read, but is rigidly dogmatic in his intellectual classification of people according to ideological criteria.

We last see Danilov in the early 1930s, noting with trepidation the shape of things to come as foreign engineers are unmasked as 'spies' and put on trial. Letunov recalls in scattered phrases his own subsequent exile in Siberia, as the Revolution swallows its children and Stalin destroys the generation that made the new world.

The novel is not only about the nature of history, but also, as Robert Russell points out, about 'the nature of memory'. Russell notes that 'running parallel to the notion that documents can reveal things that the fallible memory can not there is the counter notion that the whole truth is not accessible through documents alone, but only when the objectivity of the document is supplemented by the individual emotional involvement with the past which is contained within the private memory'.[33] Furthermore, 'everyday life only becomes real when it is subjected to the patterning of memory'.[34]

Pavel Evgrafovich, like Glebov, is unable, or unwilling, to remember details which are uncomfortable to him. Thus, only at the very end of the narrative, a year after the old man's death, we learn of his part in Migulin's trial, from a postgraduate student researching Migulin's life:

'The truth of the matter is that Pavel Evgrafovich, the kindest of men, in 1921, when asked by the prosecutor if he admitted the possibility of Migulin being part of a counter-revolutionary uprising, replied sincerely: "Yes, I do," but, of course, he had forgotten about that, not surprisingly, because everyone, or almost everyone, thought likewise at the time, there are times when truth and faith become inseparably fused together, and it is difficult to figure out which is which, but we will get to the bottom of it.' (III, 605–6)

Now we can understand the surprise expressed by Asia in her letter that opens the novel, that if anyone should write positively about Migulin, she did not expect it to be one of those who helped destroy him. Indeed, old Letunov's efforts to see Asia, to ask her why Migulin went to the front against orders in August 1919, seem a last-ditch attempt for him to appease his own conscience. He was jealous of Migulin in his youth, because he also loved Asia and he cannot understand her reply to this question, when he finally seeks her out. She is not interested in Migulin as a historical figure, but simply as the man she loved more than anyone else.[35]

Pavel Evgrafovich's memories, flashbacks and memories within memories are not arranged chronologically, but rather by association, so that, for example, the sound of gunshots outside, as the local authority kills off stray dogs, casts him back into the mayhem of 1919. Names suddenly appear, to be given faces and personalities later. Sometimes these are corpses, such as that of Volodia, Asia's brother and Pavel's friend in 1919, found with his throat cut in the old man's first recollection. We are introduced to some characters, only to be told of their future fate: Bychin is later killed, his colleague Usmar' unmasked as a White agent, Shigonstev murdered, Braslavskii executed. The disrupted flow of Letunov's memories is further illustrated with reference to Shigontsev, and his friend Egor Samsonov, head of the Petrograd Putilov militia: 'If we could have known that in three months time in Rostov, where Egor would enter with his Petrograd detachment, Shigontsev would accuse him of being soft-hearted and demand that he be turned over for trial by tribunal. And now there he was, crying, because he couldn't see Egor right away, this minute' (III, 455).

It is not only Letunov's thoughts we are a party to. Even within the old man's memories Trifonov takes us close to the feelings and perceptions of other characters, such as Shigontsev, and in the 1970s narrative, takes us into the minds of characters such as Izvarin and Kandaurov. Indeed, the 'stream of consciousness' technique is most effective in presenting Kandaurov's mind jumping from one subject to another in random association as he tries to resolve several problems at the same time. It also gives us another view of Pavel Evgrafovich, as Kandaurov sees him an old man claiming to live by his principles, that he needs nothing of material benefit, but who every day still enjoys meals specially prepared (*spetsobedy*) in a closed refectory. The image of Pavel Evgrafovich that we get from within his own frame of reference is thus subverted, for no matter how sanctimonious he may make himself out to be, he is an active contributor to injustice.

In the random flow of Letunov's memories we also get a vivid picture of the heady days of 1917, before the violence and bloodshed, with Petrograd full of people talking about freedom and idealism, with manifestoes, meetings, elections. Letunov, indeed, takes us through 1917 almost month by month, as he sells copies of *Pravda* in the Duma and stands for hours queuing for bread and firewood, and relates the fears in the capital as people prepare for General Kornilov's assault, which was ultimately to bring the Bolsheviks to power. Trifonov undoubtedly uses material from *Otblesk kostra*, in particular the diaries of Pavel Lur'e, and this documentary realism helps convey the immediacy of experience, to recreate the actual life of individuals and society, and so to bring history to life.

The novel juxtaposes past and present not only through Pavel Evgrafovich's memories. These are, after all, subjective and therefore, like Glebov's, highly selective. Sania Izvarin's memories of the past are also spurred by a chance communication, in this case a telephone call from Prikhod'ko, the director of the *dacha* co-operative. Izvarin recalls his childhood years in the co-operative thirty-five years before, his family, their neighbours the Letunovs, and his awe and respect for Pavel Evgrafovich (which contrasts sharply with Kandaurov's dismissive cynicism). He recalls other neighbours, including the son of old Prikhod'ko who was to die in the War, Prikhod'ko himself, who denounced Izvarin's father, and several others from that time. Having spoken with Prikhod'ko after a break of thirty-five years, Izvarin suddenly realises that the past never disappears: 'Aleksandr Martynovich had time in those four or five seconds to think that life was a kind of system where everything was in some enigmatic way, and in line with some higher plan, like a circle, nothing existed separately, in wisps, but stretched on and on, becoming intertwined, and not disappearing without trace' (III, 521).

Past and present are more closely 'intertwined'. Izvarin recounts the pre-revolutionary history of the *dacha* co-operative, *Burevestnik* ('Stormy Petrel'), when it was part of the landowner Korzinkina's estate, before it was burned down by peasants in 1917. There is an obvious similarity with Pavlinovo, in *Obmen*. Indeed, in the earlier work the sports complex that replaces the *dacha* settlement is called *Burevestnik*. Similarly, when Kandaurov looks at his young mistress Svetlana, he sees that 'her ancestors were probably servants of the Russian boyars. Or Tartar grandees' (III, 500).

More substantially, the novel includes another plot set in the present, revolving around the intrigues of Ruslan, Kandaurov and Izvarin to acquire a recently vacated *dacha*. As in *Obmen* the acquisition of living space is a key theme, and the image of the *dacha* as a rural haven is again laden with metaphorical suggestion.

Ruslan wants the *dacha* for himself, but his most serious rival is Oleg Vasil'evich Kandaurov, a Foreign Ministry official. In his forties, physically very fit, and with a youthful mistress Svetlana, Kandaurov abides by one principle in life: 'But one thing Oleg Vasil'evich knew for sure, and this was a principle he had long lived by, since the days of his youth, and that was: if you want to get something, exert all your power, all the means available, explore all possibilities, everything, absolutely everything... until something gives' (III, 498).

Kandaurov is unusual among Trifonov's male characters in that he is strong, but his strength lies in his total lack of scruple. He lies to everyone, including his wife and mistress, uses flattery, threats and bribery, according to the circumstance, to get what he wants, whether this be a medical certificate of good health, a prestigious trip to Mexico, or the right to own the *dacha*. He takes pleasure in recalling an incident when he was faced unexpectedly on the street with Svetlana's fiancé, and momentarily dropped him with a karate blow. Everything – from karate to yoga, knowledge of foreign languages to the ability to drop a literary quotation into a conversation (from Goethe, significantly) – is for him a means of self-assertion, used to impress, cajole, obtain. Trifonov's intellectual heroes of the Moscow stories are weak and indecisive, and typify the essential relationship of the intelligentsia to their times; the likes of Gartvig, Klimuk and Kandaurov embody the cynicism and blatant materialism that Trifonov sees as the dominant feature of the latter Brezhnev years.

Kandaurov is, like Gartvig and Klimuk, completely immersed in himself and interested only in satisfying his own selfish needs. However, he is unable to hide his real self: Svetlana knows that he lies to her when they meet for the last time before his departure, and finally his inner corruption spreads to his body when he is diagnosed as seriously ill, possibly with cancer. Given Kandaurov's strenuous efforts to keep himself sound in body as well as mind, this is, to say the least, a bitterly ironic outcome.

Still more ironic is the fate of the co-operative. All the intrigues to gain possession of a *dacha* come to naught: the Moscow City Council decide to level the whole area. The *dacha* is traditionally a place of reflection and peace: a haven of purity and wholeness. In *Starik* it is the scene of domestic squabbling, cynical manipulation, the shooting of dogs, with the air thick with smoke as fires burn nearby. The *dacha* is once more in Trifonov's fiction destroyed by the state, this time not to make way for houses or a sports stadium, but in order to construct a rest-home for state officials. The Revolutionary generation is usurped, and its values trampled underfoot to make way for the material comforts of the new generation of the political élite.

The past, again, is betrayed. Pavel Evgrafovich's life is running out, he feels increasingly that he has little time to discover the truth about Migulin's action, if only for himself. Pavel Evgrafovich's inability to understand Migulin is really his failure to face up to his own past. We recall Ol'ga Vasil'evna's words towards the end of *Drugaia zhizn'*, that in order to understand others we must first understand ourselves. With the destruction of the *dacha*, there is no past to remember, or build a future on. Time is running out for Pavel Evgrafovich in this life, just as time is running out for the *Burevestnik dacha* community, as it is running out for Oleg Kandaurov. Little wonder, then, that the passage of time is represented as a 'flow', a 'stream', water imagery in direct contrast to the fires raging in the woods around Moscow and the *Burevestnik*, and the fire and smoke with which Pavel Evgrafovich associates the year 1919 in his memories. It is an apocalyptic vision, suitably powerful and grotesque for Trifonov's last work of fiction to be published while he was alive. Significantly, Trifonov combines fire and water in the image of the 'lava flow' of time, suggesting that time not only sweeps everything along in its path, but also reduces all human striving to ash. It can be no accident, then, that Ruslan, displaying commendable civic consciousness and courage, helps to fight the forest fires, but gets quite badly burned in the process. And then hears about the decision to reduce the *dacha* co-operative to dust.

Dust and ash are emotive symbols with which to designate the Soviet present, but most of the representatives of the modern world live out spiritually barren lives.[36] Pavel Evgrafovich's unhappy daughter Vera is forced into a succession of abortions by her husband Nikolai Erastovich, a sharp contrast to the fertility of Asia Igumnova's richly endowed family before the Revolution. Prikhod'ko, a secret police informer under Stalin, organizes the shooting of stray dogs, and the gunmen are eagerly joined by the young children of the *dacha* community, including Tolia, Pavel Evgrafovich's grandson, who wants to shoot Arapka, the old man's own dog. Then there is the ultra-rationalist Kandaurov, cut down on the threshold of realizing his greatest ambition. Moscow, as elsewhere in Trifonov, is not only a locale, but both a synecdoche and a metaphor. Moscow itself seems to be ablaze as the intense August heat causes people to collapse in the street or on the Underground, and the *Vecherniaia Moskva* newspaper is full of death announcements. The new world was born in fire and smoke, and fire and smoke still characterize its contemporary development.

Starik is a work that repays detailed scrutiny, as it combines twin narrative planes, subtle psychological investigation and historical enquiry. Trifonov has stated that among all his writings, *Starik* is his favourite.[37]

Trifonov's narrative method, though, is not without its pitfalls. Because he does not explicitly offer judgment, but merely hints and alludes, he can be interpreted in differing ways, as the reactions of Mal'tsev, Efimov and Ermolaev illustrate. Many other Soviet critics have castigated him for not fulfilling one of the key demands of classical socialist realism: to state clearly the author's position *vis-à-vis* the reality he describes. On the other hand, Western critics have labelled him the writer of 'partial truth'. His texts provide material to support the view that he is at heart a socialist realist, on the one hand, or that he is sympathetic to dissident ideas, on the other. His vision of the movement of time and society is compatible with that of Engels, who saw the interrelation of all human life within the context of social evolution. But through allegory, allusions and parallels he subverts the rationality of a definitive, monolithic truth, and points to an understanding of historical continuity, even simultaneity.

However, Trifonov's accuracy as a historian is not here at issue. His marshalling and interpretation of facts are secondary factors, for Trifonov, meticulous as he is in uncovering details and facts, is first and foremost a novelist. He is intent on showing his aesthetic concept of time and man, and his vision of the historical process in general and Russia's historical development in particular. He is above all a writer of fiction, who uses actual events and personalities as the factual basis for his historical novels.

Trifonov's two historical novels are linked on several levels, and the historical theme is an integral, if often necessarily understated, part of the author's Moscow stories. Trifonov's main interest is the Revolution and its legacy, and especially the men who made it. To this end he analyses the essentials of revolutionary activity in Russia in the 1870s – 1880s, and in the years 1917–21. Here the fate of Migulin-Mironov is crucial. Trifonov admits that Migulin is not a complete representation of Mironov; rather, that the former is a 'collective' image, combining features common to Mironov and other Cossack leaders, such as Dumenko, who was also shot by the Bolsheviks. Dumenko is also 'rehabilitated' in *Otblesk kostra*. Trifonov is aware of his own Cossack lineage, and much of his writing is devoted to showing how the Bolsheviks in 1917 and their Stalinist successors have systematically destroyed the past and alienated Russians from their history. Oklianskii sees Migulin not so much as a Cossack revolutionary as a peasant rebel, a man of the soil who speaks the same language as those under his command and who is loved and respected by them. The real victors in this struggle are those who betray the Revolution by taking away those freedoms that people like Migulin-Mironov fought for.[38] Migulin's tragedy, for Letunov, is that he 'was not understood'; moreover, he is one of the great dupes of Russian history. He fought for the Bolshevik cause because he thought that it offered the greatest promise of freedom for his people. The Bolsheviks used him to win over the Cossack peasantry, and when he was no longer needed, they destroyed him. Just as they were to destroy the author's father a little more than a decade and a half later.

Trifonov, then, is begging questions not only about Russia's past, but its future, its destiny. He sees the Revolution and Civil War, and their aftermath, in a historical context, as a continuation of Russia's flirtation down the centuries with concepts of freedom and tyranny. In political terms, the October Revolution is a mirror image of the French Revolution, but the tyranny it engendered has its roots in the Russian past. It is with *Starik* that Trifonov finally realizes that his father died in vain, and that the tyranny that destroyed him is still active today. Only the power of memory can preserve truth and the striving for freedom. It is significant that Trifonov was planning to develop his researches into the history of Russian radicalism, with a projected book on German Lopatin, a nineteenth-century radical who drifted from Populism to Marxism. Lopatin would have represented a link not only between Russian Populism and European Marxism, but also between history and ideology.[39] The book, though, was not completed.

In the final analysis, Trifonov's works are about the nature of life in the modern age, where memory of the past, of continuity and of truth, is necessary to offset a 'living death'. Life and death, past and present, justice and oppression, freedom and tyranny – these are all questions that are constantly juxtaposed in Trifonov's fiction. Life is what is lived, felt, experienced, recalled by the individual; without human emotion, accountability or atonement, there can be no real life.

CHAPTER 5

Time and place
(Vremia i mesto; Ischeznovenie)

Starik marks the end of a stage in Trifonov's career not readily appreciated by critics: where history, ideas and modern urban life are interwoven. In subsequent works Trifonov becomes interested in the interaction of the writer-figure and his time, and in particular in his own experience as a mirror of the national experience.

Vremia i mesto begins where Glebov fears to tread: with memories. The first few paragraphs begin: 'Should one remember ... ?', as the author recalls details of his childhood in the 1930s, and the first chapter ends with words that give meaning and structure to the whole novel: 'Does one need to remember? Good God, that's as stupid as asking "does one need to live?" For remembering and living are of one piece, they are joined (*slitno*), the one cannot be destroyed without the other being destroyed, and together they form a verb that has no name' (IV, 260).

This first chapter also informs us that Sasha Antipov, the central character, is eleven years old, that the action is set in the 1930s, and that Antipov's father, who has left for Kiev, will never return. Sasha's biography up to this point closely follows Trifonov's own (although Trifonov's own father disappeared not on the way to Kiev, but in Moscow), and there are further parallels as the narrative progresses.

The opening chapter is set at the Antipovs' *dacha*. The importance of the *dacha* motif in Trifonov's fiction has already been discussed as being symbolic of purity and innocence, and so a metaphor for revolutionary ideals. Here it serves as a backdrop for the playing out of scenes from Sasha's childhood, happy carefree times of swimming and playing by the river. This is the idyllic, archetypical myth of Eden before the 'fall' into human history, here represented by the purges and specifically the disappearance of Sasha's father. These darker times are already looming, if as yet confined to the background: Sasha's friend Chunia relates how he saw the parents of Gal'ka Bol'shaia, another friend, burning documents on the terrace of their *dacha*. Children would perhaps not be expected to understand the full adult significance of this, but not the children of Stalin's Russia. The other boys accuse Chunia of being 'a spy', to which he retorts: 'It's you who are spies! Everyone who has a *dacha* in your area is a spy! Spies, the lot of you, spies, spies!' (IV, 258). Chunia has been in the community only a year. He is chased by the others across the river, but on the opposing bank his father is waiting. Sasha is caught and punished, old Polikarpych twisting his ear downwards until the boy is almost bent double.

There are several points of interest in this opening chapter. The appropriation of the adult realities of spying and denunciation by children not only lays bare a corrupt and debased world, but also points to its fundamental absurdity. Indeed, this world makes sense only as a children's game. Furthermore, Sasha's 'punishment' by Polikarpych, or rather the sadistic meting out of physical pain as a radio plays a popular song in the background, is a metonymic representation of the disruption of childhood and of the inherent violence of a world played out against the feigned tranquility of stability. The pursuit of Chunia, and the treatment Sasha receives from Polikarpych, are reminiscent of the scene in *Dom na naberezhnoi* where Levka Shulepnikov is attacked by his classmates, and it is young Glebov who has to face Levka's sadistic stepfather alone. Finally, the fact that this episode takes place at Sasha's *dacha* indicates a certain progression from Trifonov's usual treatment of this theme: elsewhere it may be equated with the values of the old revolutionaries, but here it is associated with pain and injustice. The idyll is no more.

The novel is Trifonov's most complex work in terms of structural and narrative technique. In *Dom na naberezhnoi*,

Neterpenie and *Starik* the author employs dual or multiple perspectives from which to view a reality that is often allegorized. In this novel we are once more presented with a narrator, the 'I' of the narrative, who does not so much comment on the actions or personality of the central character, as in *Dom na naberezhnoi*, but who rather represents a different consciousness, another, equally valid, experience of his time. The novel is about life, experience and literature, and how they interact through the years. Trifonov says that he is attracted by the 'novel of consciousness', and adds that this work represents a further progression from his earlier, 'two-dimensional' works in that it presents a multiplicity of views and experiences.[1] This multiplicity impels a move away from an all-seeing narrator who represents the author's consciousness, and to a narrative where authoritative judgment is eroded, even subverted.

The seemingly 'dialogic' form of the novel is asserted from the start: if Chapter One concentrates on Sasha as a boy, so this is balanced by Chapter Two, which describes the early childhood of the unnamed narrator. He recalls playing chess with Levka Gordeev, whose mother, Agniia Vasil'evna, is infinitely kind and compassionate: a nurse who takes in dogs with broken paws. He recalls also Levka's stepfather, Stanislav Semenovich, whom Agniia Vasil'evna rescued from hospital after his first wife had turned her back on him. Stanislav Semenovich is ill and sickly, one of life's victims, and Agniia Vasil'evna, like Sonia in *Dom na naberezhnoi*, is one of life's angels. She is in demand with the patients at the hospital where she works, who want only her to give them their injections.

The narrator also shares some details with Trifonov the writer: he lives with his grandmother, and lies when asked where his purged parents are. Trifonov therefore invests both his 'heroes' with elements from his own experience. Antipov will become a writer, the narrator a scientist; it is as if the author is striving to encompass and convey a totality and inseparability of experience, that of the intellect and that of the heart, over the subsequent decades of the narrative.

The narrator and Antipov, just like the narrator and Glebov in *Dom na naberezhnoi*, are alike in many respects. Neither, for example, is called up into active front-line service due to bad eyesight – just like Trifonov himself. Both wear glasses, both are taciturn, they are almost the same age (the narrator is six months younger), both live without their parents, and both dream of studying in the Literary Institute after the War. Furthermore, both visited the literary society of the House of Pioneers before the War, though they do not recall one another. (Here one might add that all of these details are also true of Trifonov himself, and that Sergei Baruzdin, the future editor of *Druzhba narodov*, who was to publish *Dom na naberezhnoi*, *Starik*, *Vremia i mesto* and *Ischeznovenie*, also visited the House of Pioneers literary circle with Trifonov before the War.[2]) The narrator comments: 'But I didn't like Antipov. There was something in him that made me uneasy. For a long time I couldn't understand, then I guessed: he was too much like me ... I didn't like him because I sensed my own badness in him. And there was nothing I could do. My badness, as in a radio tuned into the right wavelength, responded to his badness' (IV, 332–3).

The narrator and Antipov therefore represent a single, though disrupted, consciousness, unlike Glebov and the narrator in *Dom na naberezhnoi*. However, both are projections of the author himself, and are attempts not to contrast experience, as with Glebov and the narrator, but to synthesize and unify it.

This essential interconnectedness is well expressed in the first chapter in one of the narrator's asides, as he juxtaposes the park and the hospital, from the vantage point of his adult, present-day existence:

Everything is so tightly woven, one thing so firmly interknit with another, as if it cannot exist separately: kindness and hopelessness, euphoria and sadness, the sweetest joy and death, and so on and so on, so that it seems so distant. For example, the park and the hospital. In one people enjoy themselves, in the other they suffer, and the boundary between them is an ancient fence of metal bars. All you have to do is climb over and you're there. I realized that a long time ago. Melancholy is the bedlam of autumn beneath your feet, music, a crowd of people on the embankment, red lamps, the creak of the landing-stage. The deserted house is a wooden table, playing chess to stupefaction, a tired irritating woman with an unsightly head resembling a pear. It is someone else's pain and unwanted goodness. (IV, 264)

The phrase 'the deserted house' (*Opustelyi dom*) also belongs to the title of a novel by Lidiia Chukovskaia, which is set against the background of the purges of the 1930s. The same image applies to Trifonov's own childhood, or rather the disruption of it after both his father and his mother were arrested. Trifonov would also refer to his family home as 'overturned'.[3]

Stanislav Semenovich is writing a historical pamphlet on the Neskuchnyi garden and the First City Hospital, formerly the house of Count Orlov. We are reminded of Troitskii's historical researches in *Drugaia zhizn'*, all the more so as later, when the adult narrator reads the notebooks, it seems likely that Stanislav Semenovich feels a personal attachment to history: the original property was owned by a certain Pokhodiashin some two hundred years before, who sold it to Orlov. Pokhodiashin's father had been a simple cabman before he became a millionnaire by discovering some copper mines. Stanislav Semenovich may well be descended from Pokhodiashin on his mother's side. None of his adopted family regard his researches with any degree of seriousness, and Agniia Vasil'evna sees them as evidence that he is losing his mind. However, Levka's cousin Minka, who comes to live with them, does take an interest, and her mandolin playing is the only music to which the old man responds positively.

It is now the late summer of 1939, Germany has attacked Poland, but life in and around the parks of Moscow goes on as normal. Indeed, momentous historical events are far too distant for Levka and the narrator, as they while away their time playing chess and billiards. The author is at pains to stress the mundane, almost uneventful nature of experience, as the narrator's friendship with Levka fades. Instead, Levka becomes involved with the womanizing bully Agababov, a character reminiscent of Levka Shulepnikov in *Dom na naberezhnoi*. Time affects others: Minka leaves, Agniia Vasil'evna commits suicide, Stanislav Semenovich is taken back into hospital. The narrator merely sums up events, coldly and dispassionately, and is similarly undisturbed by the news that Levka apparently was killed during the War. Agababov, though, survived, and returned laden with medals. Minka reappears later in the narrator's life as the adult Maria Osipovna, a pianist in the local philharmonic orchestra, and it is through her that the narrator receives Stanislav Semenovich's notebooks of historical researches.

Subsequently the temporal progression of the novel is uneven: with Antipov we move from 1946 to 1953, with the narrator we move from 1941 and the defence of Moscow, to February 1944. The narrative shifts once more, as we return to Antipov in 1950 and 1951, then forward to 1957, the thaw, and the return of former prison-camp inmates. The final chapters are set in the 1970s, without much discussion of the intervening decade, and it is in 1979 that the narrator and Antipov meet, after a break of thirty years. Trifonov has therefore taken a considerable slice of social history spanning a generation, and within that span depicts various temptations and trials – sexual, professional, moral and personal. Characters, some of them merely names without faces, appear initially in the 1950s then resurface in the 1970s. One of these is the Stalinist editor Roitek, who in 1950 rejects a story by Antipov, and then reappears at Antipov's restaurant table almost thirty years later.

As Antipov progresses through life, from childhood through to the War, from his student days in the late 1940s to his attempts to break into the ranks of the writing fraternity in the early 1950s, and finally to his middle age, we learn not only of the changes in his life, but of those around him. As with Trifonov's other works, the narrative is densely populated with names and personal details. Antipov's fellow students are Miron, Vit'ka (or Viktuar) Kotov, Tolia Kvashnin: by the late 1970s Kotov is dead, Miron is married to a Bulgarian actress and is living in Bulgaria, and Kvashnin has abandoned literature to take up an administrative position of some responsibility. Yet when they were students they were inseparable; whether they were drinking, eating out, or getting involved in street brawls. The passage of time is revealed not through the depiction or enumeration of external, historical events, but through the individual's reaction to or experience of them. In 1946, for example, Antipov's mother returns to Moscow after eight years of imprisonment and exile, and the scene of their reunion is related by Trifonov with both freshness and immediacy, as experienced by both sides:

> ... and suddenly the door opened with a click of the lock, she saw in the semi-gloom of the corridor the tall, bespectacled figure of a man, she started back in surprise and whispered: 'Shurka?', and Antipov saw a small woman dressed in a padded jacket and a kerchief, a small case with a forlorn-looking canvas covering on the floor next to her, for a second he looked at the woman in silence, then offered his hand and said: 'Mother?' And their weak cries to each other betrayed a questioning tone, not because they did not recognize one another, although this would have been understandable, but because they wanted to ask all at once: How was this? How was that? How have you been these eight years? (IV, 275)

Trifonov's own mother returned to Moscow in 1946, and we can assume that the feelings experienced by Antipov as he sees his mother for the first time are based on those Trifonov himself experienced.

Antipov's mother has returned illegally from her place of exile. She relates how on the train (she has been travelling for six days) in her sleep she pulled the emergency cord. The train duly stopped, and she was terrified that she would be taken away again if her documents had been checked. She could have been returned to prison, but a soldier in her compartment protected her. To Antipov this is material for a short story: he supposes that the soldier is from a German concentration camp. The subtext of this story would suggest that the oppressed of both the Stalinist and the Nazi systems support each other against totalitarian tyranny. In Stalin's Russia Antipov declines to write the story.

The historical background is reproduced in other ways, especially with regard to the darkness of the Stalin years. Valerii Izmailovich, a neighbour, informs on Antipov by writing a letter to the director of the institute where Antipov is a student, denouncing him as having 'a hostile disposition' that consists of reading 'unnacceptable' works 'by the *émigré* Bunin', and adds that his mother is living with him in Moscow illegally (IV, 302). In 1950 Antipov takes his novel to a publisher, only to find that the editor he has previously worked with has disappeared (to be replaced by Saiasov, who reappears in a more menacing role later). Nobody in the office expects him to return, nor are they surprised. Similarly, Antipov is fond of carrying a notebook around with him in order to jot down thoughts and impressions, and is one day stopped in the Moscow Underground as he writes something down, and his documents checked. The narrator is not exempt from this pervasive fear and suspicion. As he works in an aviation factory during the the War, the old worker Terent'ich suspects him of being a management plant to inform on the rest of the work-force. Smerin, the head of security at the factory, summons the narrator when Antipov is caught with black-market tobacco that was meant for the front. Smerin sees this as subversion, an attempt to undermine front-line morale. He impresses the narrator by knowing about everyone's past: Liudmila, a hunchback, is a former nun, Terent'ich a former kulak. Smerin wonders who brought these people together in one place, and suspects that it may be part of an anti-Soviet conspiracy. The matter therefore goes beyond any simple tobacco theft, and assumes the character of a Stalinist witch-hunt, even in wartime.

The reign of Stalin is a time to be feared, the objective is simply to survive. After the dictator's death the nation's life revives, and time becomes an existential experience. An early illustration of this is immediately after Stalin's death. At the same time as Stalin's funeral, Antipov is arranging an illegal abortion for his wife Tania with the doctor Ivan Vladimirovich Gorelov. As the crowds mill and swell outside, and mass hysteria takes over, resulting in the death of hundreds of people, Antipov watches from his flat on Trubnaia Square. For him the momentous occasion of what is taking place beneath him does not compare with what is going on in the next room. Stalin's funeral is of historic importance, an event that changes history; whereas Tania's planned abortion is a small, personal event, of no importance to anyone other than those immediately involved. The abortion does not go ahead, and life, if only in this small room, triumphs over death. This episode is a good example of the *slitnost'* of the great and the small, of the inseparability of human experience, of the continuation of life amid death and change. A temporal dimension is added when Ivan Vladimirovich recalls details of his life to Antipov, first as a rebellious student in 1911, when he threw a sponge used for cleaning corpses at Kasso, the Tsarist Minister of Enlightenment. The story is completed by Antipov's aunt Ksenia who adds that Gorelov was then exiled; then came the War, internment and the Revolution. In one scene we are presented with a great historical event, a private dilemma and memory of the past.

The passage of time and history apart, the novel's main focus is on artistic creativity, censorship, and the creative process itself. As a first point of contact, Trifonov recreates the pressures experienced by a writer who has to perform according to the dictates of Zhdanovite socialist realism. In the late 1940s Antipov brings two short stories to Roitek, the literary editor of the (fictional) newspaper *Molodoi moskvich* (Trifonov's first stories were in fact published in *Moskovskii komsomolets*); but Roitek suggests, in the case of one of them in particular, certain changes. Antipov responds:

'I think that would destroy the story... You see, Roman Viktorovich, this story is about nothing. You either have to accept it or not accept it. Not everything lends itself to being redone.'

'Nonsense. Everything does! Just remember, young man, everything that is genuine can be re-done, and that which cannot is rubbish and rotten. Only something which is rotten cannot stand up to it and crumbles. Good material can always be reformed.'

Antipov thought, then said:

'No, I don't agree.'

'I believe that you study in Boris Kiianov's seminar? Let him tell you how many times he re-did *The Star Wormwood*. In its original form it was something completely different. By the way, be sure to give him my best regards!' (IV, 304)

There is a subtle, understated irony at work here. Socialist realism only recognizes as true art works which can be rewritten in accordance with its dictates: in its extreme, Zhdanovite form it would recognize no work as timeless or ineffable. And such utilitarian notions were taken by many as unalterable truths. Boris Kiianov is a case in point.

Boris Georgievich Kiianov is a teacher at the Literary Institute and in charge of Antipov's seminars. Their relationship is therefore very similar to that of Belov and Kozel'skii and Glebov and Ganchuk, and is presumably based on that of Trifonov himself and Fedin. However, the revelation that Kiianov rewrote one of his major novels in order that it be ideologically acceptable is reminiscent of the fate of Alexander Fadeev and his novel *Molodaia gvardiia* ('The Young Guard'). Fadeev's novel originally appeared in 1945, and, after some initial praise, was soon singled out for harsh criticism on the grounds that it failed to emphasize the Party's leading role in the Komsomol's resistance to the German invasion of the Kuban'. Fadeev duly rewrote the novel, and the revised version appeared in 1951. Kiianov's resemblance to Fadeev is strengthened later in the narrative when he commits suicide when the authorities begin releasing political prisoners during the post-Stalin thaw. As with Migulin in *Starik*, the figure of Kiianov combines features of two actual personages.

Kiianov's self-judgment comes as a result of his meeting Misha Teterin, a writer recently returned from the camps. Kiianov and Teterin studied together in the *gimnaziia* before the Revolution, and were fellow-writers in the 1920s before Teterin's arrest. Kotov informs us that before the War Kiianov was a second-rate writer, certainly not in the same category as Teterin. To Kotov, Kiianov's novel *The Star Wormwood* is 'devoid of substance'. When Teterin returns to Moscow he refuses to meet Kiianov. Teterin's coolness towards the prospect of meeting his old friend after almost a quarter of a century only adds to Kiianov's anxiety. It transpires that in 1934 Kiianov and Teterin had co-written a play, but after Teterin's arrest Kiianov removed Teterin's name from it. This is understandable: otherwise the work would not have been published or performed. Teterin, though, does not recall asking Kiianov to remove his name from the play. But the suspicion lingers: did Kiianov make use of Teterin's disappearance to enhance his own standing and reputation? It is Teterin who makes the telling comment on the age: 'The writer is alive, but his books have disappeared. Usually it's the other way around: the books are alive but the writer is dead' (IV, 441). Kiianov insists that he sent proceeds from the royalties to Teterin's wife Tatiana Robertovna, but she is unable to speak with or meet him. The coldness between the two men is never dissolved. We learn also that Teterin's novel *Akvarium* ('Aquarium') earned him great success at the time, and that Kiianov did not act 'one hundred per cent as a gentleman' after his arrest (IV, 361). But once more this is hearsay, a version of events and human reactions as related to Antipov, and therefore just one of many voices in the narrative. Indeed, the reader is not told who is the source of this information, simply that 'of course, everyone in the literary world knows of that' (IV, 361-2).

Kiianov is consumed by guilt following Teterin's return. Teterin refused to denounce colleagues in the 1930s, and the suspicion remains that Kiianov acted in the way he did not only to survive, but also to prosper. Kiianov's guilt is expressed in his dreams: he sees himself in a bomb-shelter-like building with the wind blowing overhead, with people passing him in blindfolds. They do not see him, though he sees them: the dead pass before him, bringing to the fore Kiianov's guilt at having survived while others perished. Kiianov tries to write a novel based on dreams: after years of self-deception, truth and fantasy become confused. Kiianov is a sad example of a writer who survived the purges, only to be accused after Stalin's death of abetting the tyranny. Whether he did or not is not made clear; but the accusation stings his conscience, and in the end he takes a drug overdose.

After his suicide Antipov is appointed to head the commission to discover the truth about Kiianov, but objective truth is impossible to find in this case. It resides in the memory of each person who knew Kiianov, and each person has his own 'truth'. Memory is selective and subjective. The only meaningful act is that of forgiveness, as Teterin forgives Kiianov. Life is difficult to categorize, truth difficult to ascertain, and we do not know if

Kiianov has actually done anything wrong that would merit forgiveness.

Kiianov's past and present stand as a counterpoint for Antipov when he is invited to act as a literary expert in a case of litigation. Old Dvoinikov is accused by Saiasov, his deputy, of plagiarism, in publishing a series of Russian classical texts. Antipov is hired to compare texts by Dvoinikov's lawyer, in order, of course, to rule in favour of Dvoinikov. Antipov is offered five hundred roubles for what should amount to a couple of evening's work. It is obviously a dishonest exercise, but Antipov needs the money. 'The Dvoinikov affair' quickly becomes even more dishonest. Dvoinikov is accused by his younger deputy Saiasov, whose brother is an editor in a publishing-house where Antipov has submitted his novel. It is made clear to him that if he testifies in favour of Saiasov, his novel will be published; if he supports old Dvoinikov, it will be rejected. Pressures are exerted on Antipov from all sides: his mother and sister advise him to drop the case, his friends Miron and Fedia Priakhin insist that he must support Saiasov for the sake of his book. Antipov looks further into the case to find out more about the two men involved, but hears conflicting views. Dvoinikov is apparently kind and generous and helps struggling writers with work. On the other hand he uses these 'defenceless' people to make money for himself. He also hears from Saiasov that Dvoinikov (as his name would suggest) is duplicitous and has instigated a reign of terror in the publishing-house where he works. Antipov learns about Saiasov's ability to betray others from both his secretary Tania, and his own subsequent experience. It is up to Antipov to decide himself, to make his own moral choice, and to take into consideration the differing aspects of Dvoinikov's character. As he muses:

Because he had nowhere to retreat to, and nothing to feel sorry about, and displaying cowardice was not his style, he realized that the only way out was to find out the truth. And he would find it out. And this is what it was: Dvoinikov did indeed aim to earn money through the efforts of others, but he also was generous in the help he gave to others. Yet how could this be combined in one man? It did, somehow. Everything was there in him... He was both brave and cowardly:

during the War he had been decorated for bravery, and yet at home he was afraid of his daughter, who at times beat him. He was both an old man and a raw youth, tormented by love and by an old man's pains, such as heart complaints.

How could Dvoinikov – whose every molecule was split in two – be made whole? (IV, 409–10)

Antipov rules in favour of Dvoinikov, sees his book 'fall' from the publisher's plan, and refuses the fee he so desperately needed. He thereby asserts his own independence and integrity, but sacrifices the prospect of material betterment and status.

From the pressures of writing according to the dictates of socialist realism, and the whims of literary editors, and from the pressures to conform and collaborate with the tyrants of the literary world, Trifonov moves on to an exploration of the creative impulse itself. Throughout the novel Antipov is writing, or thinking about writing, a short story or work. Kotov is courting a woman from the Arbat who cooks wonderful fish soup, and Antipov suddenly has the idea for a short story 'Fish Soup'. Antipov has a brief affair with a girl called Gortenziia, after helping her carry her bags and bathing with her in the river near her *dacha*. He shelters from a storm with her, and is then beaten up by her brother Lavr and a friend who mistake him for someone else. They apologize, Antipov reflects on all the chain of events leading to this, and thinks of the story 'The Chain'. Everything is interconnected, everything has its origins and its consequences. Antipov makes literature from life, transforming episodes from real life into art. When his mother returns surreptitiously from exile, and that night kisses him for the first time in eight years, Antipov decides to write the story 'The Kiss'. But this has already been done by Chekhov, so he thinks of the story 'For the Sleep to Come', but that, too, has been done already by someone, probably Hemingway. Literature is always writing and rewriting itself, in a never-ending dialogue with itself. Thus Trifonov's own *Dom na naberezhnoi* is a rewriting of *Studenty*; *Ischeznovenie* in its turn contains easily recognizable elements from *Dom na naberezhnoi*, *Vremia i mesto* and *Otblesk kostra*.

Vremia i mesto is itself a self-consciously literary narrative in which the conventions of literature are superficially taken for granted but then on a deeper level subverted. There are some pretensions to ornate descriptiveness, such as when wartime barrage balloons lying in the park are likened to huge cocoons out of which huge butterflies will appear, or the description of Antipov's first entrance into Kiianov's flat, described from Antipov's point of view as he notes with mystery and wonder the pictures on the walls, old-fashioned furniture, crumpled rugs and piles of books. This Aladdin's cave is inhabited, respectively, by a woman in a dressing-gown, a hunchback, or a least a man with no neck, and then Kiianov himself, who is introduced at first as a disembodied voice who mistakes Antipov for someone called 'Markusha'. Sentence structure, with the use of many subordinate and relative clauses which seem to pile up on one another, also adds to the flow and continuity of life itself. For example, Antipov travels to the Kuban' to write about a collective farm, and a whole paragraph consists of a single sentence detailing his arrival, the August heat, his attendance at meetings, the phrases he jots down, his smoking, drinking, and eating habits, and his travels round various villages.[4]

As with all literature, though, the novel is at root about truth and falsehood, the nature of reality and modes of perception. Although the bulk of the narrative is filtered through the consciousness of Antipov or the narrator, or related directly by the author, there are moments when we see the world through Kiianov's eyes. The most abrupt switch of viewpoint, however, occurs when the narrator recalls his time in Moscow during the War. He is helping the firemen in 1941 in the defence of Moscow, and is courting Olia Pletneva. The narrator's grandmother knows Olia's grandmother, Elizaveta Gavrilovna, from their years of Tsarist exile. Olia's family are preparing to leave Moscow, amid an atmosphere of barely subdued panic as people leave, giving away their pets, and rumours circulate that the water supply is to be cut off. Elizaveta Gavrilovna is helpless, for she is old and infirm, hardly able to move, and her daughter Ol'ga Anisimovna – Olia's mother – wants her to leave so that they can all take the train specially reserved for Old Bolsheviks and former political prisoners, for which the older woman qualifies. Both mother and daughter tolerate Elizaveta Gavrilovna as no more than an invalid who needs looking after, but then we are taken into her mind and experience her thoughts and feelings from inside. Through Elizaveta Gavrilovna's stream of consciousness emerge memories and the names of people she knew in exile. She emerges as a die-hard radical who condemns human weakness in others, including her own family, and for whom the great cause of the Revolution is more real than any simple human truth. As her family prepares to leave Moscow Elizaveta Gavrilovna recalls herself and her friend Dasha, who died in the Ukraine in 1921, as they attempted to escape from Siberia dressed as nuns. Elizaveta Gavrilovna is a type dear to the author, and is reminiscent of his own maternal grandmother, T. A. Slovatinskaia (compare, too, the figure of Aunt Pasha in *Drugaia zhizn'*). But there is here also a condemnation of the old woman's blind rationalism and Nechaev-like abnegation of human feelings.

There are several examples of Trifonov's parallel narrative technique in the work. Mention has been made of the narrator-Antipov dualism, of Dvoinikov and the Saiasov brothers. Other similarities include the figure of Kiianov, the *alter ego* of both Teterin and Antipov as a writer-figure who also embodies the tyrant-victim dichotomy of his age. The narrator works in the aviation factory with Liudmila, a hunchback; her physical disability corresponds to that of Grisha, the hunchback Antipov sees in Kiianov's flat. Such dualism applies to the time: the larger events in the outside world are of secondary importance compared to the internal life of characters. This is perfectly expressed in the scene of Stalin's funeral, when the historical moment, and the mass hysteria of the mourning crowds outside, are nothing to Antipov as his wife prepares to have an abortion in the next room.[5] Similarly, the narrator, Antipov, Liudmila and their workmates from the aviation factory throw a party, at which everyone is happy despite the misery and hardship of wartime. Indeed, reality to these people consists of the simple pleasures of vodka, tea, potatoes and beetroot. These seeming banalities are more vital, more immediate, than the victories of the Red Army as reported in the Ukraine, or the tasks of making radiators for aeroplanes. The personal becomes the irrational and eclipses the historic, the impersonal.

Reality itself is examined in the novel, as successive layers are laid bare and authoritative discourse is subverted. Dream and reality are confused, and not only by Kiianov. Antipov dreams that Susanna Vladimirovna, the departmental secretary, is trying to seduce him – but she has a moustache. He spurns her advance, and she taunts him with remarks about his virginity. The moustache is transferred to her from an unnamed circus performer, the partner of Natasha, a young girl Antipov has just met. The grotesqueness of the dream is a mirror-image of actuality. Susanna is about forty years old, and her sexual assertiveness in Antipov's dream corresponds to the rude joke told by Natasha, a girl half the age of Susanna, which takes Antipov's breath away and which he sees as sexual encouragement. Antipov's fear of women as threatening and domineering, and also what the future holds, are hinted at: Antipov will lose his virginity to Susanna. Tat'iana Robertnova, wife of Teterin, dreams of a goat in her bedroom which speaks to her. Her husband tells her that she needs to learn how to milk it; then, awake, she learns that the last thing her husband did before his arrest was to go to the village Kozino (from the word 'koza': a goat). Antipov has another dream in which Valerii Izmailovich, the neighbour who denounces Antipov's mother for living in Moscow illegally, falls down on his knees and begs forgiveness. Dream and reality are not that far apart; indeed, dream acts as a presentiment of the future. Views, opinions, dreams are all subjective, and the reader never gets a final, authoritative 'truth'. We see Antipov through his own eyes, and through the eyes of others, such as the narrator and Kiianov. Their views are their own, their 'truth', like that of Elizaveta Gavrilovna, has its own legitimacy. We never get to know whether Teterin did actually ask Kiianov to remove his name from the play they wrote together; we never find out the 'objective' truth of the Dvoinikov – Saiasov case. In both instances individuals make their decisions on the basis of the objective information they possess, as well as their subjective feelings and impressions. Like the truth of the past in Trifonov's historical works, subjective feelings and objective facts combine to form a *slitnost'* of experience and perception. Reality, then, becomes refracted through a myriad of human experience, individual, each viewpoint valid, each truth with its own importance. Subjective experience, like Tania's planned abortion, becomes more immediate and meaningful than the seemingly greater historical experience. As Antipov muses: 'Man can split the atom, investigate the most minute details of the world and is close to destroying the world with the sum of his knowledge, but he trembles helplessly before the mystery of whether this is real or not' (IV, 483). Reality, as with Rebrov and Troitskii, is the totality of experience, the merging of the objective and the subjective.

The book, then, is about experience. There are enough allusions to suggest or occasionally paint in detail the changing social and political environment as Antipov and the narrator progress through the years and decades: the purges, the War, post-war cultural repression (Kiianov, like Ganchuk and Kozel'skii before him, is denounced and attacked in the press), the thaw and the release of political prisoners, the 1970s. Human experience is inseparable from the historical experience which frames it, and the dualism of the novel as a whole suggests that Antipov's progression in the novel from childhood to middle age, which is very similar to Trifonov's own life, is also a refracted potted history of Soviet society itself, moving from youthful idealism through to terror and fear in its middle years before coming to rest in the cynicism and materialism of the present. *Byt* here is important, for the tests it sets him are the very fabric of Antipov's life: his many brawls, his friends, his sexual experiences, his attempts to record experience in literary form, the temptations to compromise principle for material gain. The links and cross-links in everyday life become more apparent in middle age: Antipov's son courts Roitek's daughter, becomes a doctor, and treats the narrator's daughter Katia in the last chapter of the novel. It is, indeed, through this latter link that Antipov and the narrator meet again after more than quarter of a century.

Another link of past and present is the curious figure of

Markusha, whom we first meet as the brother of Olia, the narrator's girlfriend during the War. He is also acquainted with Kiianov, and reappears in the 1970s, when, after the death of Antipov's mother, it is he who visits Antipov more frequently than anyone else. Markusha is another ambivalent character: a black-marketeer in books, he is described as 'a schizophrenic' and seen by Antipov as like a clock from Salvador Dali, ticking off the hours as Antipov finds himself in his own surreal time and place. Markusha cuts across both Antipov's and the narrator's worlds, and unites both past and present. He stands at the centre of the novel's temporal and structural framework.

The passage of time is counterbalanced by the permanency of place in the novel. Most of the action is set in Moscow, and many chapter headings indicate the actual place where the action of that chapter takes place: the Central Park, Tverskoi Boulevard, Iakimamka, the side-street behind Belorusskii Station, Trubnaia Square, Bol'shaia Bronnaia Street, the suburbs. Even when place-names change, as when Bol'shaia Kaluzhskaia becomes Leninskii Prospect, people's homes still remain. Antipov travels to the Kuban' and to Mongolia, the latter reminiscent of Trifonov's own travels East, to Turkmenia, as well as to Czechoslovakia. In each case experience – social, cultural and sexual – leads to him writing a story.

Literature as an integral part and a mirror of the everyday life of society is nowhere better demonstrated than in Antipov's novel *Sindrom Nikiforova* ('The Nikiforov Syndrome'). This is the great work Antipov comes to in his later years, and the culmination of Trifonov's novel. Nikiforov, Antipov's central character, is a writer living in Antipov's own time, a resident of Moscow, middle-aged and, like Antipov, not very successful. He is painstakingly writing a book about himself, or, as Antipov expresses it, 'an analysis of a life that didn't make out' (*analiz nesochinivsheisia zhizni*)' (IV, 468). Antipov's book is greeted with suspicion in his publishing-house, as internal reviewers and editors doubt the wisdom of writing a book about a fairly unsuccessful, not very talented or well-known writer. And, in true socialist realist spirit, 'if he was talented, but with limited success, it was necessary to show the social origins of his failure against a background of the life of the country' (IV, 468). Antipov asserts that there are origins and a background, but not those as demanded by socialist realism.

Nikiforov is a writer who is himself writing about another writer, who is in turn writing about a writer, who is also writing about a writer, and he is writing about a writer who is writing about some little-known nineteenth-century writer who is writing about a writer close to the Freemasons and the Novikov circle. We have therefore a series of 'mirrors, stretching across almost two centuries' (IV, 469), linking different historical epochs. Those who read the manuscript assume that Nikiforov, the creator of this 'chain', is the *alter ego* of Antipov, who is also, of course, the *alter ego* of Trifonov himself. Antipov has largely based Nikiforov on the figure of Kiianov, whose literary credo, borrowed from Dostoevskii, was that literature was about suffering. Antipov's novel is like a labyrinth, a Russian doll in which one writer is hidden inside another.

The writers are as follows: Ryndich, a Freemason; Ryndich is created by Klembovskii, consumed by anguish and guilt at having supposedly incriminated his friends and trying to come to terms with this feeling of guilt through writing. Klembovskii is the hero of Syromiatnikov, a writer in the nineteenth-century radical journal *Sovremennik*. Syromiatnikov is the subject of a novel by Vsevolodov, written in 1910 in exile, on the eve of Vsevolodov's flight to England. *The Nikiforov Syndrome* devotes most space, apart from Nikiforov's own life from the 1930s to the 1950s, to Vsevolodov. Vsevolodov was a thinker and terrorist, a poet and a merchant seaman who returned to Russia in 1917 and who was killed two years later in the Urals. He thus, like most of Trifonov's characters in this novel, combines seemingly paradoxical features. Nikiforov made his acquaintance in Iaroslavl' in 1918. Nikiforov has spent many years writing this novel, leaving it in order to write short plays or do lucrative translation work, or altering it in line with his own changing views and the changing times. All the writers are trying to find meaning in their writer-hero's death, to seek its relationship with the life he led.

A particular place in Nikiforov's life is occupied by his wife

Georgina Vasil'evna, or Goga. She is the subject of polarized views: some consider that she ruined Nikiforov as a writer, while others assert that she saved his life, especially in 'the difficult years'. Again, truth is double-edged. Goga saved Nikiforov by becoming the mistress of Iarbor, his interrogator. But Goga did much for Nikiforov after his death by publishing eight of his books and looking after his literary legacy. Indeed, Nikiforov would not be unusual in Soviet literature as a writer who published more posthumously than in his lifetime. Also, his widow is reminiscent of the great widows of Soviet literature, such as those of Mandel'shtam, Bulgakov, Platonov, Abramov and Tendriakov (and Trifonov's own, of course), who have preserved and then published their husband's work posthumously in more favourable political circumstances. Antipov is fascinated by Goga's personality. He is at the time having an affair with Irina, a film producer whom he first met in Czechoslovakia, and it is Irina he uses as a basis for developing Goga's personality and role.

Trifonov 'reproduces' whole pages from Antipov's novel, and we are introduced to several characters from this novel-within-a-novel.[6] Goga's first husband is Saenko, who returns to Moscow after several decades with his new family and asks her to help him 'correct his shaky affairs' (IV, 484). What these 'shaky affairs' exactly are we do not find out. Goga has a friend Lialia, from whom she learns of the death of Iarbor (Iaroslav Borisovich). Iarbor, we learn, died in 1955. He was very intelligent, wore glasses, played tennis: a tyrant, but also with features of the author Trifonov himself. The mirrors, then, proceed from Trifonov to Antipov, Antipov to Nikiforov, then to Nikiforov's characters, and come to rest with Iarbor. All represent mirrored experiences, and represent the chain of being, the interconnectedness of literature, and the interaction of man, his time and his place. Furthermore, the actions of Iarbor's widow following his death are in direct contrast to those of Goga. She sells his belongings immediately, moves to the south and abandons their flat.

Antipov's novel fails, because it is not the result of the artist's suffering. As he explains to his mother: '"It failed probably because I began something that was beyond me,' said Antipov. 'I wasn't up to it, you see. I can't dig deep enough, as you have to. You have to dig right down to the bottom, and get out the last reserves, and I only realised that by the end, when it was too late. Anyway, it doesn't matter. Don't get upset. I'll write something that won't fail"' (IV, 496).

Antipov's novels within novels are thus ultimately about the process of literary creativity itself, about the human emotions of love and pain, happiness and sadness which bring into life a work of art. Emotion is a creative force. When Antipov sits on a bench in an unnamed street, the old woman sitting next to him, whose face he does not even see, acts as a Greek chorus when she says that there is no joy in the world 'because man must love and be loved. Nothing else has any meaning' (IV, 502). The novel *Vremia i mesto* is not only about Trifonov's own literary craft and experience, it is also his most self-referential work of fiction.

The novel is about the relationship of individuals to the environment in which they live, work, love and write. But its terms of reference are broader, as elsewhere in Trifonov's writings. Russian art and literature are juxtaposed with Western art. Markusha is likened to the clock in Salvador Dali; Modigliani's orange woman with her blue but blind eyes is the point of comparison for Iuliia Fedorovna, an acquaintance of the narrator's daughter Katia. Links and associations stretch across cultural as well as national boundaries. The novel, like all art, is about life and death, the experience of living and creating, and the individual's relationship with his time.

Ischeznovenie is Trifonov's last large-scale work to be published, appearing almost six years after his death. Although it is incomplete, it has a curious unity. In particular, it contains many features common to both *Dom na naberezhnoi* and *Vremia i mesto*, and some motifs can be traced back to *Studenty*. The novel can be seen as a bridge stretching across the three decades of his *oeuvre*.

The first chapter of *Ischeznovenie* contains the seed of Trifonov's dialogue with time, the point of departure for all his other works:

Once I lived in this house. No – that house has long since died, disappeared, I lived in another house, but within these huge, concrete, dark grey, fortress-like walls. The house towered over a small two-storey building, detached houses, small churches, bell-towers, old factories, embankments with granite parapets, flanked on both sides by the river. It stood on an island and resembled a ship, heavy and absurd-looking, without masts, a helm or funnels, a cumbersome box, an ark, packed with people ready for disembarkation. Where to? No-one knew, no-one thought about that. To those people on the street walking past its walls twinkling with the lights of hundreds of small fortress windows the house seemed indestructible and eternal, like a cliff: over a span of thirty years its walls did not lose their dark grey hue.

But I for one knew that the old house was dead. It died long ago, when I left it. That's what happens with houses: we leave them, and they die.[7]

The physical description of the house takes us back into the territory of *Dom na naberezhnoi*: the large, imposing house on the embankment, the home of Levka Shulepnikov, Sonia Ganchuk, Anton Ovchinnikov, and the narrator, overlooking the dingy two-storey house where Glebov lived in his communal apartment. The metaphysical reflection on death brings us nearer to *Vremia i mesto*. And the death of the home is the seminal event from which Trifonov the writer is born. The *slitnost'* of Trifonov's themes is by now self-evident.

The narrative method of the novel is familiar: multiple viewpoints, parallel time scales, a central character who has many features common to Trifonov himself. This is sixteen-year-old Igor' Baiukov (Gorik), boarding a train in 1942 to return from Tashkent to Moscow, to work in a factory manufacturing radiators for military aeroplanes. As he changes trains in Kuibyshev, his luggage is stolen, and he has to make the rest of the journey without any belongings or food. Some fellow-passengers take pity and share their food with him, and in the background he overhears a conversation about the course of the War, the defence of Stalingrad and Mozdok, and the Anglo-American offensive in Libya. The battle of Stalingrad serves as a reference point throughout the text, as news of the progress of the fighting several times intrudes into the narrative, and into Igor''s consciousness, culminating in the news of the Soviet victory.

While aboard the train he has a dream. I have discussed the relevance of dreams with reference to other works, and this novel is no exception. Igor' dreams of his old apartment in Moscow, the layout of the rooms, and recalls how a mirror smashed without anyone touching it, just before New Year. Not only does the breaking of the mirror herald bad luck; it is a metonymic symbol for the eventual destruction (or 'overturning') of the home itself.

This dream prompts the first major flashback in the novel. Igor' recalls the happy times of his childhood, only a few years previously. This carefree time is particularly associated with the family *dacha* in Serebrianyi bor. The motif of the *dacha*, as we have seen, serves as a particular metaphor in Trifonov's writing. As in his Moscow stories this pristine setting is usurped by the modern urban world, so here, too, the realities of the adult world increasingly encroach upon Igor''s juvenile consciousness, as members of his family discuss the disappearance of friends. It is now 1937.

Throughout the novel snatches of overheard conversations provide the means of filling in the factual background to the narrative. As in Trifonov's other works, the temporal backdrop is drawn in almost elliptically, as if what is important is not the event, but the individual's response to it. Children disappear from Igor''s school, presumably, as in *Dom na naberezhnoi*, because of the misfortunes visited upon one or both parents. The young Igor' hears news from the front of the Spanish Civil War, and about the visit to Russia of the leftist German writer Lion Feuchtwanger. The death of Ordzhonikidze, Stalin's commissar for heavy industry, as reported by Igor''s father, also helps to establish authentic events as part of the backdrop.

In this work Trifonov strives for authenticity, both through memory and grasp of technical detail. His painstaking description of Igor''s work in the aviation factory is similar to the preoccupation with industrial processes in *Utolenie zhazhdy*. The various characters the reader comes across represent a cross-section of the work-force: Igor''s fellow-workers, such as the old man Uriuk, the young tearaway Kol'ka, the thirty-year-old Nast'ia, who has to work shifts in order to feed her three children; foremen such as Chuma, so called because he is always issuing orders frantically, shouting, cajoling, and never seems to be standing still (*chuma* in Russian means 'plague'), and the more deliberate Kolesnikov; and Avdeichik, head of the work-section (a less sinister version of Smerin in *Vremia i mesto*). These three layers are symbolic: the workers, watched over by 'supervisors' who, like the *liftery* in *Dom na naberezhnoi*, assume the role and functions of the secret police, with the autocratic figure in overall command.

The factory as microcosm is further evident in the atmosphere of fear within it. When he applies to work there, Igor' has to hide the fact of his father's arrest as an 'enemy of the people', and is later called in to Avdeichik's office. He goes with trepidation, fearing that his secret has been discovered. But Avdeichik has merely heard that Igor' has attended art classes, and wants him to draw up factory slogans. Igor' does so, but makes a spelling mistake: instead of the word '*shturmovik*' ('battle-plane') he writes '*shturmik*' ('little storm'), thereby, in the ever-vigilant eyes of those looking for any hint of subversion, denigrating the solemnity and vigour of the labour onslaught. This is not simply an orthographical oversight on his part; he realises that with his suspect background there could be a 'political undertone' (*politicheskaia podopleka*) evident to anyone who wished to look further.

These scenes from 1942 contrast sharply with those recalled by Igor' from five years previously. The family scenes in the *dacha*, with Igor''s sister Zhen'ka, his mother and father, grandmother, uncle Misha (based on Evgenii Trifonov) and his son Valera, and his uncle Serezha, are done with effortless ease. They are reminiscent of Chekhov's family scenes, and their relaxed tea-drinking on the balcony has about it an air of *fin-de-siècle* nonchalance. The love and closeness of the family is soon to be shattered by the imminent cataclysm.

Contrasted to this is Igor''s life when he returns to Moscow from evacuation in Tashkent. He returns not to his grandmother's apartment on Bol'shaia Kaluzhskaia (she has remained in Tashkent), but to the flat of her cousin, Vera, who lives in a communal apartment with her daughter Dina and granddaughter Marina on Strastnoi Boulevard, in the centre of Moscow. The joy of Igor''s return to Moscow, the familiarity he feels back in the streets of his childhood, is reproduced with the same feeling for the capital as was evident in *Studenty*. But life in the communal apartment is hard: there is not enough to eat, and not enough space. The *byt* of everyday life in a communal flat in war-torn Moscow is described as dark and chilling. There are none of the moral or ethical dilemmas of peacetime, this is a struggle merely to survive.

Igor' also recalls his Tashkent evacuation with his sister and grandmother (both his mother and father have been arrested). They are there with the half-senile David Shvarts, whose real-life prototype Aron Sol'ts was a great friend and comrade of Valentin Trifonov, and about whom Trifonov the son writes warmly as the 'conscience of the party' in *Otblesk kostra*. The picture we have of Shvarts here is a pathetic contrast to the dashing, fearless figure he once was: he wishes dearly to return to Moscow, and is reluctant to wash or shave until he does so: 'in his sick consciousness there was a connection here with the vows of his youth, when he would announce himself on hunger strike in prisons or would refuse to reply to the interrogator'. Shvarts is totally helpless, and depends on Igor''s grandmother. Without her, she knows, he would perish. The changes the years have wrought on Shvarts are not merely a manifestation of time's effects on individuals; there is also a political statement here. Shvarts in Tashkent is a sad shadow of his former self, and his shabby appearance and mental deterioration symbolize the physical degeneration of the ideals of the Revolution.[8] The moral degeneration of the times is personified more chillingly in their neighbour Siniakova, a vicious, prying old woman who despises as 'opportunists' what is left of the family after the purge, is continually exchanging cruel words with the grandmother and denouncing them or complaining about their presence to the authorities. When Igor' is back in Moscow, his grandmother writes to him about her hopes for a speedy return to Moscow, an outbreak of influenza in Tashkent and Shvarts' unchanging poor health, in a code they have invented themselves, a reflection of the conspiratorial role into which they have been thrown by the times.

If we return to Igor''s memories of his childhood, his schooldays are recounted with as much vividness as are his schoolfriends – characters with whom we are familiar from *Dom na naberezhnoi* and *Vremia i mesto*. Lenia Karas' is an obvious reproduction of Anton Ovchinnikov and Levka Gordeev, all based on the real-life Levka Fedotov. Similarly, Katia Florinskaia seems a distant relation of Sonia Ganchuk, although her father here is not an academic, but an important figure in the security service. Other characters such as Sapog, Chepets and Marat recall the likes of Morzh, Min'ka Byk and Khimius. Significantly, there is no character in this novel corresponding to Levka Shulepnikov. Adventures identical to those we know from previous works are related: the tyranny of a local gang, similar to the Bychkovs, where even the formulaic challenge to a fight, '*po kha ne kho?*', an abbreviation of '*po khare ne khochesh*'?' ('wouldn't you like a fist in your mug?') features in *Dom na naberezhnoi*. Lenia's 'testing of the will' is displayed when he shows Igor' and Marat round some caves he had explored alone, much to the amazement and awe of his friends (this event is alluded to in *Dom na naberezhnoi*).[9] There is also much description of school-days: the Pushkin competition, held in 1937 in connection with the centenery of the poet's death, which pupils in all classes are invited to enter, with portraits, scrapbooks, sculptures and so on (the first prize goes to a boy in the eighth-grade for his plasticine statue 'The Young Stalin reads Pushkin'). Igor' is terribly disappointed, because he thought that his scrap-book of portraits and pictures cut out from various magazines, newspapers and even books would win at least third prize. He also valued highly his own ability to remember more lines by heart from *Evgenii Onegin* than anyone else in the family, including his mother's brother Sergei, a student at Moscow university. The various antics to upset the teacher, the view from the class-room window – all details recreate the atmosphere of school-days.

It is not only Igor''s memories of a few years previously that are in the centre of the narrative. His grandmother's cousin Vera, rather like old Nila in *Dom na naberezhnoi*, tells him of her own past, her husband and the husband of Igor''s grandmother, both of whom died in the years of the Revolution. Her husband was executed 'by mistake', like Migulin, and Igor''s grandfather was killed in Baku. It is Vera who expresses one of the fundamental tenets of Trifonov's view of human society. Igor' reproaches her for sorting out grains of rice with a magnifying glass, accusing her of doing 'the labour of Sisyphos', after the Corinthian king who was sentenced to slavery in the underworld, eternally rolling a boulder up a mountain-side, only to let it roll down again near the top. She remarks: 'Just like every person. At first he's a king, then a slave.'[10] Here we have crystallized the author's view of life in Stalin's Russia, where man is either a tyrant or one of the oppressed, and can fall from his state of grace at any time. Shulepnikov, for example, in *Dom na naberezhnoi* begins his adolescence and adult life as a king, and by the end of the narrative is at the humblest level of human society; Glebov's progression is in the opposite direction. Characters such as Shvarts and Igor''s father also topple from the pedestal of eminence.

A more significant switch of viewpoint is when we see events through the eyes of Sergei, Igor''s uncle. We are still in the year 1937 when he recalls the recent dismissal of professor Uspenskii as 'a Trotskiist and ideological deviant': the echoes of *Studenty* and *Dom na naberezhnoi* are obvious. He is the lover of Ada, a young artist whose much older husband is an academic and the editor of a philosophy journal. The husband, Volovik, is a furious unmasker of 'spies' and 'enemies', about to suffer the same fate as those he has denounced. Sergei is always apprehensive of visiting her at home because of his fear of the all-seeing doorman who inspects everyone coming and going: another echo of *Dom na naberezhnoi*. Sergei is convinced that the mounting danger around Volovik will come to nothing, that Volovik himself is not threatened: 'He is one of those who do the hitting, but who is not hit himself,' he says.[11] But Volovik is arrested, and the apartment is searched, when Ada and Sergei have fallen asleep after making love (the description of their coupling is as elliptical as the would-be steamy scenes in *Starik*, when Kandaurov and Sveta share a shower, or in *Dom na naberezhnoi*, when Glebov sleeps with Sonia for the first time). The search, carried out by half a dozen stony-faced men in military uniform, is related as Sergei, shocked, embarrassed, uncomprehending, sees it. The thoroughness and sheer impersonality of the search, which lasts more than three hours, is a concise metonymic expression of the relentlessness of the Stalinist machine as it destroys human lives. We are not introduced to Volovik, we merely hear unfavourable things about him from Sergei and Ada, but this diffuseness merely heightens the pathos of Ada's subsequent rejection of Sergei. She displays loyalty toward her husband, and sets off for the famous building on Kuznetskii Most to join the long queue of similar women, all waiting for news of their arrested husbands.

A word should be reserved for the depiction of female characters in this novel, which in this respect is a marked departure from Trifonov's previous works. Characters such as Ada and Igor''s grandmother are made strong by the times they live in, by the sudden calamities visited on them. Igor''s mother, we learn, could not disown her husband following his arrest, despite the pressure put on her to do so. Dina tries to cope with wartime deprivation and maintain her human dignity as best she can. She disowned her own husband when he was arrested, out of consideration for her remaining family, and Marina helps the adolescent Igor' recover from a beating by unknown thugs with kisses and caresses. Igor''s workmate Nast'ia also has to work and look after three children and a sick mother. Old Vera still retains a sharp mind and clear ethical and moral priorities, and expresses some of the author's basic themes. Almost all the women in the novel (Siniakova is a significant exception) are portrayed as strong moral characters who assume responsibility for the fate of others when visited by misfortune. Not only must they survive, but they have to protect others. Most of the men have been, or are about to be, arrested, or are fighting at the front, and it is on the women that the burden of living and protecting the rest of the family falls. These images contrast sharply with the self-seeking opportunists of Trifonov's modern city, the likes of Lena and her mother in *Obmen*, Rita in *Predvaritel'nye itogi*, Mara Klimuk in *Drugaia zhizn'*.

Ischeznovenie, Trifonov's last fictional work to be published, is also, fittingly perhaps, the work in which the figure of his father is most clearly drawn. Igor''s father, Nikolai Grigor'evich, is the most positive figure in the novel, and it is to him that the most important statements about time and ideals belong. In the figure of Nikolai Grigor'evich Trifonov gives his most detailed and affectionate portrait of his own father. It is the son's last, loving farewell to a father whose life and ideals inspired him so much. It is no accident, then, that Nikolai Grigor'evich expresses views on the course of history and the passage of time that Trifonov the author himself holds dear.

Thus, for instance, he reflects on the changing times when asked to help an old Bolshevik friend:

With each year Nikolai Grigor'evich was more and more hard put to handle such matters: those he knew when he worked in the collegiate no longer existed, some had died, others had disappeared, some had been edged out, and others, although they still worked at the same place had changed so drastically that it was no longer possible to appeal to them. Only David had not changed.[12]

Nikolai Grigor'evich is aware of the emergence of the new breed of Soviet functionary, as the old Bolsheviks like himself and David Shvarts are being removed from positions of power. A perfect example of the 'new' Soviet man is Arkadii Florinskii, a neighbour whom he meets on his way back from Shvarts' flat. Florinskii is a highly placed official in the secret police, and much more cold and menacing than Shulepnikov senior in *Dom na naberezhnoi*. He bears grudges from the past, has a good memory for slights, even those that happened in the Civil War over fifteen years previously, and he gets a perverse enjoyment from destroying people. In Florinskii we see the pleasure and the corruption of power, the privileged life-style he leads, and the secret contempt he holds for all those under his control – which is almost everyone. We see Florinskii and his huge apartment not only through the eyes of Nikolai Grigor'evich, but from his own point of view, thus increasing the narrative possibilities of the novel. We also see Nikolai Grigor'evich through his eyes, and we are left in no doubt that the latter's days are numbered.

On his return from Florinskii's, Nikolai Grigor'evich reflects further:

> He thought of how many houses there had been in his life, beginning with Temernik, Saratov, Ekaterinburg, and then Osypki, Petersburg, Line Fourteen, Moscow and the 'Metropol'', sleeper carriages, Helsingfors on Albertsgatan, Dairen, God knows where else, but nowhere had there been a home, it was all vague, had sloped off somewhere, an eternal sleeper carriage. This feeling had arisen only here, Liza and the children, life coming to a close, it has to come about sometime, for it is after all on behalf of it, on behalf of this feeling that revolutions are made, but suddenly it had seemed to him with momentary and insane force that this pyramid of comfort shining forth in the night, this lampshade-like tower of Babylon was also temporary, was also cast up in the air, like dust on the wind. Residents switch off the lights in the rooms and, delighting in the darkness, fly off somewhere into another, even larger, room. This is what occurred for a second to Nikolai Grigor'evich before he went to bed, as he stood by the window.[13]

Nikolai Grigor'evich has two important conversations in the novel, one with Shvarts, the other with his brother Misha. With Shvarts he discusses the case of Nikodimov, Dina's husband, a man with considerable services to the Revolution behind him and with whom he had shared some years in Siberian exile. Nikodimov was implicated in the Vickers and Industrial Party spy trials of the early 1930s, and has now been arrested again, as a 'counter-revolutionary'. Nikolai Grigor'evich reads Nikodimov's diaries from 1931–2, and discovers that he had signed a confession then. Not because he was guilty, but, like Tolstoi's Hadji-Murat, he had put his trust in people who had betrayed it. And now he was paying the price for his 'cowardice'. Another analogy is that of Peter, who thrice denied Christ, not out of cowardice, but, like Hadji-Murat, 'confusion and bewilderment'.[14] As in all of Trifonov's writing, reference to other literary works, both from the Russian classical heritage and European literature, places the central drama of the narrative in a broader context.

The difference between Shvarts and Igor''s father is that Shvarts cannot bring himself to accept that anyone who signed a confession of guilt, and with it had named another fourteen people, especially someone who had stood up to Tsarist policemen and warders with such courage, could do it knowing that it was 'untrue', 'a lie' (*nepravda, lozh'*). Shvarts is unable to accept that the regime for which he had fought and suffered so much in the past could now be generating falsehoods. Nikolai Grigor'evich's name could also be on the list of the fourteen betrayed by Nikodimov: the assumption of his friend's guilt strikes Shvarts as 'wild and ridiculous'. But Nikolai Grigor'evich is deeply implicated: he had recently recommended Nikodimov for a trip to England. Shvarts' subsequent breakdown is understandable. He has already been removed from positions of power and influence by the State Prosecutor Vyshinskii, and now spends his time writing articles on the past. He is torn between two 'truths': either he, too, has been living a 'lie', or everything that has happened has been, as with Ganchuk, 'correct', and his friends and former comrades were enemies and spies.

Nikolai Grigor'evich, like Danilov in *Starik*, can see the movement of time even though he is in the middle of its flow, as all around him more and more people vanish. He is afraid not for himself, but for his family and 'for that on behalf of which his life had been spent'.[15] His past comes alive when he receives a letter from Mariia Poluboiarova, whom he has not seen for twelve years but who is associated chiefly with his time in Rostov in 1920. He saved her from being shot, when other members of the tribunal were reaching for their Mauser pistols, although she had family connections with counter-revolutionaries: 'he believed her eyes and her voice'.[16] Like Danilov, he tries to use human, not ideological, criteria for judging people; unlike him, he succeeds in saving people. Also, the unexpected letter from the past is reminiscent of the letter Pavel Evgrafovich receives from Asia Igumnova at the beginning of *Starik*.

Poluboiarova comes to Moscow to see Nikolai Grigor'evich, not to plead with him to intercede for her recently arrested husband, but because he is the only person she knows who can explain what is happening. Her husband is accused of being a Japanese spy, but Nikolai Grigor'evich can only try to soothe her with words to the effect that the wave of arrests is a 'fascist provocation', 'the wave is coming to an end' and that there is information that 'some people are being released'. He muses further on the nature of the times: 'People believe in the guilt of others too easily – "there is something" – and are therefore too relaxed about their own person. This was a cruel fact, and did not presage any good.'[17]

The second important conversation is with his brother Mikhail. Both Nikolai Grigor'evich and his brother have known Stalin personally in the past, regarded his coming to power with apprehension, especially after the siege of Tsaritsyn in 1918, but their opposition to Trotskii ('he with the short black beard and pince-nez') was stronger. Mikhail, already ill, predicts that neither will see out the end of the year. Mikhail rejects the explanation his brother had given Poluboiarova, that the Fascists are to blame. He is accustomed 'in every movement to see logic, a beginning and an end', and gives Stalin's terror a greater historical dimension: 'This is, perhaps, of our own national making. And with ancient traditions. It is a question of power.'[18] The relationship of people and power, the cruelty and despotism that has marked Russian history for centuries, from Ivan the Terrible to the Cossacks to Peter the Great and Stalin, is once more the context for the debate over the 'times'.

The novel reaches both its narrative and symbolic culmination at the end, on the eve of the May Day parade of 1937. Nikolai and his brother go out for some air, and see the preparations for the parade the next day: soldiers, tanks, and huge aerial portraits of Stalin, Marx, Engels and Lenin, trailed by aeroplanes. Stalin's portrait is larger than the others. As the planes disappear, one huge portrait of Stalin remains suspended over the Kremlin, hung 'on an invisible thread': 'It shone in the black sky like a cinema screen of incredible proportions. Its suspension in the air seemed supernatural, it was a miracle.'[19] The symbolism is clear: Stalin has assumed deity-like proportions, and embodies both the supernatural and the miraculous as his effigy rises over the population. Young Igor' the next day senses 'with his heart' that this is the last May Day he and his father will see together.

The May Day parade brings Trifonov's work to a close not only with the huge portrait of Stalin looming out of the darkness. It brings to his *oeuvre* a curious symmetry. His first novel ends on an intensely optimistic note, as the tenets of Stalinist socialist realism are affirmed: all the students participate in the May Day parade, singing songs, laughing, keenly aware of the correctness of their lives and their futures. Here we have an eleven-year-old boy feeling intuitively that his father, a Don Cossack who fought in the Civil War, represented the State abroad, and who was later an eminent and respected state functionary, will not witness another parade like this, the symbolic celebration of socialism. The future is in doubt, governed by images of darkness. The final words of the work make us aware of another temporal perspective for the first time: 'But many years passed...'[20] This last, incomplete sentence reveals Trifonov the author for the first time, standing above his text rather like Stalin's image hovers over Moscow, and relating all from a temporal distance of 'many years'. We take leave of the work as the events it relates recede into the past, as if we are looking through the wrong end of a telescope.

Ischeznovenie displays signs that it is not part of the writer's 'idealistic' period. In this work, as in *Otblesk kostra*, the father-figure is hero and martyr, embodying a strict morality and adherence to idealism and the values of the Revolution. In the later *Starik* the father-figure is unable to prevent injustice and murder. Furthermore, Trifonov's focus is the year 1937, the year of the purge of the Party, but not the years when the people suffered in their millions, such as the years of collectivization. Only in later works does he address the post-war purges of intellectuals, or hint at the disappearance of large numbers of ordinary people. Only in works such as *Dom na naberezhnoi* and *Starik* do the ills of the present become rooted in the abuses of the past, and in *Neterpenie* and *Starik* Trifonov explores the philosophical origins of these abuses. *Ischeznovenie* may belong to Trifonov's earlier historical period, when he still believed in the ideals of October, but it serves as a synthesis of the structural and autobiographical elements of his work.²¹ It is *Vremia i mesto*, however, with its exploration of the creative impulse and its linkage of the artist and his time, that offers the clearest path indication of Trifonov's creative evolution, and it is this work which is closest to the reflective and self-appraising *Oprokinutyi dom*.

Conclusion: unity through dislocation (Oprokinutyi dom)

After a discussion of the contrasts, mirror images and parallelism at the structural and thematic heart of Trifonov's fiction, it seems particularly apposite to introduce Trifonov's accounts of his later travels, published posthumously in 1981 under the title *Oprokinutyi dom* ('The Overturned House'). These are seven accounts which vary considerably in style and content, but which are united by the author's persona, present in each, as well as his attempts to link places as superficially disparate as Las Vegas, Helsinki, Rome, Sicily, Paris and the Austrian Tyrol.[1] Throughout the stories past and present come together, and places become linked within the author's own inner world. The author's contextualization of Russia and its conflicts within spatial and temporal parameters stretching across national boundaries and even continents is evident as early as *Obmen*. Here the Dmitrievs' two-storeyed *dacha* in Pavlinovo is said to be not at all like a Russian *dacha*, 'rather like a factory house somewhere in the forests of Canada, or a hacienda in the Argentinian savannah' (II, 32). These stories are all narrated in the first person, and are the most explicitly personal of Trifonov's later work. Trifonov may well have traversed the globe in his later years, but the stories are just as much about internal movement: the overcoming of ideologically imposed barriers of suspicion and division to embrace new concepts of belonging to one world: *slitnost'*.

The first two stories in the collection, 'Koshki ili zaitsy?' ('Cats or Hares?') and 'Vechnye temy' ('Eternal Themes'), are set in Italy. Past and present are lodged side by side in the author's consciousness as he recalls being in Rome eighteen years previously. The first few sentences express his sense of time past, the contrast between the 'now' and the 'then':

Then I was thirty-five, I could run, jump, play tennis, I was an avid smoker, I could work nights, now I am fifty-three, I don't do any running or jumping, I don't play tennis, I don't smoke and I can't work at night. Then I came to Rome in a crowd of tourists, now I am alone. Then all around me were friends, now I am surrounded by Italians whom I hardly know, who have their own affairs to worry about. I understand them. (IV, 193)

From reflection on his own past and present Trifonov quickly moves to a juxtaposition of time and human history:

Here, in Rome, millennia are confused, the times are mixed up, and exact time is difficult to pinpoint. It is not needed here. For this is an Eternal City, and eternity doesn't care if you're late. You live in a nineteenth-century house, descend an eighteenth-century staircase, emerge into a fifteenth-century street and get into a twenty-first-century car. (IV, 193)

Trifonov the observer is looking at the history of Rome as a Muscovite who has seen and depicted most of his native city's old buildings ruthlessly pulled down to make way for modern, monolithic high-rise blocks. The durability of the past in present-day Italy is therefore all the more poignant and at the same time dramatic for such an observer, and provides a counterpoint from which to view his own society's recent development.

Trifonov travels to the small town of Genzano di Roma, the one place outside the city where he had been eighteen years before, and had penned a short story, 'Vospominanie o Zhentsano' ('A Memory of Genzano'). There he meets Russo, who had spent two years in a Soviet camp, and recalls his visit to the trattoria Pistamentuccia, where he had eaten fried hare-meat and drunk Chianti. The town has not changed at all in the interim, but the trattoria has changed hands, as the old owner had been accused of frying up not hares, but cats. He had eventually been exonerated, but nevertheless sold up his business and moved on. Trifonov had praised this meat in his story, and is startled by the thought that what he had written may have been false. There is a hint of allegory here, that perhaps the writer had been involved in falsehoods before, and had been misled, but 'Good Lord, but what a feeling of happiness there was!' (IV, 196). It is the happiness of ignorance, of suspension of reality, and a naive belief in the benevolence of what others serve up to you, be it fried cutlets or political hegemony.

If in this story the author is reunited with places from his past, in other stories he comes across people from the past. In 'Vechnye temy', for example, again set in Rome, he meets a former editor who twenty-two years ago had rejected his short stories because they expressed 'eternal themes'. In the intervening years there had been no hostility between them, but on the other hand there had been no occasion to bring them together. They are linked, though, through their acquaintances, as the editor had known the first husband of Trifonov's wife. They had also once been on holiday together in Yalta, but now 'everything had become entangled' (IV, 200). The editor is now a man with his own share of sorrow and suffering, and the two meet in a restaurant while the neighbourhood is cordoned off by police after a weapons cache has been found nearby. As elsewhere in Trifonov's fiction (for example, Stalin's funeral in *Vremia i mesto*), personal feelings are played out against a background of momentous political and social events.

In 'Nedolgoe prebyvanie v kamere pytok', the author again comes across a figure from his past, in a similarly personal context. The author recalls the year 1964, when he was reporting on the Winter Olympics in Innsbruck. The Trifonov of the present who is recounting this can barely remember the outwardly important details of who won and who lost, or even the names of the sportsmen who competed. But he does remember the personal, subjective impressions: the blinding whiteness of the snow, the blue sky, the fresh air, the smell of coffee, and the gruff owner of the hotel, whose only communication would be to frown and mutter 'Morgen' in greeting. In this hotel he once more meets N., whom he had last seen fourteen years previously. In 1950 Trifonov had been threatened with expulsion from the Komsomol at the Literary

Institute when it was discovered that his father was 'an enemy of the people'. N. spoke at the meeting called to discuss Trifonov's case, Trifonov was duly expelled, but subsequently reinstated by the city committee 'with a severe reprimand and a warning'. When N. and Trifonov meet up, it is in the torture-chamber of a medieval castle outside Salzburg they are viewing as tourists. To the author, N.'s testimony seemed crucial for the expulsion order to be passed; N., however, insists that his speech in fact ultimately saved him from expulsion. The author then muses: 'Yes, I had forgotten, I couldn't remember, I had confused everything, it had all receded into darkness. He extended me an uncertain hand, and I uncertainly shook it' (IV, 211). The episode is similar to the scene in *Vremia i mesto* when Teterin does not recall asking Kiianov to remove his name from the title of the script they wrote together back in the 1930s. Memory is defective and unreliable as a source of truth. There is only the truth of the spirit, which demands reconciliation with others.

The unreliability of subjective truth is further illustrated in a digression, when Trifonov recalls travelling in 1947 with N. and N.'s future wife Nadia to the Caucasus. They were all students at the Literary Institute at the time and were travelling in order to write about the Sevan Hydro-Electric Station. Trifonov and N. protected Nadia from the attentions of the local youths, who threatened to attack and abduct her, almost getting into a fight.[2] Trifonov was convinced that Nadia would choose him as her sexual partner, but she eventually chose N. Trifonov's 'truth' then did not coincide with the objective truth of the situation.

The fundamental unity of time and place is asserted in the setting of this latest confrontation. The medieval torture-chamber where two would-be antagonists settle their differences is likened to that torture-chamber of fourteen years ago when Trifonov was attacked from the podium and threatened with dismissal, and consequent isolation and penury. Trifonov then proceeds from past to present to future, informing us briefly that N. died eight years after this meeting (i.e. 1972), but he does not know what has become of Nadia.

In 'Smert' v Sitsilii' ('Death in Sicily') Trifonov is back in Italy. He is in the town of Mondello in Sicily for a prize-winning ceremony eventually won by 'a Czech from Paris' (Milan Kundera, who as an exile could not be named in the Soviet Union at that time) (IV, 220). The story differs from those that have preceded it in the collection by beginning in a traditional travelogue fashion, with descriptive passages of the local fishing community, the sea, the heat and the evening coolness. As with the living history of Rome, the comparison with grey and prosaic Moscow is apparent. Trifonov also shows an awareness of the island's history, and the influences of those who have colonized it: the Phoenicians, the Carthaginians, Romans, Arabs, Ostrogoths, and the Normans, right up to the reign of Roger I in the eleventh century.

In Sicily he makes the acquaintance of Margarita Maddaloni, a woman of Russian parentage who left Russia at the age of seventeen in 1920. It turns out that she and Trifonov have much in common: she, too, is of Cossack extraction, from Novocherkassk, like Trifonov's father. Two Russians with the same roots meet in Sicily, two people whose adult lives have been determined by the Revolution and its aftermath. Although their fathers were on opposite sides – hers was with the Whites, his the Reds – their acquaintance brings about a peculiar unity through, or perhaps despite, their current dislocation. Margarita still reveres the past, and keeps some of her mother's belongings. To her the most terrifying thing is to die in Sicily. *Slitnost'* here consists of an *émigré* Russian yearning to bury her bones in Russia, and a Russian writer seeking links between apparent opposing entities, Russia and the West.

'Oprokinutyi dom', the story that provides the title for the whole collection, is another highly individualized story, which differs from those preceding it by its more detached and reflective style. We can instantly recognize a Trifonov sentence, with the accumulation of detail and the relentless succession of relative and subordinate clauses, that lasts a whole page, in which the author lists the places and main impressions of his two-month stay in the USA: the Arlington military cemetery in Washington, dolphins in San Diego, a rodeo in Kansas, Indians smoking marijuana in Lawrence, and many more. He provides us with a kaleidoscope of life in its infinite variety. There is a peculiar unity here, too: it is American reality refracted through a Russian consciousness, and with an emphasis on a Russian context: Professor Tamerlan Chingizkhanovich, a Bunin expert in Oberlin, and the table in the student refectory where only Russian is spoken. American realia are not only 'made strange' in the Formalist fashion, but, are, moreover, assimilated into a parallel discourse. Once more a unity of place, Russia and America, is achieved through the author's contextualization.

As the author recalls his own past and people from it, such as the year 1954, with Colonel Gusev, Boria, and Sergei Timofeevich, the latter a convinced Stalinist who died soon after Khrushchev's 'secret' speech, so he juxtaposes his own personal place and time with that of present-day America: 'I can see my house, but it is upside-down. It seems to be spilling out and flaking as if it is reflected in water. In front of the house was a small garden with apple trees whose fruit was sour and of poor quality, and further down was a road which was impassable in autumn. Autumn begins early here, earlier, for some reason, than in Moscow' (IV, 223).

The link between places becomes more apparent as the author observes his American friends, their love, their squabbles, all set against a background of one-armed bandits, casinos and the desert: 'It occurred to me that the thread which connects two such dissimilar places is very straightforward: it consists of love, death, hopes, disappointments, despair and happiness, albeit fleeting, like a gust of wind' (IV, 230).

In other words, the link is human life and everyday concerns: *byt*. Everyday, yet profoundly important for individuals. Everywhere people are connected by the same concerns, the same worries and joys, despite their external differences. Each person is responsible for his own life (compare Glebov's reasoning), a person is 'the blacksmith of his own happiness' (IV, 231), as his friend Ruth reminds him in a letter at the end of the story. This type of ending is similar to that of *Obmen*: we are told that the events of the narrative took place three years before, and Ruth's letter bridges the temporal gap by relating details of what has happened to Lola, Bobchik, Suzy and Steve in that time.[3]

Time and place are linked again in 'Poseshchenie Marka Shagala' ('A Visit to Marc Chagall'), where Trifonov is in Paris, visiting the *émigré* artist who is now in his nineties. He recalls his father-in-law Iona Aleksandrovich (a fictional name thinly disguising his father-in-law from his first wife, Amshei Markovich Niurenberg). Iona Aleksandrovich knew Chagall when he was in Paris in 1910, and defended Chagall against orthodox socialist realist critics at the height of the Stalinist repression, and, like Georgii Maksimovich in *Drugaia zhizn'*, destroyed many of his early works after being accused in the press and at meetings of 'Chagallism'. The grim ironies of the Stalinist terror are emphasized: Kugel'man, the main instigator of these attacks, himself perished in the Gulag five years later. So the Moscow of the early 1950s and Paris of the early years of the century are linked through art. Trifonov himself recalls the Moscow art scene of the early 1950s, providing his own subjective link between places and times. These recollections are conveyed in long sentences, full of details of the house he and his wife lived in on Maslovka, the other artists who lived and worked there, inspired and enthusiastic for their craft despite their poor living conditions. He recalls the theft from Iona Aleksandrovich's flat of a Chagall lithograph, and the subsequent difficulties this caused: Iona Aleksandrovich could not go to the police, as any connection with the *émigré* modernist in 1951 would have provoked the suspicion of the political authorities. The lithograph was eventually traced to Afanasii, a model who would terrorize the artists through his shady links with the KGB, and was returned to its rightful owner by Afanasii's widow in the mid-1950s. The fate of the lithograph becomes a metaphor for the change in the cultural climate after Stalin's death.

Iona Aleksandrovich died in an old people's home two years before the narrative. Everyone from the Maslovka period is now dead. Only Chagall remains, and Trifonov, a modern-day Moscow writer, muses once more on the unseen interactions of times, places and people: 'One has to overcome the ramshackle time that scatters people about: someone is left behind in Vitebsk, another is hurled into Paris, and someone else to Maslovka, into an old house built in the Constructivist style now inhabited by people I do not know' (IV, 239).

'Seroe nebo, machty i ryzhaia loshad'' ('The Grey Sky, Masts and a Red Horse'), the story which concludes the collection, is the most personal, as it touches on Trifonov's childhood. Trifonov is in Finland, where he spent some of his early childhood when his father was head of the Trade Mission in the Helsinki embassy in 1926–8.[4] Trifonov's sister Tania was born here. He recalls the house on Albertsgattan (No. 25) where they lived, and, as he was with his mother walking through the port, a chestnut-coloured horse, a grey sky and the snow. The house no longer exists: it was destroyed by a bomb in 1941. Further recollections include the three Finnish knives his father brought back to Moscow, for it was only after his father's arrest that he felt 'free' to handle them. This is a poignant memory, for the eleven-year-old boy did not then appreciate the full brutality of the adult world; only later did he experience grief.

Trifonov is in Jyväskylä for a book exhibition, and is keen to seek out people who can remember the years 1917–18, the Finnish Revolution, the German attack and the Red Guard. He speaks to one old man who recalls a German attack mounted from Loviisa on Kotka and Lahti, and recalls that his family had their *dacha* at Loviisa. This sudden memory links past and present; but it also links places, for the *dacha* at Loviisa had the same wooden frame and smell of pitch as their subsequent *dacha* at Serebrianyi bor. He also meets Elena Ivanovna, a ninety-four-year-old woman who used to work in the Soviet embassy and who remembers his father. Her table-lamp is exactly the same as the one Trifonov recalls in his own home in the 1930s, and the table-cloth and chairs are similar, too. Elena Ivanovna can only recall that Valentin Trifonov treated his underlings very well, and that the handyman Anderson had a chestnut-coloured horse. He also speaks to Silvia, a former Red Guard, and is spurred on to reflect on the fallibility of memory: 'Memory, like the artist, selects details. There is nothing whole, united (*slitnyi*) in memory, although it does strike up sparks: it can see the neck of a bottle on a dam, gleaming in the moonlight, as did Chekhov's Trigorin, when he described a summer's night' (IV, 246).⁵ Trifonov's meetings with these people from the past recall Troitskii's encounter with old Koshel'kov in *Drugaia zhizn'*, and the feeling of joy he experiences when establishing this living connection with history is one that Trifonov the author also shares.

Trifonov everywhere seeks links between cultures and nations. In *Obmen* Dmitriev's uncle Nikolai had lived and worked in Japan and China, and, like Valentin Trifonov, had worked with the Soviet Ministry of Foreign Trade. He had brought back to Russia the Chinese game of mah-jong. Trifonov here relates how his father had also brought back mementoes from a foreign land, the three Finnish knives. These knives he remembers as a source of mystery during his later childhood years, but they also serve to provide a curiously morbid symmetry: one of the knives was appropriated by his stepbrother Andrei, who was later killed on the Finnish front.

On the streets of Jyväskylä he notes Japanese and Swedish shops, Soviet cars, factories, the university, supermarkets, bookshops. His own home in Moscow and this small and distant part of his past are thus linked. It is, like the other travels in this collection, a journey of discovery, not so much of another culture, but of his own past, and in particular his own father; he may not learn any new information about his father but the small, seemingly insignificant details related by others enable him at least to understand a little better the father he lost at the age of eleven. History is a personal quest where every detail is part of a wider experience. Everything has its place to form a whole, a totality with its origins and consequences. As he muses on his way back to Moscow on the train: 'This is what is strange: everything has its place within the circle. In the beginning was the horse, and then it reappeared totally unexpectedly. Everything else is in the middle' (IV, 250).

The cycle *Oprokinutyi dom* provides a suitable culmination to this study of Trifonov's writing. His fiction is characterized by the interaction of Soviet man and his environment, always within a historical context. Throughout his fictional and documentary writings he has sought to explore the personal dramas of his characters and the links between people, times and states. *Oprokinutyi dom* explicitly expands these links beyond Russia and the USSR, and even beyond Europe. Moreover, in this work the author's persona is in the foreground; in this personalized text he needs no narrator or protagonist, he is expressing his own views, his own personal vision of the world.

Trifonov has been described as 'a historian of the present', that is, a writer who gives historical depth to his depiction of the present, everyday lives of his characters.[6] In his works incidents and characters in the present are seen as either direct parallels or consequences of the past. Nowhere is this dualism more apparent than in *Vremia i mesto*, where contrast, parallelism and juxtaposition serve to convey the concept of totality: *slitnost'*.

But Trifonov also expresses in his subtext the essential characteristics of the times he has lived through. In both *Studenty* and *Dom na naberezhnoi* he shows how men of talent and originality are hounded out of their jobs by mediocrities and careerists. The two works are separated by the times: in the Stalin Prize-winning novel the author does not condemn Kozel'skii's persecution; in the later novel he puts Ganchuk's dismissal into a broader historical and literary context, where the works of Goethe, Dostoevskii and Bulgakov are used to allude to the darkness of Glebov's soul, and the horror of the times he lives through. In *Utolenie zhazhdy* he is reflecting the changing political atmosphere, the steady release of creative energy, and the hopes of a new generation following Stalin's death. *Obmen*, though, relates the failure of those hopes, as the idealism of the Revolution is swept away and replaced by the pragmatism, even the banality, of getting through life with its many minor temptations to compromise, corrupt, or hurt others. In *Obmen* in particular Trifonov crystallizes the actuality of Soviet life as it is experienced by the vast majority of the population: all striving and ambition, and the values of honour and freedom by which the old revolutionaries lived, are reduced to the desire, the need, for extra living space. The pressures of everyday life, the collapse of all moral authority when a family abandons all ethical principles, and the personal crisis of a literary intellectual are the themes of *Predvaritel'nye itogi*, again conveyed within a specific literary and spiritual context.

In *Dolgoe proshchanie* Rebrov's idealism gets him nowhere in material terms, and he only becomes successful by espousing the popular acclaim he once spurned. Troitskii in *Drugaia zhizn'* is similarly idealistic, but the task of seeking historical truth when it is opposed by officialdom is too much. This work also brings two approaches to historical truth in conflict: Troitskii's search for links and continuity through the ages, and Klimuk's official view of history as already determined, not by any immutable laws, but by ideology. The work also shows the futility of resisting the Klimuk approach.

When we come to Trifonov's historical works, we go beyond the writer's own personal experience. However, the figure of his father looms large in *Starik*, where the injustices and the terror of the victors in the Civil War have obvious consequences for the Soviet present. Men of principle and vision, such as Danilov, and Nikolai Grigor'evich in *Ischeznovenie*, do not survive long in the new world, where slavish adherence to 'historical expediency' is the main requirement the all-powerful State demands of individuals. In *Neterpenie* Trifonov traces the roots of political terror back to the *Narodnaia Volia* but broadens his vision in both works to encompass Russian historical development from the time of Ivan the Terrible, focusing in particular on the parallel themes of the destruction of freedom and the striving for freedom, with the resulting establishment of an authoritarian autocracy. The principles of terror and autocracy Trifonov sees as fundamental features of Russian history, and are above all else responsible for Russia's political severance from Europe for centuries, despite the historical and cultural links between the two. It is also the use of terror which provides a parallel, or rather a perspective, within which to view the Bolshevik take-over in 1917, and the subsequent terror and dictatorship.

There is thus an evolution of Trifonov's perception of the Revolution, from the hope, inspired by de-Stalinization, to rehabilitate his father and to find out the truth, to the fearful realization, in *Starik*, that the Civil War was won by men who had little regard for principles of honour, justice and democracy. In *Otblesk kostra* and *Obmen*, the revolutionary generation is idealized, and the values its representatives live by are not open to question. In *Starik* men of honour are irrelevant, the new world is created by terror and brutality, and it is men such as Florinskii in *Ischeznovenie* who come to enact the will of Stalin in the 1930s.

In his works from the late 1960s Trifonov moves away from an interpretation of history and his times towards a subjective experience of them. Perhaps he had realized the futility of a Troitskii-like rebellion against the current, and concentrated on the individual's perception of the times he has lived through. Also, Trifonov goes back more obviously into his own past, his own childhood, in *Vremia i mesto*, *Ischeznovenie* and *Oprokinutyi dom*. (He had also used experiences from his own childhood in *Dom na naberezhnoi*.) It is in these works, and especially *Vremia i mesto*, that Trifonov comes closest to modernist, as opposed to realist writing, when reality is refracted through various viewpoints, and literature itself becomes reality, and a form of dialogue with time. Personal, private experience becomes the essence of history; external events, no matter how momentous, assume secondary importance when compared to the significance and immediacy of private feelings, thoughts and personal lives.

Indeed, Trifonov's novel can be seen as a continuation, and perhaps a conscious one, of *Doctor Zhivago*. In Pasternak's novel we are also presented with a writer-hero observing and becoming involved in the dilemmas of his time. Here too the writer's response to events and changes in his own life is to transform life into literature, to express and interpret what he sees, feels and knows as poetic or artistic experience. Here, too, irrationality and coincidence are dominant formative influences in the life of the writer. And here too the importance of experience lies not in history, but in the evolution of the individual artistic consciousness. Significantly, Pasternak's hero dies in 1929; is it a Pasternakian coincidence that Zhivago's odyssey is continued by Sasha Antipov through the 1930s, the purges, War, repression, and up to the time of Brezhnev.

It could be argued that Trifonov is retreating from the challenge he set himself in his earlier works of the Moscow cycle, that of attacking the ethos of his age, by withdrawing into personal experience in his later works. On the contrary, these last few works set themselves new tasks, for Trifonov is trying to integrate man, his time and his place. They offer evidence of further evolution of Trifonov's fundamental credo, expressed as early as *Studenty*: the unity of time and place, and man's role within these categories. His picture of man and society 'in its revolutionary development' accords with the formal demands of socialist realism, but his later themes do not. Nor does his later depiction of time as fractured and personalized.

Trifonov stresses the importance of memory, individual and collective, for in memory lies the key to truth and history: history not as the government of his country would interpret it, but rather the people's history, the history of their suffering, their losses, their hopes, their experience. His works are not only landmarks to the 'moral resistance', as Grigorii Svirskii puts it, to tyranny, but also as individual statements on the nature of man's constant struggle with existential time.[7] Many critics have said that *Obmen* could serve as the title for all of Trifonov's major works, as they all revolve around the temptation to 'exchange' one set of values for another. However, all of his titles could be just as relevant, for people 'take stock' of their lives as they go through changes, they say 'goodbye' to one life and start 'another life', and everyone, be it Levka Shulepnikov, Grisha Rebrov or Sasha Antipov, in the course of their lives discovers their 'time and place'. Their 'place' is specific, perhaps their home 'on the embankment', or their home may be disrupted by time, 'overturned', where values and a way of life once held dear 'disappear'.

The period of *glasnost'* in the Soviet Union in the late 1980s and the early 1990s has seen an upsurge in nationalist sentiment. It is a time when national identity and Russia's future, or destiny, as the Russians themselves like to call it, is discussed. Trifonov's significance for Russian literature is his awareness of the historical context of the contemporary moment, his examination of the past for clues to the future. His works are imbued with an awareness of freedom, and the tyranny that can easily usurp noble aims. Iurii Trifonov can be seen as a true precursor of *glasnost'* literature in his analysis of the modern condition, his historical enquiry, and his striving, however concealed in his writing, for truth.

Notes

INTRODUCTION

1 Valentin Trifonov's career is comprehensively related in *Otblesk kostra*, and also discussed in the story 'Seroe nebo, machty, i ryzhaia loshad'' ('A Grey Sky, Masts, and a Red Horse'), part of the *Oprokinutyi dom* cycle. See chapter 4 and the Conclusion.
2 Iurii's return to Moscow and his wartime experiences are described in detail in *Ischeznovenie* ('The Disappearance', 1987) and *Vremia i mesto* ('A Time and Place', 1981). See chapter 5.
3 *Druzhba narodov*, 1989, no. 10, p. 17. This memoir could only be published in full in the *glasnost'* era. It appeared in abridged form in Trifonov's collection *Prodolzhitel'nye itogi*, and again in the 1984 collection *Kak slovo nashe otzovetsia*. The restored version relates in detail Tvardovskii's battles with the literary conservatives in the 1950s and 1960s. He devotes much space to the increasing attacks on *Novyi mir* in the late 1960s, and the role played by Solzhenitsyn in the journal's fortunes. Less than half the memoir was published in 1975. There is further biographical information in Lev Levin's memoir, *Voprosy literatury*, 1988, no. 3, especially pp. 183–91.
4 In 'Zapiski soseda' Trifonov names Mikhail Bubennov, Fedor Panferov and Leonid Sobolev as those who were vehement in their demands that Trifonov be punished. Marietta Shaginian, in particular, wanted the Prize rescinded. See *Druzhba narodov*, 1989, no. 10, p. 17. Inna Goff, *Oktiabr'*, 1985, no. 8, pp. 94–106, and Sergei Baruzdin, *Druzhba narodov*, 1987, no. 10, pp. 255–62, both fellow-students of Trifonov's at the Literary Institute, recall him at the time.
5 Iurii Oklianskii, *Iurii Trifonov: Portret-vospominanie* (M: Sovetskaia Rossiia, 1987) p. 53.
6 Tvardovskii was editor of *Novyi mir* from 1950 to 1954, when he was dismissed in a reaction against the first post-Stalin thaw, and in particular his publication in November 1953 of Pomerantsev's

article 'Ob iskrennosti v literature' ('On Sincerity in Literature'). Tvardovskii was reinstated as editor in 1958, but forced to resign in 1970. For further discussion see Edith Rogovin Frankel, *Novyi mir: A Case Study in the Politics of Literature*, 1952–1958 (Cambridge University Press, 1981); Dina R Sprechler, *Permitted Dissent in the USSR: Novyi mir and the Soviet Regime* (New York: Praeger, 1982); and Alexander Solzhenitsyn, *The Oak and the Calf* (London: Collins-Harvill, 1980).

7 'Roman s istoriei', in *Kak slovo nashe otzovetsia*, pp. 327–8.
8 *Druzhba narodov*, 1989, no. 10, p. 35. Trifonov was introduced to Solzhenitsyn by Boris Mozhaev in 1970, at the height of the campaign to save Tvardovskii and *Novyi mir* (p. 37).
9 See the bibliographical entries for Sinel'nikov, 'Ispytanie povsednevnost'iu', Sokolov, 'Rasshcheplenie obydennosti', Andreev, 'V zamknutom mirke', Brovman, 'Izmereniia malogo mira'; Hughes, '*Bol'shoi mir* or *zamknutyi mirok*', p. 471.
10 *Voprosy literatury*, 1972, no. 2, pp. 66–7.
11 *Shestoi s"ezd pisatelei SSSR. 21–25 iiunia 1976 g. Stenograficheskii otchet* (M: Sovetskii pisatel', 1976), p. 10.
12 'Kazhdyi chelovek – sud'ba', in *Kak slovo nashe otzovetsia*, p. 293
13 'Roman s istoriei', in *Kak slovo nashe otzovetsia*, p. 327.
14 'V kratkom – beskonechnoe', in *Kak slovo nashe otzovetsia*, pp. 242–3.
15 'Pisat' na predele vozmozhnogo', in *Kak slovo nashe otzovetsia*, pp. 336–7.
16 'Voobrazit' beskonechnost'', in *Kak slovo nashe otzovetsia*, p. 281.
17 'Kak slovo nashe otzovetsia', in *Kak slovo nashe otzovetsia*, p. 311.
18 See also S. Eremina and V. Piskunov, *Voprosy literatury*, 1982, no. 5, p. 59.

1 FROM MOSCOW STUDENTS TO THE TURKMENIAN DESERT

1 'Roman s istoriei', in *Kak slovo nashe otzovetsia*, p. 326. However, Lev Levin quotes a letter of Trifonov's from 1970 where the author is less sanguine, remarking in particular that the picture of student life, the lyrical scenes between Belov and Lena and the feeling for Moscow were 'successful' (*Voprosy literatury*, 1988, no. 3, p. 190).
2 *Kontekst* – 1977, Moscow, 1978, pp. 45–6.
3 Vera Dunham, *In Stalin's Time: Middleclass Values in Soviet Fiction* (New York: Cambridge University Press, 1976), p. 44. *Studenty* is further discussed pp. 87–90, 207–10.
4 Katerina Clark observes: 'Like Germany and several other

countries in this period, the Soviets focused on the primordial attachments of kinship and projected them as the dominant symbol for social allegiance. Soviet society's leaders became "fathers" (with Stalin as the patriarch); the national heroes, model "sons"; the state, a "family" or "tribe". The new root metaphor for society provided the state with a single set of symbols for enhancing its increasingly hierarchical structure by endowing it with a spurious organicity' (Katerina Clark, *The Soviet Novel: History as Ritual*, (Chicago and London: University of Chicago Press, 1985), p. 114).

5 Geoffrey Hosking, *Beyond Socialist Realism*, pp. 180–1.
6 A 'panamist' is a corrupt or dishonest person, a swindler. The word is derived from the Panama Canal scandal in France in 1889–93, in which many high-placed public officials were implicated in acts of bribery and embezzlement.
7 Natal'ia Ivanova makes the point that the accusations of Kozel'skii's 'indifference' to Soviet literature are patently absurd: 'Kozel'skii is a specialist in classical literature, and it is difficult to imagine a lecture on Turgenev that switches over to Soviet literature, but neither the author nor his "mouthpiece-heroes" take that into consideration.' N. Ivanova, *Proza Iuriia Trifonova* (M: Sovetskii pisatel', 1984), p. 21.
8 This scene is also discussed by Levin, *Voprosy literatury*, 1988, no. 3, p. 193.
9 Trifonov himself, in a letter of 1975, remarked that he saw the book's 'main weakness' in the conflict between Belov and Kozel'skii. *Voprosy literatury*, 1987, no. 4, p. 184.
10 *Druzhba narodov*, 1985, no. 3, p. 236.
11 'Doktor, student i Mitia', in Trifonov, *Utolenie zhazhdy: Roman i rasskazy* (M: Politizdat, 1979), p. 383.
12 Trifonov relates how he had to study many subjects for this novel, and learn about such diverse specialisms as land reclamation, hydrology, botany, construction, ethnography and geography. *Druzhba narodov*, 1985, no. 3, p. 236.
13 Iurii Oklianskii, on the other hand, sees Nagaev as a positive character who 'would appear to enjoy working more than earning' (Oklianskii, *Iurii Trifonov*, p. 76).
14 *Vecherniaia Moskva*, 11 July 1964.

2 MOSCOW LIFE, 1966–1975

1 M. Hayward and L. Labedz (eds.), *On Trial: The Case of Sinyavsky (Tertz) and Daniel' (Arzhak)* (London: Collins and Harvill, 1967), p. 36.

2 A. Solzhenitsyn, 'Zakhar-Kalita', *Novyi mir*, 1966, no. 1, pp. 69–76; 'Matrenin dvor', *Novyi mir*, 1963, no. 1, pp. 42–63; V. Belov, 'Privychnoe delo', *Sever*, 1966, no. 1, pp. 7–92; B.Mozhaev, 'Iz zhizni Fedora Kuz'kina', *Novyi mir*, 1966, no. 7, pp. 42–118.
3 Seemingly minor details and personal memories play a major role in this story, where the researcher is intent on establishing objective truth, and Ol'ga Robertnova recalls the personal, subjective things in her life with her husband. See in particular Robert Russell, 'Time and memory in the works of Yury Trifonov', *Forum for Modern Language Studies*, 24, 1 (January 1988), pp. 44–5.
4 See also L. Loseff, *On the Beneficence of Censorship: Aesopian Language in Modern Russian Literature* (Munich: Otto Sagner, 1984), pp. 106–7, and T. Patera, *Obzor tvorchestva i analiz moskovskikh povestei Iuriia Trifonova* (Ann Arbor: Ardis, 1983), pp. 41–84. In his 1972 essay 'Zapiski soseda' Trifonov reveals that this story was in fact submitted to *Novyi mir* for publication in 1966 along with 'Vera i Zoika' and 'Byl letnii polden'', but was rejected and accepted two years later. See *Kak slovo nashe otzovetsia*, p. 171. In the restored version of this essay there is a more open account of this story's publication history, and the fears it aroused among editors (especially the character of Brykin and the arrest of Boris Evgen'evich). See *Druzhba narodov*, 1989, no. 10, pp. 27–8.
5 In 1974 Trifonov stated that his 'third period of literary practice' began with the publication of these short stories, ('again short stories!'), which were 'the beginning of something new' in his work. See his interview with A. Bocharov, 'V kratkom – beskonechnoe', in *Kak slovo nashe otzovetsia*, p. 242.
6 'Vybirat', reshat'sia, zhertvovat'', in *Kak slovo nashe otzovetsia*, pp. 86–7
7 'Vybirat', reshat'sia, zhertvovat'', in *Kak slovo nashe otzovetsia*, p. 85.
8 'Kak slovo nashe otzovetsia', in *Kak slovo nashe otzovetsia*, p. 316.
9 To this could be added Carolina de Maegd-Soëp's words: 'The *dacha* appears often as the symbol of true beauty, freshness, youth and peace. For certain of Trifonov's heroes *dacha* life is in fact the sole refuge where they can escape from the difficult conditions of the city' ('The theme of "byt" – everyday life – in the stories of Iurii Trifonov', in *Selected Papers from the Second World Congress for Soviet and East European Studies: Russian Literature and Criticism*, edited by Evelyn Bristol (Berkeley: Berkeley Slavic Specialties, 1982), p. 53). This is undoubtedly true, but, moreover, the *dacha* in this story can also be seen as a metaphor for the idealism, freshness and vitality of those who created the Revolution. Indeed, the *dacha* village used to be inhabited exclusively by Red Partisans. It is thus

no accident that here, as in Trifonov's other works, the *dacha* is demolished to make way for urban development. It is not hard to see an affinity with the symbolism of village prose here.

10 M. Bulgakov, *Tri romana: Belaia gvardiiya; Teatral'nyi roman; Master i Margarita* (M: Khudozhestvennaia literatura, 1973), p. 541. On further links between Trifonov and Bulgakov, see R. Schröder, *Literaturnoe obozrenie*, 1987, no. 8, p. 97.
11 'V kratkom – beskonechnoe', in *Kak slovo nashe otzovetsia*, p. 254.
12 The irony of publishing in Central Asia a story about Moscow life, when he had published his Central Asian stories in Moscow, could be seen as a veiled comment on the inanities of the literary censorship, as alluded to in the story itself.
13 *Prostor*, 1970, no, 7, p. 80.
14 'V kratkom – beskonechnoe', in *Kak slovo nashe otzovetsia*, p. 265.
15 'Neskonchaemoe nachalo', in *Kak slovo nashe otzovetsia* p. 95.
16 Sigrid McLaughlin has studied the work's allusions to Kafka, Dostoevskii and Chekhov in *The Russian Review*, 66, 1987, pp. 19–34.
17 Natal'ia Ivanova states that 'with her meekness and sympathy Niura brings together that which Gartvig destroys: the home' (*Proza Iuriia Trifonova*, p. 129).
18 Andrew Durkin: 'The inclusion of an outsider, even one from another culture, in the family, and the acceptance of responsibility for others contrasts sharply with Gennadii Sergeevich's own family, in which no-one is willing to assume the responsibility for the family's devoted and exploited maid when she is found to be mentally ill' ('Trifonov's "Taking Stock": The role of Čexovian subtext', *Slavic and East European Journal*, 28, 1 (Spring 1984), p. 37).
19 'Neskonchaemoe nachalo', in *Kak slovo nashe otzovetsia*, p. 97, and 'Voobrazit' beskonechnost'', in *ibid.*, p. 289.
20 See his letter to Lev Levin, *Voprosy literatury*, 1988, no. 3, pp. 189–90.
21 See the discussion of 'machine' and 'garden' metaphors by Katerina Clark in her seminal analysis of Soviet fiction during industrialization in the early 1930s, in *The Soviet Novel*, pp. 93–113.
22 A Kantonist was the son of a soldier registered for military service from birth. The term refers originally to the Prussian military, but the practice was widespread in Russia in the first half of the nineteenth century.
23 'Roman s istoriei', in *Kak slovo nashe otzovetsia*, p. 328.
24 The details of Georgii Maksimovich's life are based on those of Amshei Niurenberg, Trifonov's father-in-law from his first wife.

There is no suggestion that Niurenberg also capitulated when under pressure in the 1930s.
25 See Oklianskii, *Iurii Trifonov*, p. 59. After Nina Nelina's death in 1966, Trifonov married Alla Pastukhova in 1972, although that marriage was short-lived. His third and final marriage was in 1979 to Ol'ga Miroshnichenko.
26 *Voprosy literatury*, 1982, no. 5, p. 49; *Times Literary Supplement*, 6 December 1985, p. 138.
27 See also, for example, Trifonov's article 'Voobrazit' beskonechnost'', in *Kak slovo nashe otzovetsia*, especially p. 288: 'But time, after all, is that in which we are immersed every day, every minute ... I wanted readers to realize that the mysterious "connecting thread of time" that passes through you and me is the nerve of history.' Compare Shulubin's words to Kostoglotov in Solzhenitsyn's *Rakovyi Korpus*: 'Not all of me shall die ... Not all of me shall die ... Sometimes I have a very clear sense that what is inside me is not all of me. That there is something there quite indestructible, quite sublime! Some fragment of the Spirit of the Universe. Don't you have this sense?' (A. Solzhenitsyn, *Rakovyi Korpus* (Paris: YMCA, 1970), pp. 404–5).
28 Edward J. Brown comments: 'Few things in contemporary Russian literature can touch that scene in its elevation of the tiny detail to the place of universal significance. The scene illustrates once more Trifonov's special talent for synecdoche, for giving us "v kratkom, beskonechnoe"' (Edward J. Brown, 'Trifonov: The Historian as Artist', in *Soviet Society and Culture: Essays in Honor of Vera S. Dunham*, edited by Terry L. Thompson and Richard Sheldon (Boulder and London: Westview Press, 1988), p. 114).
29 For further deliberations on 'the bog' in this story, see R. Schröder, *Literaturnoe obozrenie*, 1987, no. 8, p. 98.
30 Trifonov says of his preoccupation with the *neudachniki*: 'I am interested by characters. And among them, as a subject of investigation, are the so-called "failures", those who have been unable to attain or achieve something. Drama is ever-present in their lives ... I seek the answer to the question: why is he a failure? The reasons can differ: perhaps he cannot settle down in the city which is itself heaving with people, perhaps he has chosen the wrong profession, perhaps his family life is not harmonious ... His life is made up of dissatisfaction, incompleteness, unhappiness, lack of emotion' ('Gorod i gorozhane', in *Kak slovo nashe otzovetsia*, p. 301).
31 Barbara Heldt, *Terrible Perfection: Women and Russian Literature*

(Bloomington and Indianapolis: Indiana University Press, 1987), p. 2.

32 On the 'embedded' plot in Trifonov, Edward J. Brown claims that Trifonov's 'dominant mode' is metonymy rather than metaphor, where 'the narrative plot of each of his novels is embedded in a larger plot: the unidirectional movement of history itself, the threads of which he is trying to identify and disentangle from the random chaos of experience' ('Trifonov: The Historian as Artist', p. 112). However, I have endeavoured to show that Trifonov is equally adept at using metaphor to express the flow of time, and, moreover, that time for him does not only move forward, but backwards.

3 THE HOUSE ON THE EMBANKMENT

1 *Beyond Socialist Realism*, pp. 180–1, The new *glasnost'* of Gorbachev's Russia has enabled more information to emerge on the troubles this work met with in the literary and political establishment. In an article published in 1987 to greet the appearance of the fourth and final volume of Trifonov's collected works, Sergei Baruzdin, editor of *Druzhba narodov*, who was responsible for publishing Trifonov's fiction from 1976 until his death, denied that the journal had much trouble actually getting Trifonov into print. Certainly, he asserts, not as much as they had with Boris Mozhaev's relatively uncontroversial short novel 'Poltora kvatratnykh metra', which came out in the April 1982 issue. On the critical silence that greeted Trifonov's work, Baruzdin reveals that 'the critics were silent because somewhere someone, as they said at that time, 'on high', was displeased by the journal's publication of that *povest'*. That is also why it was not subsequently published in a separate edition, but was included in a Trifonov collection (published by 'Sovetskaia Rossiia') with a miserable edition of 30,000' (*Druzhba narodov*, 1987, no. 10, p. 257). Perhaps this 'someone' was Markov, who, judging by his comments on the work at the Sixth Writers' Congress, was clearly displeased by it.

2 This is how Trifonov recalls Fedotov: 'he tried his hand at many disciplines, especially mineralogy, palaeontology, oceanography, he drew extremely well, his water-colours were exhibited and printed in the journal 'Pioneer', he was in love with symphony music, and wrote novels in thick general-use exercise books with calico covers. I grew attached to that tedious business – writing novels – thanks to Leva. Apart from this, he would harden himself up physically – in winter he walked around without a coat and in short trousers, and had mastered ju-jitsu' ('Dobro, chelovechnost',

talant', in *Kak slovo nashe otzovetsia*, pp. 187–8). In the same article Trifonov reveals that he has Lev's school diaries in his possession (just as the narrator of *Dom na naberezhnoi* admits to visiting Anton's mother and being given Anton's pre-war diaries. Trifonov includes material from these diaries in his stage adaptation of *Dom na naberezhnoi*, produced at Moscow's Taganka theatre. Compare *Teatr pisatelia* (M: Sovetskaia Rossiia, 1982), especially pp. 135–6, and *Kak slovo nashe otzovetsia*, pp. 188–9. Also on Fedotov, see Trifonov's article 'Istoriia bolezni', written in 1961, *Kak slovo nashe otzovetsia*, especially p. 200.

3 There is an apparent inconsistency, though, in Trifonov's presentation of the narrator's persona: he looks up Ganchuk several years later, and he seems to have forgotten him. This despite the fact that they would have been neighbours in the big house, and we already know that the narrator visited the Ganchuks often as a child.

4 'Octopeds' and 'omnivores' are terms used by Anton and his closest friends to denote two kinds of schoolboy: those who actively pursue knowledge for intellectual self-enrichment and self-understanding (octopeds), and those who only learn what they need to know in order to pass exams (omnivores). The terms are also used by Gorik, Lenia and their friends in *Ischeznovenie*.

5 F. Björling asserts that the narrator is separate from the author ('Jurij Trifonov's *Dom na naberezhnoi*: fiction or autobiography?', in *Svantetit*, 9, 1 (1983), p. 25). There is, however, an essential contiguity between *siuzet* and *fabula*: the author is in control of the text, and through the use of contrast and juxtaposition, he ensures that the reader gets exactly the impression of Glebov that he, Trifonov, wants. The narrator's function is merely to provide additional facts, provide another, though not radically different, perspective. Like *Starik*, the novel is concerned with the nature of memory as a facet of human existence.

6 Sigrid McLaughlin sees a connection between this work and Dostoevskii's *Crime and Punishment*, especially in the figures of Sonia Ganchuk and Sonia Marmeladova: 'Sonia Ganchuk shares not only first name and physical appearance with her Dostoevskian namesake – both are pale, blue-eyed, and homely – but also such essential character traits as meekness, compassion and self-sacrificing love ... Both Sonias are, in fact, infinitely giving; the two men receive and take; Raskol'nikov makes her share the burden of his murders, Glebov that of his own unscrupulousness and moral paralysis' (S. McLaughlin, 'Iurii Trifonov's *Dom na naberezhnoi* and Dostoevskii's *Prestuplenie i nakazanie*', *Canadian Slavonic Papers*, 25, 2 (June 1983), p. 279).

7 J. W. Goethe, *Faust*, lines 1334–6.
8 Oklianskii, *Iurii Trifonov*, p. 121.
9 Sigrid McLaughlin notes: 'Ganchuk's commentary unmasks Marxist philosophy as an inadequate guide for moral conduct and an insufficient tool for the comprehension of human motivation (S. McLaughlin, 'Iurii Trifonov's *Dom na naberezhnoi* and Dostoevskii's *Prestuplenie i nakazanie*, p. 282).
10 'But he [Trifonov] does not write to condemn or praise his characters; he provides an ethical measuring stick of crime and punishment and the coordinates for us to place them in' (Sigrid McLaughlin, 'Jurij Trifonov's *House on the Embankment*: Narration and Meaning', *Slavic and East European Journal*, 26, 4 (Winter 1982), p. 432).

4 TERRORISM, CIVIL WAR AND THE PRESENT

1 On how the novel came to be written, see Trifonov's interview 'Sovremennost' – splav istorii i budushchego', *Literaturnaia gazeta*, 19 June 1974, p. 5.
2 *Literaturnaia gazeta*, 25 August 1971, p. 3. See also the following: 'The present day also carries the burden of past years. In order to understand today, we have to understand yesterday and the day before yesterday. Nothing of what we have lived through disappears without trace' ('Iadro pravdy', p. 235).
3 See 'Knigi, kotorye vybiraiut nas', in *Kak slovo nashe otzovetsia*, pp. 272–74.
4 Benjamin Disraeli, the Earl of Beaconsfield, was British Prime Minister 1874–80. He attended the Congress of Berlin in 1878, which reduced Russian influence in the Balkans in the wake of the Russo-Turkish War of 1877–8.
5 'Sovremennost' – splav istorii i budushchego', in *Kak slovo nashe otzovetsia*, p. 233.
6 Trifonov: 'In my novel I wanted to show that with the use of terror it is impossible to attain true social goals. In the modern world terrorists of all calibres and shades follow Nechaev's line, which means that they try to achieve their ends by any means', ('Roman s istoriei', *Kak slovo nashe otzovetsia*, p. 323). See also his article 'Nechaev, Verkhovenskii, i drugie', when he likens Verkhovenskii to the international terrorist Carlos, and unfavourably compares Ulrike Meinhof to Sergei Nechaev, *Kak slovo nashe otzovetsia*, pp. 51–2. In a 1978 interview with the Italian newspaper *Paese sera*, at the height of the Aldo Moro affair, Trifonov pointed out that the 'vital difference' between the terrorists of today and those of a

hundred years ago was that the latter were 'the most genuine idealists', characterized by 'a humanistic consciousness and ethic' who baulked at the idea of killing people. See *Kak slovo nashe otzovetsia*, p. 345. Trifonov also stated soon after the novel was completed that he could have entitled it 'Beskorystie' ('Unselfishness'): 'Sovremennost' – splav istorii i budushchego' in *Kak slovo nashe otzovetsia*, p. 235.

7 *Russkaia mysl'*, 27 September 1979, p. 6. K. Shenfel'd expanded this idea as follows: 'Perhaps the hypothesis is correct, that in this work Trifonov was trying to find an answer to the question of his own attitude to the Soviet opposition of today. Indeed, did not the author want to say that the Soviet dissidents also show impatience, by trying to change the course of events in the country to their own advantage?' ('Iurii Trifonov – pisatel' chastichnoi pravdy', *Grani*, 121 (1981), p. 115).

8 'Sovremennost' – splav istorii i budushchego', in *Kak slovo nashe otzovetsia*, p. 236.

9 'Sovremennost' – splav istorii i budushchego', in *Kak slovo nashe otsovetsia*, pp. 236–7.

10 *Iz-pod glyb*, edited by A. Solzhenitsyn and I. Shafarevich (Paris: YMCA Press, 1974).

11 See Trifonov's letters from 1973–7 dealing with his researches on *Neterpenie*, in *Voprosy literatury*, 1987, no. 7, pp. 170–85.

12 R. A. Shatseva, a Leningrad-based editor of the *Biblioteka poeta* series, wrote to Trifonov in 1973 pointing out that there were several inaccuracies of his mapping out of the geography of St Petersburg a hundred years before. See his reply, *Voprosy literatury*, 1987, no. 7, pp. 171–2. Trifonov was assiduous in correcting inaccuracies for later book editions of the novel: see V. Tvardovskaia, *Voprosy literatury*, 1988, no. 2, p. 193.

13 Trifonov: 'I deliberately overloaded the book with the names of people who were not closely connected with the subject-matter, for I wanted to achieve the maximum historical authenticity.' ('Sovremennost' – splav istorii i budushchego', in *Kak slovo nashe otzovetsia*, p. 235). He is undoubtedly successful in this. However, he includes in the narrative a key event which is not historically documented: the meeting between Nechaev and Zheliabov. Furthermore, he admits that his picture of Kletochnikov is largely his own, claiming the absence of any historical sources. See *Voprosy literatury*, 1987, no. 7, p. 176.

14 *Voprosy literatury*, 1987, no. 7, p. 173.

15 To Trifonov, the significance of Zheliabov's break with his family is immense: 'Here the future leader of the 'People's Will' crossed

the boundary of the personal and set out on the path of self-sacrifice, the path of revolution. That is why the book begins with a detailed description of Zheliabov's Odessa period' ('Sovremennost' – splav istorii i budushchego', *Kak slovo nashe otzovetsia*, p. 234).

16 In particular, the book contains extensive quotations from the diary of Pavel Lur'e, the brother of Trifonov's grandmother. Lur'e was to serve as the prototype for Pavel Evgrafovich in *Starik*. There are some omissions in the book, such as passages on the revolutionary credentials of Valentin Trifonov (*Znamia*, 1965, no. 3, p. 156) and Dumenko (*Znamia*, 1965, no. 3, pp. 174–5). But essentially the journal contains mere factual material, while the book is fleshed out with various personal reminiscences and first-hand accounts. The 1966 book edition was republished only in 1987 and again in 1988.

17 The fickle relationship between truth, time and political expediency is further laid bare in a vivid episode Trifonov recalls in the narrative: 'And I remember in 1956, after the Party's Twentieth Congress, I went to see a respected historian and showed him the protocol of the 'initiatory five'. I supposed I was doing a good thing, presenting a specialist with valuable material not yet studied by anyone. The respected historian, after leafing through the papers, shook his head in doubt: "But are these documents genuine?" He should have known that they were genuine, for they were from the archive of one of the leaders of the Red Guard. But in actual fact the respected historian was troubled by something else: "But are the events of the Twentieth Party Congress genuine? And is Valentin Trifonov's posthumous rehabilitation genuine?" I left him with a heavy heart: I suddenly realized how slowly and with what amount of difficulty the ossified untruth would crumble, and how so many people would defend it in order to defend themselves' (IV, 68).

18 See, for example, the bibliography for his articles in *Literaturnaia gazeta* of 1 November and 5 December 1967.

19 'The business-like tone of this piece of paper, on which the lives of two people depended, is striking. V. Trifonov has not the shadow of moral doubt: he is thinking above all about the good of the cause.

'The document here exposes the contradictory nature of V. Trifonov's character and actions about which the authorial text remains silent' (Ivanova, *Proza Iurii Trifonova*, p. 90).

20 In the 1988 edition of his new (1984) translation of *And Quiet Flows the Don*, Robert Daglish has gone back to the 1933 edition of the

novel to restore Mironov to the text 'not mechanically but in such a way that the reader will at least know on whose side he and his men were fighting' ('Translator's Introduction' to Mikhail Sholokhov, *Quiet Flows the Don: a Novel in Two Volumes* (M: Raduga, 1988) I, 7 (n.)).

21 'Zapiski soseda', *Druzhba narodov*, 1989, no. 10, p. 26.
22 'Dela kazhdodnevnye', *Literaturnaia gazeta*, 13 June 1973, p. 2.
23 Iu. Mal'tsev, 'Roman Trifonova', *Russkaia mysl'*, 19 October 1978, p. 11; I. Efimov, 'Pisatel' raskonvoirovannyi v istoriki', *Vremia i my*, 71 (1983), pp. 152–3; H. Ermolaev, 'Proshloe i nastoiashchee v "Starike" Iuriia Trifonova', *Russian Language Journal*, 128 (1983), p. 143.
24 Sergei Starikov and Roy Medvedev, *Philip Mironov and the Russian Civil War*, translated by Guy Daniels (New York: Knopf), 1978, p. 34. This book has now appeared in the USSR under the title *Zhizn' i smert' komandarma Mironova*, *Pod"em*, 1989, no. 1, pp. 3–26; no. 2, pp. 86–103; no. 3, pp. 3–24; no. 4, pp. 97–123; no. 5, pp. 102–16. Trifonov knew of this text, and was acquainted with it. He was a good friend of Roy Medvedev. See Carolina De Maegd-Soëp, *Trifonov and the Drama of the Russian Intelligentsia* (Ghent State University: Russian Institute, 1990), pp. 64–5.
25 Starikov and Medvedev, *Philip Mironov*, p. 44.
26 Starikov and Medvedev, *Philip Mironov*, p. 111. Herman Ermolaev concludes: '*Starik* was printed in the Soviet Union because its author, or the censors, concealed the authorship of the Orgbiuro directive, removed or altered its most barbarous points, and deleted the sharpest criticisms of Communists from Mironov's letters and proclamations. All these revisions made it possible to interpret Bolshevik terror in accordance with the current official view that neither Lenin, nor Sverdlov, nor the Party, had anything to do with the directive and that its architects and implementors were Trotskii, the Trotskiites, the Donbiuro, and various shady persons who had wormed their way into the Party' (H. Ermolaev, 'The Theme of Terror in *Starik*, in *Aspects of Modern Russian and Czech Literature: Selected Papers of the Third World Congress for Soviet and East European Studies*, edited by Arnold McMillin (Columbus, Ohio: Slavica, 1989), p. 106).
27 The terrorists in *Neterpenie* also refer to the destruction of Carthage in the editorial of one of their newspapers: 'Delenda est Carthago' (III, 172).
28 See *Druzhba narodov*, no. 1, 1987, especially p. 90.
29 Herman Ermolaev does not agree, and sees the novel as an attack on revolutionary morality *per se*: 'The conclusion is inevitably

reached that, in consistently juxtaposing the French Terror with that of the Bolsheviks, Trifonov brings us round to the idea that the arbitrariness of the Bolsheviks is rooted not in the Russian national character, not in Ivan the Terrible, but in the revolutionary class approach, based as it is on the murderous experience of the Jacobin dictators' ('Proshloe i nastoiashchee v "Starike" Iuriia Trifonova', *Russian Language Journal*, 128 (1983), p. 133).

30 Starikov and Medvedev, *Philip Mironov*, p. 177.
31 Iurii Trifonov, *Vechnye temy* (M: Sovetskii pisatel', 1985), p. 68. The sentence beginning 'And against this background' is missing from the *Sobranie sochinenii* edition.
32 Shigontsev is very close to Nechaev's self-definition, as expressed in his 'Catechism of a Revolutionary'. Trifonov quotes this document extensively in his article 'Nechaev, Verkhovenskii, i drugie'. Of particular relevance is the following: 'A revolutionary is a man with a destiny. He does not have personal interests, activities, feelings, attachments, property, even a name. Everything in him is consumed by a single, exclusive interest, a single idea, a single passion: the revolution' (*Kak slovo nashe otzovetsia*, p. 42).
33 Russell, 'Time and memory in the works of Yury Trifonov', *Forum for Modern Language Studies*, 24, 1 (January 1988), p. 44.
34 Russell, 'Time and memory in the works of Yury Trifonov', p. 46.
35 Josephine Woll sees the novel as 'essentially concerned with the nature of truth and man's perception of truth'. She asks: 'Is the pursuit of truth important, and if so why? Indeed, is there such a thing as objective truth, or is truth the proverbial elephant in the hands of the blind man? To what extent and in what ways do circumstance, point of view, emotional involvement, ideological commitment and historical exigencies influence one's perception of truth?' ('Trifonov's *Starik*: The Truth of the Past', *Russian Literature Triquarterly*, 19 (1986), p. 246). Thus Pavel Evgrafovich's search for 'the truth' behind Migulin's unauthorized advance is first of all a search for self-understanding, to come to terms with his own ambivalent feelings toward Migulin (his personal truth), and the desire to establish an objective truth for future generations (historical truth). She concludes: 'In *Starik* the truth of the past, which in turn becomes the truth of the present, is an amalgam of memory, of documents, of impressions, of words and thoughts, and sensations. Pavel Evgrafovich never claims that it will be comforting to know the truth. Merely that it is imperative' (*ibid.*, p. 256).
36 Trifonov explained the significance of the heat: 'I placed the situation in the summer of 1972. The image of that terrible

Moscow heat, when the sky was obscured by a smoky gloom, was absolutely necessary in this work. It squeezed everything, like a hoop. In the finale the heat dies away. The hoop falls apart. By using this detail I escaped the temptation to write a separate story about that difficult Moscow August' ('Gorod i gorozhane', *Kak slovo nashe otzovetsia*, p. 304).
37 'Kazhdyi chelovek – sud'ba', in *Kak slovo nashe otzovetsia*, p. 296.
38 Oklianskii, *Iurii Trifonov: Portret-vospominanie*, p. 121.
39 'Pisat' na predele vozmozhnogo', in *Kak slovo nashe otzovetsia*, p. 335. German Lopatin was born into the gentry, and was considered a friend of Marx and Engels. He translated parts of *Das Kapital* into Russian, and was active in Populist circles in the 1870s and 1880s, helping Petr Lavrov to escape from exile and trying to free Nikolai Chernyshevskii from Siberian imprisonment.

5 TIME AND PLACE

1 'Roman s istoriei', in *Kak slovo nashe otzovetsia*, p. 326. James Woodward also writes on the significance of the twin narrative planes: 'Thus the novel establishes a direct correlation between literature, morality and sensitivity to the "links" which exist at once between individuals and generations, and it therefore follows that Antipov's development as a writer in the work is to be seen as reflecting his development as a man. The "dots" of the "line" which the narrator traces are joined by the theme of his gradual conversion from the "calculator" or "mathematician" of the early chapters into a writer who triumphs over his "time and place" by exposing himself fully to the "test" they set, by boldly confronting its divisive effects, and by retaining in the process the moral integrity which is the necessary basis of human relationships' ('The "Dotted Line" of Jurij Trifonov's Last Novel', *Die Welt der Slaven*, 36 (N. F. 15), 1991, 1–2, pp. 340–1).
2 See S. Baruzdin, 'Neodnoznachnyi Trifonov', *Druzhba narodov*, 1987, no.10, pp. 255–62.
3 L. Chukovskaia, *Opustelyi dom* (Paris: YMCA, 1965). This has since appeared in the USSR: *Neva*, 1988, no. 2, pp. 51–93.
4 Colin Partridge remarks of Trifonov's style: 'Trifonov's prose captures the questioning rhythm of his protagonists' forlorn self-interrogations; his long sentences contrive to an echo-chamber wherein they meditate in a private space that is also, through Trifonov's adroit use of the Russian verb's tenses and aspects, a public forum for anguished speculation. His skill with verbs continues an "endlessness" – a sense that the questions and

perceptions articulated personally and presently are part of all humanity's problems, and hence timeless. They are not confined to the illusions and disillusions of particular Soviet citizens in the period of Trifonov's observations' (C. Partridge, *Yury Trifonov's The Moscow Cycle* (Lewiston, Queenston, Lampeter: The Edwin Mellen Press, 1990), p. 19).

5 Edward J. Brown notes of this passage: 'The passage is quite possibly Trifonov's most powerful historical synecdoche, a microcosm that beautifully contains and shadows forth the macrocosm. Before the massive and mysterious movement of history – monstrous, menacing, indifferent – which the individual human being can neither understand nor control, the only refuge in which he can create a reality of his own is his separate, personal life. The scene is a summing up of Soviet history almost Tolstoyan in its sweep and thrust. Two lonely people try to preserve something of their own through all the weird misery of revolution, socialist construction and reconstruction, purge and rehabilitation, war and peace' ('Trifonov: The Historian as Artist', p. 121).

6 Sigrid McLaughlin notes: 'With the help of his embedded novel, Trifonov illustrates that fearlessness and persistence are the most essential qualities a writer must possess because these qualities make knowledge accessible, and knowledge is the precondition for conveying the truth. The artist, then, must be a person of conscience and compassion, who takes the responsibility of conveying the truth, even though constrained by circumstances' ('Antipov's *Nikiforov Syndrome*: The Embedded Novel in Trifonov's *Time and Place*', *Slavic and East European Journal*, 32, 2 (Summer 1988), p. 246).

7 *Druzhba narodov*, 1987, no.1, pp. 6–7.

8 *Ibid.*, p. 54. Compare Trifonov's own recollection of Sol'ts when he met him in his last days, from *Otblesk kostra*: 'I saw Sol'ts not long before his death, during the War. His reason really had dimmed. All the time he would write endless rows of figures on long sheets of paper. I don't know what it was. Possibly he was writing something important in his old underground code ... Sol'ts was too lonely and too ill' (IV, 24).

9 Sigrid McLaughlin sees Lenia as a 'small-scale Stalin', and thinks that 'the relationship of Gorik and the select boys of the secret society to their leader Lenya mirrors, as a microcosm, that of the Party élite to Stalin' ('A Moment in the History of Consciousness of the Soviet Intelligentsia: Trifonov's Novel *Disappearance*', *Studies in Comparative Communism*, 21, 3–4 (Autumn-Winter 1988), p. 309).

10 *Druzhba narodov*, 1987, no.1, p. 65.

11 *Ibid.*, p. 80.
12 *Ibid.*, p. 31.
13 *Ibid.*, p. 39.
14 *Ibid.*, p. 33.
15 *Ibid.*, p. 84.
16 *Ibid.*, p. 85.
17 *Ibid.*, p. 87.
18 *Ibid.*, p. 90. At the siege of Tsaritsyn Stalin took over military command without authority from Moscow, and thus came into conflict with Trotskii as War Commissar. Stalin was eventually recalled to Moscow, but only after the White forces had been beaten back. Many saw Tsaritsyn as the first sign of Stalin's desire for greater personal power. Stalin was himself to claim the credit for the victory at Tsaritsyn.
19 *Ibid.*, p. 92.
20 *Ibid.*, p. 95.
21 Sigrid McLaughlin, though, sees the book as a 'key' to Trifonov's other works: '*Disappearance* is about the loss of home, home being a symbol for beliefs, ideals, justice, order, meaning and elementary well-being and belongingness [*sic*]. It is also about the mentality of conformism and obedience which produced the personality cult and was, in turn, reinforced by it. And it is about memory as the antidote to this mentality. It is about the Russian intelligentsia and its relation to Russian history. It is about the psychology of memory which retains trivia that stand for a larger totality. It is about the difficulty of knowing one's time and place. It is about the "exchange" of the high ideals of the revolutionaries for the creature comforts of the petit bourgeois. And it is about the irony and irrationality of history, which destroys those very actors who believed in its logic and acted in its name' ('A Moment in the History of Consciousness of the Soviet Intelligentsia: Trifonov's novel *Disappearance*', p. 304).

CONCLUSION

1 Only six of the stories appeared in the original publication. The seventh, 'Nedolgoe prebyvanie v kamere pytok', appeared in 1986. It was restored to its place in the cycle in Trifonov's 1985–7 collected works (volume IV).
2 This account is almost identical to a scene in *Drugaia zhizn'*, where the young Sergei and Vlad protect Ol'ga and Rita from hot-blooded Caucasions when they holiday together in Gagry on the Black Sea.

3 Trifonov's picture of America is also discussed by Sally Thompson, 'Reflections of America in Trifonov's *Oprokinuty dom*', in *The Waking Sphinx: South African Essays on Russian Culture*, (Witwatersrand: University of Witwatersrand Library, 1989), pp. 23–39.
4 See also the illuminating discussion of this story in Paul M. Austin, 'From Helsingfors to Helsinki: Jurij Trifonov's Search for his Past', *Scando-Slavica*, 32 (1986), pp. 5–15.
5 Trigorin is a writer in Chekhov's play *The Seagull*.
6 *Voprosy literatury*, 1982, no 5, p. 44.
7 Grigorii Svirskii, *Na lobnom meste (Literatura nravstvennogo soprotivleniia, 1946–1976 gg.)* (London: Overseas Publications Interchange, 1979).

Iurii Trifonov (1925–1981): Bibliography

This bibliography, of course, does not pretend to be exhaustive. Rather, it concentrates on Trifonov's major literary works as discussed in this monograph, most of his journalistic articles and interviews, and the most notable, to my mind, secondary criticism and comment. It omits, on the other hand, many of his reflections on sporting themes, and critical articles in provincial newspapers such as *Turkmenskaia iskra*. Similarly, references to his early plays of the 1950s (which received universally bad reviews) are not included, nor is his screenplay for the film *Khokkeisty* ('The Hockey Players', 1964), nor his translations. Most of these items relate to the 1950s and early 1960s, and so are of minimal interest to this study. I have included English translations of his works. I trust that the items referred to below include Trifonov's significant fictional and non-fictional writings from the mid-1960s, and that the secondary literature includes most recent criticism and comment published in English, Russian, German and French, up to 1991. Items are listed in chronological order. Critical articles are of a general nature, unless otherwise indicated.

TRIFONOV'S WRITINGS

BOOKS

Studenty. Povest', M: Molodaia gvardiia, 1951
Studenty. Povest', Kursk: Kurskoe oblastnoe knizhnoe izdatel'stvo, 1952
Studenty. Povest', Magadan: Sovetskaia Kolyma, 1952
Studenty. Povest', M: Molodaia gvardiia, 1953
Students. A Novel, translated by Margaret Wettlin and Ivy Litvinova, M: Foreign Languages Publishing House, 1953
Studenty. Roman, Omsk: Omskoe oblastnoe knizhnoe izdatel'stvo, 1954
Studenty. Roman, M: Moskovskii rabochii, 1956
Pod solntsem. Rasskazy, M: Sovetskii pisatel', 1959
Studenty. Povest', M: Sovetskii pisatel', 1960

V kontse sezona. Rasskazy, M: Fizkul'tura i sport, 1961
Utolenie zhazhdy. Roman, M: Goslitizdat, 1963 (*Roman-gazeta*, 20 (296))
Utolenie zhazhdy. Roman, M: Sovetskii pisatel', 1963
Kostry i dozhd'. Rasskazy, M: Sovetskaia Rossiia, 1964
Fakely nad Flaminio. Rasskazy i ocherki, M: Fizkul'tura i sport, 1965
Utolenie zhazhdy. Roman, M: Sovetskii pisatel', 1965
Otblesk kostra, M: Sovetskii pisatel', 1966
Utolenie zhazhdy. Roman, M: Khudozhestvennaia literatura, 1967
Kepka s bol'shim kozyr'kom. Rasskazy, M: Sovetskaia Rossiia, 1969
Utolenie zhazhdy. Roman, M: Sovetskii pisatel', 1970
Igry v sumerkakh. Rasskazy i ocherki, M: Fizkul'tura i sport, 1970
Rasskazy i povesti, M: Khudozhestvennaia literatura, 1971
Neterpenie. Povest' ob A. Zheliabove, M: Politizdat, 1973; second corrected edition 1974
Dolgoe proshchanie. Sbornik povestei i rasskazov, M: Sovetskaia Rossiia, 1973 (Contains 'Obmen', 'Predvaritel'nye itogi', 'Dolgoe proshchanie', 'Beskonechnye igry', stories)
Prodolzhitel'nye uroki. Ocherki, M: Sovetskaia Rossiia, 1975
Drugaia zhizn'. Povest', M: Sovetskii pisatel', 1976
Obmen. P'esa, M: VAAP, 1977
The Long Goodbye. Three Novellas, translated by Helen P. Burlingame and Ellendea Proffer ('The Exchange', 'Taking Stock', 'The Long Goodbye'), Ann Arbor: Ardis, 1978
The Impatient Ones, translated by Robert Daglish, M: Progress, 1978
Povesti, M: Sovetskaia Rossiia, 1978 (Contains 'Obmen', 'Predvaritel'nye itogi', 'Dolgoe proshchanie', 'Drugaia zhizn'', 'Dom na naberezhnoi')
Izbrannye proizvedeniia v dvukh tomakh, M: Khudozhestvennaia literatura, 1978 (vol.I: 'Neterpenie', stories; vol. II: 'Obmen', 'Predvaritel'nye itogi', 'Dolgoe proshchanie', 'Drugaia zhizn'', essays and articles)
Drugaia zhizn'. Povesti, rasskazy, M: Izvestiia, 1979 (Contains 'Drugaia zhizn'', 'Obmen', 'Predvaritel'nye itogi', 'Dolgoe proshchanie', short stories)
Starik. Roman, M: Sovetskii pisatel', 1979
Utolenie zhazhdy. Roman i rasskazy, M: Profizdat, 1979
Starik; Drugaia zhizn', M: Sovetskii pisatel', 1980
Teatr pisatelia. Tri povesti dlia teatra, M: Sovetskaia Rossiia, 1982 (Contains 'Beskonechnye igry', 'Obmen', 'Dom na naberezhnoi')
Dom na naberezhnoi, Ardis: Ann Arbor, 1983
Neterpenie. Starik, M: Izvestiia, 1983
Izbrannoe. Roman, povesti, Minsk: Vysheisha shkola, 1983 (Contains

'Starik', 'Obmen', 'Predvaritel'nye itogi', 'Dolgoe proshchanie', 'Drugaia zhizn'')
Vechnye temy. Romany, povesti, M: Sovetskii pisatel', 1984 (Contains 'Starik', 'Vremia i mesto', 'Drugaia zhizn'', 'Oprokinutyi dom')
Kak slovo nashe otzovetsia... M: Sovetskaya Rossiia, 1985
Predvaritel'nye itogi: Roman, povesti, rasskazy, Kishinev: Literatura artistike, 1985 (Contains 'Obmen', 'Predvaritel'nye itogi', 'Dolgoe proshchanie', 'Starik', 'Beskonechnye igry', stories)
Sobranie sochinenii v chetyrekh tomakh, M: Khudozhestvennaia literatura, 1985–7 (vol. I (1985): 'Studenty', 'Utolenie zhazhdy'; vol. II (1986): 'Obmen', 'Predvaritel'nye itogi', 'Dolgoe proshchanie', 'Drugaia zhizn'', 'Dom na naberezhnoi'; vol. III (1986): 'Neterpenie', 'Starik'; vol. IV (1987): 'Otblesk kostra', 'Vremia i mesto', 'Oprokinutyi dom', stories and articles)
The House on the Embankment, translated by Michael Glenny, Tunbridge Wells: Abacus, 1985
Another Life, translated by Michael Glenny, Tunbridge Wells: Abacus, 1985
Iadro pravdy: Stat'i, interv'iu, esse, M: Pravda, 1987
Otblesk kostra; Ischeznovenie, M: Sovetskii pisatel', 1988
Moskovskie povesti, M: Sovetskaia Rossiia, 1988 (Contains 'Obmen', 'Predvaritel'nye itogi', 'Dolgoe proshchanie', 'Drugaia zhizn'', 'Dom na naberezhnoi')
Vremia i mesto: Povest', romany, M: Izvestiia, 1988 (Contains 'Vremia i mesto', 'Ischeznovenie', 'Dom na naberezhnoi')
Neterpenie: Povest' ob A. Zheliabove, M: Sovetskii pisatel', 1988; also Politizdat, 1988
Otblesk kostra; Starik; Ischeznovenie, M: Moskovskii rabochii, 1988
Otblesk kostra; Ischeznovenie, M: Sovetskii pisatel', 1988
Otblesk kostra; Starik, M: Izvestiia, 1989
Beskonechnye igry: O sporte, o vremeni, o sebe, M: Fizkul'tura i sport, 1989 (Contains also short stories and essays)
Dom na naberezhnoi, Alma-Ata: Zhasushy, 1989 (Also contains *Starik*)
Ischeznovenie; Vremia i mesto; Starik, M: Sovremennik, 1989

FICTION PUBLISHED SEPARATELY

'Shirokii diapazon. Fel'eton', *Moskovskii komsomolets*, 12 April 1947
'Znakomye mesta. Rasskaz', *Molodoi kolkhoznik*, 1948, no. 4, pp. 12–13
'Studenty. Povest'', *Novyi mir*, 1950, no. 10, pp. 56–175; no. 11, pp. 49–182
'Vstrechi na Volge', *Smena*, 1951, no. 21, pp. 9–11

'Fedor Kuz'mich iz konservatorii. Rasskaz', *Ogonek*, 1955, no. 39, pp. 25–7
'Doktor, student i Mitia. Rasskaz', *Molodaia gvardiia*, 1956, no. 1, pp. 54–76
'Nepriznannyi. Rasskaz', *Smena*, 1956, no. 9, p. 3
'Neokonchannyi kholst. Rasskaz', *Neva*, 1957, no. 3, pp. 87–94
'Daleko v gorakh. Rasskaz', *Fizkul'tura i sport*, 1957, 11, pp. 37–40
'Puti v pustyne. Rasskazy', *Znamia*, 1959, no. 2, pp. 70–99 (Stories include 'Polet'; 'Pesochnye chasy'; 'Ochki'; 'Piat' let nazad ...'; 'Odinochestvo Klycha Durdy'; 'Beseda s gerpetologami'; 'O vode'; 'Festival' v Mery'; 'Pod solntsem')
'V bufete aeroporta ... Rasskaz', *Fizkul'tura i sport*, 1959, no. 7, pp. 36–8
'Odnazhdy dushnoi noch'iu', in V. Koblikov, N. Otten, N. Panchenko and others (eds.), *Tarusskie stranitsy. Literaturno-khudozhestvennyi illiustrirovannyi sbornik* (Kaluga: Kaluzhskoe knizhnoe izdatel'stvo, 1961), pp. 202–3
'Ispanskaia Odisseia. Rasskaz', *Fizkul'tura i sport*, 1963, no. 1, pp. 37–9
'Utolenie zhazhdy. Roman', *Znamia*, 1963, no. 4, pp. 81–118; no. 5, pp. 3–39; no. 6, pp. 3–68; no. 7, pp. 3–88
'Vospominaniia o Dzhentsano. Rasskaz', *Molodaia gvardiia*, 1964, no. 4, pp. 114–19
'Deti doktora Grishi. Rasskaz', *Vokrug sveta*, 1964, no. 7, pp. 58–9
'Otblesk kostra', *Znamia*, 1965, no. 2, pp. 142–60; no. 3, pp. 152–77 (extract in *Smena*, 1966, no. 10, pp. 18–20)
'Kepka s bol'shim kozyr'kom. Rasskaz', *Prostor*, 1966, no. 8, pp. 47–50
'Dva rasskaza: Vera i Zoika; Byl letnii polden'', *Novyi mir*, 1966, no. 12, pp. 75–91
'Dva rasskaza: Samyi malen'kii gorod; Golubinaia gibel'', *Novyi mir*, 1968, no. 1, pp. 74–88
'Pobeditel'. Rasskaz', *Znamia*, 1968, no. 7, pp. 122–5
'V gribnuiu osen'. Rasskaz', *Novyi mir*, 1968, no. 8, pp. 67–75
'Obmen. Povest'', *Novyi mir*, 1969, no. 12, pp. 29–65
'Beskonechnye igry', *Prostor*, 1970, no. 7, pp. 52–82
'Predvaritel'nye itogi', *Novyi mir*, 1970, no. 12, pp. 101–40
'Pereulok zabytykh lits. Rasskaz', *Trud*, 10 December 1970, p. 4
'Dolgoe proshchanie. Povest'', *Novyi mir*, 1971, no. 8, pp. 53–107
'Neterpenie. Roman', *Novyi mir*, 1973, no. 3, pp. 44–116; no. 4, pp. 35–112; no. 5, pp. 8–90; extracts in *Literaturnaia Rossiia*, no. 4, 1973, pp. 8–10; *Nedelia*, 11–17 September 1972, pp. 6–7; *Nedelia*, 18–24 September 1972, pp. 6–7
'Drugaia zhizn'. Povest'', *Novyi mir*, 1975, no. 8, pp. 7–99
'Dom na naberezhnoi. Povest'', *Druzhba narodov*, 1976, no. 1, pp. 83–167

'Starik. Roman', *Druzhba narodov*, 1978, no. 3, pp. 27–153
'Oprokinutyi dom. Rasskazy', *Novyi mir*, 1981, no. 7, pp. 58–87
'Vremia i mesto. Roman', *Druzhba narodov*, 1981, no. 9, pp. 72–148; no. 10, pp. 22–108
'Nedolgoe prebyvanie v kamere pytok. Rasskaz', *Znamia*, 1986, no. 12, pp. 118–24
'Ischeznovenie. Roman', *Druzhba narodov*, 1987, no.1, pp. 6–95; extracts in *Knizhnoe obozrenie*, 1986, no. 38, pp. 8–9; no. 39, pp. 8–9

INTERVIEWS AND OTHER WRITINGS

'Mysli pered nachalom', *Smena* 1950, no. 21, p. 4 (on Second All-Union meeting of young writers)
Untitled speech at Moscow's Lenin Pedagogical Institute, at a students' discussion of 'Studenty', *Novyi mir*, 1951, no. 2, p. 228
'Posle soveshchaniia', *Literaturnaia gazeta*, 29 March 1951 (co-author with N. Evdokimov)
'Povest' o stalevarakh', *Novyi mir*, 1951, no. 5, pp. 238–9 (on N. Evdokimov's *Vysokaia dolzhnost'*)
'Denisov i drugie', *Literaturnaia gazeta*, 7 April 1954 (on G. Bakalanov's *V Snegiriakh*)
'Rozhdenie gorodov. Zametki pisatelia', *Literaturnaia gazeta*, 21 June 1955, p. 2
'Rasskazy o molodykh', *Literaturnaia gazeta*, 25 December 1956 (on F. Koluntsev's *Dorogi zovut*)
'Zametki o zhanre', *Literaturnaia gazeta*, 3 December 1959, p. 3 (on N. Tarasenkova's stories *Cherez les*)
'Cherez vsiu zhizn'', *Literaturnaia gazeta*, 28 January 1960, p. 5 (on Chekhov)
'Puti, kotorye my vybirali', *Literaturnaia gazeta*, 6 October 1960, p. 3
'Ne tol'ko detiam', *Literaturnaia gazeta*, 24 August 1961, p. 3 (on V. N. Ordzhonikidze's stories *Dolgie u kraia pustyni*)
'Nel'zia otniat' u liudei', *Literaturnaia gazeta*, 9 September 1961 (on the occasion of the celebration of Bulgarian liberation)
'A koster gorit', *Literaturnaia gazeta*, 19 December 1961, p. 4 (on the occasion of meeting Second World War partisans and soldiers in Bulgaria)
'Oni zhivut v peskakh', *Vecherniaia Moskva*, 17 October 1962, p. 3 (on *Utolenie zhazhdy*)
'O tekh, kto nachinal ...', *Literaturnaia gazeta*, 23 February 1963, pp. 1, 4 (on the organization of the Red Guard in St Petersburg, with reference to Valentin and Evgenii Trifonov; subsequently incorporated into *Otblesk kostra*)

'Iskusstvo prinadlezhit narodu. Pisateli o traditsiiakh i novatorstve. Otvet na anketu', *Voprosy literatury*, 1963, no. 2, pp. 61–2

'Pisateli za rabotoi. Otvet na anketu', *Voprosy literatury*, 1964, no. 2, p. 248

Untitled review of A. Bitov's book *Bol'shoi shar, Iunost'*, 1964, no. 4, p. 74

Untitled review of K. Vanshenkin's short novel *Bol'shie pozhary, Znamia*, 1964, no. 11, pp. 247–8

'Detstvo, shkola, voina', *Literaturnaia gazeta*, 16 March 1965, p. 3 (on V. Amlinskii's *Tuchi nad gorodom vstali*)

'Mal'chik vel dnevnik ... ', *Literaturnaia gazeta*, 6 November 1965, pp. 2, 4 (on the diary of Pavel Lur'e, February – October 1917, in St Petersburg; subsequently incorporated into the book edition of *Otblesk kostra*)

'Pisateli o kritike. Otvet na anketu', *Voprosy literatury*, 1966, no. 5, pp. 42–3

'Pristal'noe vnimanie k cheloveku', *Moskovskii komsomolets*, 22 June 1966, p. 4

'O svoikh tvorcheskikh planakh', *Moskovskaia pravda*, 27 July 1966

'Trud intelligenta', *Literaturnaia gazeta*, 20 September 1966, p. 2 (co-author with P. Novikov, S. Klorik'ian)

'Sila dokumental'nosti', *Moskva*, 1967, no. 2, pp. 201–2 (on L. Ginzburg, *Bezdna. Povestvovanie, osnovannoe na dokumentakh A. V. Ginzburga*)

'Kakoi literaturnyi geroi vam naibolee blizok? Otvet na anketu', *Moskva*, 1967, no. 11, p. 217

'Khudozhnik i revoliutsiia. Otvet na anketu', *Voprosy literatury*, 1967, no. 11, pp. 101–2

'Maiak skvoz' gody', *Literaturnaia gazeta*, 1 November 1967, p. 10 (on Rikhard Ansuaard, Estonian-born veteran of the Revolution)

'Neobkhodimye dobavleniia k ocherku', *Literaturnaia gazeta*, 5 December 1967, p. 12 (continuation of preceding article)

'Glashatai novoi epokhi', *Voprosy literatury*, 1968, no. 3, p. 16 (on the centenery of Gor'kii's birth)

'O futbole. Sub"ektivnye zametki', *Literaturnaia gazeta*, 12 June 1968, p. 13

Untitled foreword to the short novel by Vl. Gusev, *Zhizn'. Dvenadtsat' mesiatsev, Druzhba narodov*, 1969, no. 1, p. 118

'Otblesk istorii', *Literaturnaia Rossiia*, 7 March 1969, p. 15 (about work on a new novel)

'Vozvrashchenie k "prosus"', *Voprosy literatury*, 1969, no. 7, pp. 63–7

'Rabochii klass i literatura', *Druzhba narodov*, 1970, no. 3, pp. 268–9

'Nash drug Dolzhinsuren', *Literaturnaia gazeta*, 23 December 1970, p. 4

'Zrelost' talanta', *Literaturnaia Rossiia*, 5 February 1971, p. 5 (on the sixtieth birthday of Anatolii Rybakov)
'Geroi "Narodnoi Voli"', *Literaturnaia gazeta*, 25 August 1971, p. 3 (interview)
'Vechnozelenoe puteshestvie', *Voprosy literatury*, 1971, no. 12, pp. 96–9 (on his links with Bulgaria)
'Vybirat', reshat'sia, zhertvovat'', *Voprosy literatury*, 1972, no. 2, pp. 62–5
'Uroki mastera', *Literaturnaia gazeta*, 31 May 1972, p. 6 (on the eightieth birthday of Konstantin Paustovskii)
'Dela kazhdodnevnye', *Literaturnaia gazeta*, 13 June 1973, p. 2 (on his latest plans)
'Neskonchaemoe nachalo', *Literaturnaia Rossiia*, 21 December 1973, pp. 8, 9 (on his work as a writer)
'Sovremennost' – splav istorii i budushchego', *Literaturnaia gazeta*, 19 June 1974, p. 5 (interview)
'Na polkakh folianty... (o roli starykh knig v zhizni i tvorchestve)', *Literaturnaia gazeta*, 27 July 1974, p. 3
'V kratkom – beskonechnoe', *Voprosy literatury*, 1974, no. 8, pp. 171–94 (interview)
'Zhguchie voprosy vzroslomu cheloveku. Otvet na anketu', *Komsomol'skaia pravda*, 25 October 1975
'Knigi, kotorye vybiraiut nas', *Literaturnaia gazeta*, 10 November 1976, p. 6
'Voobrazit' beskonechnost'', *Literaturnoe obozrenie*, 1977, no. 4, pp. 98–102 (interview)
'Proizvoditel'nost' talanta', *Literaturnaia Rossiia*, 12 August 1977, p. 11 (on Iurii Kazakov's fiftieth birthday)
'Interv'iu o kontaktakh', *Inostrannaia literatura*, 1978, no. 6, pp. 243–51 (on his recent trip to the USA)
'Vospominaniia o mukakh nemoty: Fedinskii seminar sorokovykh godov', *Druzhba narodov*, 1979, no. 10, pp. 185–94; reprinted in K. Vanshenkin (ed.), *Vospominaniia o Litinstitute* (M: Sovetskii pisatel', 1983), pp. 245–60
'Pisatel' i kritika. Otvet na anketu', *Voprosy literatury*, 1979, no. 12, pp. 290–2
'Mir derzhitsia na beskorystnykh', *Sputnik*, 1980, no. 6, pp. 150–2 (interview)
'Slavim cherez shest' vekov', *Literaturnaia gazeta*, 3 September 1980, p. 6 (on the 600th anniversary of the Battle of Kulikovo Field)
'Pamiati L'va Ginsburga', *Literaturnaia gazeta*, 1 October 1980, p. 15
'Gorod i gorozhane', *Literaturnaia gazeta*, 25 March 1981, pp. 4, 5 (interview)

'Kak slovo nashe otzovetsia ... ; Zagadka i providenie Dostoevskogo',
  Novyi mir, 1981, no. 11, pp. 233–44
'Roman s istorii', *Voprosy literatury*, 1982, no. 5, pp. 66–77
'Interv'iu s Iuriem Trifonovym', *Obozrenie*, no. 6 (September 1983),
  pp. 28–34
'Iadro pravdy. Rabochie zapisi', *Druzhba narodov*, 1985, no. 3,
  pp. 235–8
'"Sopriazhenie istorii s sovremennost'iu" (Iz pisem ob istorii)',
  Voprosy literatury, 1987, no. 7, pp. 170–85
'Zapiski soseda', *Druzhba narodov*, 1989, no. 10, pp. 7–43

SELECTED CRITICISM

Agurskii, M., 'Polemika s dissidentami Iuriia Trifonova', *Russkaia mysl'*, 27 September 1979, p. 6
Akchurin, S., 'Zvonite v liuboe vremia (Iz vospominanii o Iu. V. Trifonove)', *Literaturnaia ucheba*, 1982, 6, pp. 230–3
Akmuradova, A., 'Nekotorye khudozhestvennye osobennosti romana Iu. Trifonova "Utolenie zhazhdy"', *Izvestiia AN SSSR. Seriia obshchestvennykh nauk*, 1974, no. 5, pp. 64–70
Aleksandrov, L., 'Vremia rabotat' vslast'', *Literaturnaia Rossiia*, 25 October 1963, p. 14 (review of *Utolenie zhazhdy*)
Aleskerova, E. A., 'V poiskakh sobstvennoi temy', *Uchenye zapiski Azerbaidzhanskogo pedagogicheskogo instituta russkogo iazyka i literatury*, 1974, no. 2, pp. 94–9 (on *Studenty*)
  'Roman "Utolenie zhazhdy"; opyt osvoeniia zhizni', *Uchenye zapiski Azerbaidzhanskogo pedagogicheskogo instituta russkogo iazyka i literatury*, 1975, no. 3, pp. 113–19
  '"Moskovskie" povesti Iu. Trifonova', *Uchenye zapiski Azerbaidzhanskogo pedagogicheskogo instituta russkogo iazyka i literatury*, 1976, no. 3, pp. 50–3
Amlinskii, V., 'O dniakh edinstvennykh', *Literaturnoe obozrenie*, 1982, no. 1, pp. 42–5 (on *Oprokinutyi dom*)
Amusin, M., 'Voprosy, poiski, obreteniia', *Zvezda*, 1982, no. 11, pp. 182–91; on Trifonov: pp. 184–6 (review of *Vremia i mesto*)
Anar, 'Za gran'iu obydennosti', *Druzhba narodov*, 1976, no. 4, pp. 278–80 (on *Drugaia zhizn'*)
Andreev, Iu., 'V zamknutom mirke', *Literaturnaia gazeta*, 3 March 1971, p. 5
  'Sovremennik: delo i slovo', *Literaturnaia gazeta*, 12 July 1978, p. 4 (on *Drugaia zhizn'*)
Anninskii, L., 'Spor dvukh talantov', *Literaturnaia gazeta*, 20 October 1959, p. 3 (on *Pod solntsem*)
  'Pisatel' za rabochim stolom', *Vecherniaia Moskva*, 11 July 1964

Iadro orekha, M: Sovetskii pisatel', 1965, pp. 123–32 (on *Utolenie zhazhdy*)

'Neokonchatel'nye itogi. O trekh povestiakh Iu. Trifonova ('Obmen', 'Predvaritel'nye itogi', 'Dolgoe proshchanie')', *Don*, 1972, no. 5, pp. 183–92

'Ochishchenie proshlym', *Don*, 1977, no. 2, pp. 157–60 (on *Drugaia zhizn*' and *Dom na naberezhnoi*)

'Intelligenty i prochie', in his *Tridsatye-semidesiatye. Literaturno-kriticheskie stat'i*, M: Sovremennik, 1977, pp. 199–227

'Rassechenie kornia. Zametki o publitsistike Iuriia Trifonova', *Druzhba narodov*, 1985, no. 3, pp. 239–46; reprinted in Iu. Trifonov, *Kak sovo nashe otzovetsia*, pp. 3–20

Austin, P. M., 'From Helsingfors to Helsinki: Jurij Trifonov's Search for his Past', *Scando-Slavica*, 32 (1986), pp. 5–15

Babaev, E., 'Rasskazy romanista', *Novyi mir*, 1970, no. 9, pp. 268–72 (on *Kepka s bol'shim kozyr'kom*)

Baruzdin, S., 'Neodnoznachnyi Trifonov', *Druzhba narodov*, 1987, no. 10, pp. 255–62 (on four-volume edition of Trifonov's work, with memoir); also in his *Pisatel'-zhizn'-literatura*, M: Sovetskii pisatel', 1990, pp. 286–302

Bauer, J., 'Die Trifonov-Rezeption in der westlichen deutschsprachigen Presse', in N. Franz and J. Meichel (eds.), *Russische Literatur der Gegenwart. Themen. Tendenzen. Porträts*, Mainz: Liber Verlag, 1986, pp. 13–32

Bazhenov, G., 'Kakoi ei byt', zhizni?', *Oktiabr'*, 1975, no. 12, pp. 210–12 (on *Drugaia zhizn*')

Bednenko, V., Kirnitskii, O., 'Prezhdevremennye itogi', *Molodaia gvardiia*, 1971, no. 10, pp. 305–9 (on *Predvaritel'nye itogi*)

Belaia, G., *Khudozhestvennyi mir sovremennoi prozy*, M: Akademiia Nauk SSSR, Nauka, 1983, pp. 151–84

'O "vnutrennei" i "vneshnei teme"', *Nauchnye doklady vysshei shkoly. Filologicheskie nauki*, 1983, no. 2, pp. 10–17 (on *Drugaia zhizn*')

'Nepovtorimoe odnazhdy: Filosofsko-eticheskaia tema v proze Iu. Trifonova', *Literaturnoe obozrenie*, 1983, no. 5, pp. 7–12

Björling, F., 'Jurij Trifonov's *Dom na naberezhnoi*: Fiction or Autobiography?', *Svantetit*, 9, 1 (1983), 9–30; reprinted in Jane Gary Harris (ed.), *Autobiographical Statements in Twentieth Century Russian Literature*, Princeton: Princeton University Press, 1990, pp. 172–92

Björling, F., 'Morality as History: an Analysis of Jurij Trifonov's Novel *Starik*', in P. A. Jensen and B. Lönnqvist (eds.), *Text and Context: Essays in Honor to Nils Åke Nilsson*, Almqvist and Wiksell International, Stockholm, 1987, pp. 154–69

Bocharov, A., 'Kanal – eto v sushchnosti, zhizn'', *Druzhba narodov*, 1963, no. 12, pp. 267–70 (on *Utolenie zhazhdy*)
  'Sovremennik – krupnym planom', *Voprosy literatury*, 1965, no. 12, pp. 95–6 (on *Utolenie zhazhdy*)
  'Vremia v chetyrekh izmereniiakh', *Voprosy literatury*, 1974, no. 11, pp. 33–68 (on *Predvaritel'nye itogi*)
  'Voskhozhdenie', *Oktiabr'*, 1975, no. 8, pp. 203–11
  'Vremia kristallizatsii', *Voprosy literatury*, 1976, no. 3, pp. 29–57 (on Trifonov: pp. 42–8; on *Drugaia zhizn'*)
  'Strast' bor'by i igrushechnye strasti', *Literaturnoe obozrenie*, 1978, no. 10, pp. 64–7 (on *Starik*)
  'Energiia Trifonovskoi prozy', in Iu. Trifonov, *Povesti*, M: Sovetskaia Rossia, 1978, pp. 507–23
  'Listopad', *Literaturnoe obozrenie*, 1982, no. 3, pp. 45–8 (on *Vremia i mesto*)
  'Kontrapunkt: Obshchee i individual'noe v proze Iu. Trifonova, V. Shukshina, V. Rasputina', *Oktiabr'*, 1982, no. 7, pp. 190–9; on Trifonov, pp. 192–7
Borshchagovskii, A., 'Chelovek i ego delo', *Trud*, 10 March 1971, p. 3 (on *Predvaritel'nye itogi*)
  'Poisk v puti. O proze Iu. Trifonova', *Literaturnaia Rossiia*, 29 August 1975, p. 16
Brovman, G., *Problemy i geroi sovremennoi prozy*, M: Khudozhestvennaia literatura, 1966, pp. 97–102 (on *Utolenie zhazhdy*)
  'Izmereniia malogo mira', *Literaturnaia gazeta*, 8 March 1972, p. 5
Brown, D., *Soviet Russian Literature since Stalin*, Cambridge, London, New York, Melbourne: Cambridge University Press, 1978; on Trifonov: pp. 167–9
Brown, E. J., *Russian Literature since the Revolution*, second edition, revised and enlarged, Cambridge, Mass., and London: Harvard University Press, 1982; on Trifonov: pp. 313–19
  'Trifonov: the Historian as Artist', in Terry L. Thompson and Richard Sheldon (eds.), *Soviet Society and Culture: Essays in Honor of Vera S. Dunham*, Boulder and London: Westview Press, 1988, pp. 109–23
Burkhart, D., 'Historisches Ereignis und Aesthetisches Zeichen. Zu Iurij V. Trifonovs Roman "Neterpenie"', *Russian Literature*, 6, 2 (April 1978), pp. 155–74
De Maegd-Soëp, C., 'The Theme of "byt" – Everyday Life – in the Stories of Iurii Trifonov', in E. Bristol (ed.), *Selected Papers from the Second World Congress for Soviet and East European Studies: Russian Literature and Criticism*, Berkeley: Berkeley Slavic Specialties, 1982, pp. 49–62

'Trifonov et "Le reflet du brasier",' *Slavica Gandensia*, 12 (1985), pp. 69-76
'Iurii Trifonov and his Novel *The Impatient Ones*,' *Slavica Gandensia*, 13 (1986), pp. 337-45
'The Moscow Stories of Yury Trifonov,' *Slavica Gandensia*, 15 (1988), pp. 7-15
Trifonov and the Drama of the Russian Intelligentsia, Ghent State University, Russian Institute, 1990
Demidov, A., 'Minuvshee', *Teatr*, 1981, no. 7, pp. 97-107 (on Liubimov's production of *Dom na naberezhnoi* at Moscow's Taganka theatre)
Dobrenko, E. A., 'Siuzhet kak "vnutrennee dvizhenie" v pozdnei proze Iu. Trifonova', *Voprosy russkoi literatury*, 1987, no. 1, pp. 44-50
Druzhnikov, Iu., 'Sud'ba Trifonova', *Vremia i my*, 108 (1990), pp. 247-78
Dudintsev, V., 'Stoit li umirat' ran'she vremeni?', *Literaturnoe obozrenie*, 1976, no. 4, pp. 52-7 (on *Drugaia zhizn'*)
'Velikii smysl – zhit'', *Literaturnoe obozrenie*, 1976, no. 5, pp. 48-52 (on *Dom na naberezhnoi*)
Dumrath, F., *Die Funktion des Präsens im Roman "Starik" von Jurij V. Trifonov: Mit einer Zeitgestaltungsgrafik*, Hamburg: Buske, 1982
Durkin, A., 'Trifonov's "Taking Stock": The Role of Čexovian Subtext', *Slavic and East European Journal*, 28, 1 (Spring 1984), pp. 32-41
Dymshits. A., 'Vospityvat' v cheloveke cheloveka', *Literaturnaia Rossiia*, 19 February 1965, p. 7 (on *Utolenie zhazhdy*)
Efimov, I., 'Pisatel', raskonvoirovannyi v istoriki', *Vremia i my*, 71 (1983), pp. 139-53 (on *Starik*)
El'iashevich, A., 'Gorod i gorozhane', *Zvezda*, 1984, no. 12, pp. 170-85; considerably expanded and reprinted in his *Gorizontali i vertikali: Sovremennaia proza – ot semidesiatykh k vos'midesiatym*, M: Sovetskii pisatel', 1984, pp. 255-366
Eremina S., Piskunov, V., 'Vremia i mesto prozy Iu. Trifonova', *Voprosy literatury*, 1982, no. 5, pp. 34-65
Ermilov, V., 'Nekotorye voprosy teorii sotsialisticheskogo realizma', *Znamia*, 1951, no. 7, pp. 167-8 (on *Studenty*)
Ermolaev, H., 'Proshloe i nastoiashchee v "Starike" Iuriia Trifonova', *Russian Language Journal*, 128 (1983), pp. 131-45
'The Theme of Terror in *Starik*', in Arnold McMillin (ed.), *Aspects of Modern Russian and Czech Literature: Selected Papers of the Third World Congress for Soviet and East European Studies*, Columbus, Ohio: Slavica, 1989, pp. 96-109

Evtushenko, E., 'Besposhchadnost' k "besposhchadnosti"', *Sovetskaia kul'tura*, 6 July 1976, p. 4 (on the Taganka theatre's production of *Obmen*)

Fink, L., 'Zybkost' kharaktera ili zybkost' zamysla?', *Literaturnaia gazeta*, 29 October 1975, p. 4 (on *Drugaia zhizn'*)

Galanov, B., 'Nachalo puti', *Znamia*, 1951, no. 1, pp. 171–4 (on *Studenty*)

Geideko, V., 'Liudi na rabote', *Zvezda*, 1964, no. 12, pp. 196–203 (on *Utolenie zhazhdy*)

Gillespie, D. C., 'Time, History and the Individual in the Works of Yury Trifonov', *Modern Language Review*, 83, 2 (April 1988), pp. 375–95

'Unity through Disparity: Trifonov's *The Overturned House*', *Australian Slavonic and East European Studies*, 5, 1 (1991), pp. 45–58

Goff, I., 'Vodianye znaki: Zametki o Iurii Trifonove', *Oktiabr'*, 1985, no. 8, pp. 94–106 (memoir)

Golovskoi, V., 'Nravstvennye uroki trifonovskoi prozy', *Russian Language Journal*, 128 (1983), pp. 147–61

Gorlovskii, A., 'A chto v itoge?', *Literaturnaia Rossiia*, 19 March 1971, p. 11 (on *Predvaritel'nye itogi*)

Gusev, V., 'Usloviia vstrechi', *Literaturnaia gazeta*, 4 February 1970, p. 6 (on *Kepka s bol'shim kozyr'kom*)

'Prostranstvo slova: o dvukh stilevykh tendentsiiakh sovremennoi prozy', *Literaturnoe obozrenie*, 1978, no. 6, pp. 24–7; reprinted in *Kriticheskii dnevnik 'Sovremennika'*, M: Sovremennik, 1979, pp. 200–9; and in V. Gusev, *Pamiat' i stil'*, M: Sovetskii pisatel', 1981, pp. 324–33

Hosking, G., 'Yury Trifonov', in his *Beyond Socialist Realism: Soviet Fiction since Ivan Denisovich*, London, Toronto, Sydney, New York: Paul Elek and Granada Publishing, 1980, pp. 180–95

'*Byt* by *byt*', *Times Literary Supplement*, 6 December 1985, p. 1386 (on the appearance in English translation of *Another Life* and *The House on the Embankment*)

Hughes, A. C., '*Bol'shoi mir* or *zamknutyi mirok*: Departure from Literary Convention in Iurii Trifonov's Recent Fiction', *Canadian Slavonic Papers*, 22, 4 (December 1980), pp. 470–80

Iakimenko, L., 'Lik vremeni', in Iu. Trifonov, *Utolenie zhazhdy* (M: 1967), pp. 5–13

'Literaturnaia kritika i sovremennaia povest'', *Novyi mir*, 1973, no. 1, pp. 238–50; on Trifonov: pp. 245–8 (*Dolgoe proshchanie*)

Il'ina, N., 'Iz rodoslovnoi russkoi revoliutsii', *Neman*, 1976, no. 12, pp. 170–5 (on *Neterpenie*)

'Iu. V. Trifonov. Nekrolog', *Izvestiia*, 31 March 1981, p. 6; *Litera-*

turnaia gazeta, 1 April 1981, p. 3 (with contributions by S. Baruzdin, S. Zalygin)

Ivanova, N., 'Postupok i slovo, ili Obraz pisatelia v proze Iuriia Trifonova', *Literaturnaia ucheba*, 1983, no. 2, pp. 149–57

Proza Iuriia Trifonova, M: Sovetskii pisatel', 1984

'Uporstvo vozvrashcheniia', in Iu. Trifonov, *Vremia i mesto: Povest', romany* (M: 1988), pp. 555–72

Karasev, Iu., 'Povest' o studentakh', *Ogonek*, 1951, no. 12, p. 24

Kardin, V., 'Legendy i fakty', *Novyi mir*, 1966, no. 2, pp. 237–50; on Trifonov: pp. 237–8 (*Otblesk kostra*)

'Proroki v svoem otechestve', *Druzhba narodov*, 1974, no. 8, pp. 267–71 (on *Neterpenie*)

'Vremena ne vybiraiut... Iz zapisok o Iurii Trifonove', *Novyi mir*, 1987, no. 7, pp. 236–57

Obretenie: Literaturnye portrety, M: Khudozhestvennaia literatura, 1989, pp. 6–67

Khmara, V., 'Protivostoianie', *Literaturnaia gazeta*, 28 June 1978, p. 5 (on *Starik*)

Khoreva, E., 'Kazhdyi chelovek – sud'ba', *Sovetskaia kul'tura*, 10 October 1980, p. 6

Khort, A., 'Vysokaia temperatura', *Literaturnaia Rossiia*, 28 June 1974

Klado, N., 'Prokrustovo lozhe byta', *Literaturnaia gazeta*, 12 May 1976, p. 4 (on *Dom na naberezhnoi*)

Kolesnikoff, N., 'Jurij Trifonov as a Novella Writer', *Russian Language Journal*, 118 (1980), pp. 137–44

'Trifonov's *Vremja i mesto*: Compositional and Narrative Structure', *Russian Language Journal*, 41 (140) (1987), pp. 167–74

'The Temporal and Narrative Structure of Trifonov's Novel *Starik*', *Russian Literature*, 28, 1 (July 1990), pp. 23–32

Yury Trifonov: A Critical Study, Ann Arbor: Ardis, 1991

Kozhinov, V., 'Problema avtora i put' pisatelia', in N. Gei (ed.), *Kontekst – 1977*, M: Nauka, 1978, pp. 23–47; reprinted in V. V. Kozhinov, *Stat'i o sovremennoi literature*, M: Sovremennik, 1982, pp. 212–34 (comparison of *Studenty* and *Dom na naberezhnoi*)

Kramov, I., 'Sud'ba i vremia', *Novyi mir*, 1967, no. 3, pp. 252–4 (on *Otblesk kostra*)

Kriachko, L., 'Pozitsiia tvortsa i besplodie meshchanina', *Oktiabr'*, 1964, no. 5, pp. 216–17 (on *Utolenie zhazhdy*)

Kutmina, O. A., 'Vnutrennii monolog v povesti Iu. Trifonova "Drugaia zhizn'"' (nekotorye aspekty)', in *Problemy psikhologizma v khudozhestvennoi literature*, Omskskii gosudarstvennyi universitet, 1980, pp. 44–9

'Avtorskoe "ia" v povesti Iu. Trifonova "Drugaia zhizn'"', in

M. V. Kuznetsova (ed.), *Khudozhestvennyi metod i tvorcheskaia individual'nost' pisatelia*, Tomsk: Gosudarstvennyi universitet, 1982, pp. 102–10

Kuznetsov, F., 'Nastuplenie novoi nravstvennosti', *Voprosy literatury*, 1964, no. 2, pp. 5–10, 18, 22–6 (on *Utolenie zhazhdy*)

'Byt' chelovekom', *Oktiabr'*, 1975, no. 2, pp. 193–203 (on *Obmen*)

'V bor'be za cheloveka', in Iu. Trifonov, *Sobranie sochinenii v chetyrekh tomakh*, vol. I, pp. 5–20

Kuznetsova, N., 'I komissary v pyl'nykh shlemakh', *Kontinent*, 53 (1987), pp. 391–6 (on *Ischeznovenie*)

Lanshchikov, A., 'Geroi i vremia', *Don*, 1973, no. 11, pp. 169–78 (on *Dolgoe proshchanie*)

Laychuk, J. L., 'Yury Trifonov's Male Protagonists in the "Test of Life"', *New Zealand Slavonic Journal*, 1989–90, pp. 109–25

Lebedev, A. A., 'Neterpimost'', in A. A. Lebedev, *Stat'i*, M: Sovetskii pisatel', 1980, pp. 193–246 (on *Neterpenie*)

Leech-Anspach, G., 'Bemerkungen zum Verständnis von Zeit und Erinnerung in Romanen Boris Pasternaks, Andrej Bitovs und Jurij Trifonovs', *Zeitschrift fur Slavische Philologie*, 46 (1986), pp. 218–29

Leiderman, N., 'Potentsial zhanra', *Sever*, 1978, no. 3, pp. 101–9 (on *Dom na naberezhnoi*)

Lemkhin, M., 'Zheliabov, Nechaev, Karlos i drugie', *Kontinent*, 49 (1986), pp. 359–69 (on *Kak slovo nashe otzovetsia*)

Levin, L., 'Vosem' stranits ot ruki', *Voprosy literatury*, 1988, no. 3, pp. 183–98 (memoir)

Levinskaia, G. S., '"Dom" v khudozhestvennom mire Iuriia Trifonova', *Filologicheskie nauki*, 1991, no. 2, pp. 3–11

Lezina-Kurochkina, A. V., 'Ideal geroicheskoi lichnosti v romane "Andrei Kozhukhov" C. M. Stepniaka-Kravchinskogo i "Neterpenie" Iu. Trifonova', in M. Ia. Ermakova (ed.), *Traditsii i novatorstvo v khudozhestvennoi literature*, Gor'kii: Gosudarstvennyi pedagogicheskii institut, 1983, pp. 100–6

Loseff, L., *On the Beneficence of Censorship: Aesopian Language in Modern Russian Literature*, Munich: Otto Sagner, 1984, pp. 106–7 (on 'Golubinaia gibel'')

Lur'e, A., 'Uroki zhizni i tvorchestva', *Neva*, 1978, no. 4, pp. 179–81

McLain, M., 'Trifonov's *The Exchange* at Liubimov's Taganka', *Slavic and East European Arts*, 3, 1, (1985), pp. 159–69

McLaughlin, S., 'Jurij Trifonov's *House on the Embankment*: Narration and Meaning', *Slavic and East European Journal*, 26, 4 (Winter 1982), pp. 419–33

'Iurii Trifonov's *Dom na naberezhnoi* and Dostoevskii's *Prestuplenie i nakazanie*', *Canadian Slavonic Papers*, 25, 2 (June 1983), pp. 275–83

'Literary Allusions in Trifonov's "Preliminary Stocktaking"', *The Russian Review*, 46 (1987), pp. 19–34

'Antipov's *Nikiforov Syndrome*: The Embedded Novel in Trifonov's *Time and Place*', *Slavic and East European Journal*, 32, 2 (Summer 1988), pp. 237–50

'A Moment in the History of Consciousness of the Soviet Intelligentsia: Trifonov's Novel *Disappearance*', *Studies in Comparative Communism*, 21, 3/4 (Autumn/Winter 1988), pp. 303–11

Mal'tsev, Iu., 'Roman Trifonova', *Russkaia mysl'*, 19 October 1978, pp. 10–11 (on *Starik*)

Markish, S., 'K voprosu o tsenzure i nepodtsenzurnosti: gorodskie povesti Iu. Trifonova i roman F. Kandelia "Koridor"', in Georges Nivat (ed.), *Odna ili dve russkikh literatury?*, Lausanne: L'Age d'Homme, 1981, pp. 145–55

Markov, G., 'Sovremennost' i problemy prozy', *Literaturnaia gazeta*, 24 May 1967, p. 3 (on *Utolenie zhazhdy*)

Mednikov, A., 'Zhazhda istiny (vospominaniia o Iurii Trifonove)', *Iunost'*, 1985, no. 10, pp. 98–102

'Obsuzhdaem novye povesti Iu. Trifonova': see articles under V. Sokolov, M. Sinel'nikov (1972), and Trifonov's reply 'Vybirat', reshat'sia, zhertvovat''

'Obsuzhdenie povesti Iuriia Trifonova "Studenty"' (by students of Moscow's Lenin Pedagogical Institute)', *Novyi mir*, 1951, no. 2, pp. 221–8

Oklianskii, Iu. M., *Iurii Trifonov: Portret-vospominanie*, M: Sovetskaia Rossiia, 1987

Orekhova, N., 'Vybirat' pozitsiiu...', *Neva*, 1979, no. 10, pp. 195–6

Oskotskii, V., 'Nravstvennye uroki "Narodnoi voli". Zametki o romane Iu. Trifonova "Neterpenie"', *Literaturnoe obozrenie*, 1973, no. 11, pp. 55–61

Ozerov, V., 'Formirovanie kommunisticheskoi lichnosti i sotsial'no-nravstvennye problemy v zhizni i v literature', *Literaturnaia gazeta*, 30 June 1976, p. 4 (on *Dom na naberezhnoi*)

Pankin, B., 'Po krugu ili po spirali? O povestiakh Iu. Trifonova "Obmen", "Predvaritel'nye itogi", "Dolgoe proshchanie", "Drugaia zhizn'", "Dom na naberezhnoi"', *Druzhba narodov*, 1977, no. 5, pp. 238–53; reprinted in his *Strogaia literatura: Literaturno-kriticheskie stat'i i ocherki*, M: Sovetskii pisatel', 1980, pp. 123–64, and (under the title 'Ne po krugu, po spirali!') in his *Strast' k nastoiashchemu*, M: Detskaia literatura, 1983, pp. 126–62

Pankov, A., 'Zaboty zhizni i puti literatury', *Druzhba narodov*, 1985, no. 10, pp. 217–29 (on Trifonov: pp. 220–2 (*Starik*))

Pankov, V., 'Istoricheskii parol'', *Ogonek*, 1964, no. 2, pp. 24–5 (on *Utolenie zhazhdy*)

Partridge, C., *Yury Trifonov's The Moscow Cycle*, Lewiston, Queenston, Lampeter: The Edwin Mellen Press, 1990

Patera, T., *Obzor tvorchestva i analiz moskovskikh povestei Iuriia Trifonova*, Ann Arbor: Ardis, 1983

Paton, S., 'The Hero of his Time', *Slavonic and East European Review*, 64, 4 (October 1986), pp. 506–24

Pertsovskii, V., 'Proza vmeshivaetsia v spor', *Voprosy literatury*, 1971, no. 10, pp. 27–48 (on *Obmen*)

'Ispytanie bytom', *Novyi mir*, 1974, no.11, pp. 236–51 (on *Dolgoe proshchanie*)

'"Avtorskaia pozitsiia" v literature i v kritike', *Voprosy literatury*, 1981, no. 7, pp. 65–105 (on Trifonov: pp. 97–105)

Platonov, B., 'Literaturnoe obozrenie. Zametki o russkoi sovetskoi proze 1950 goda. Stat'ia Vtoraia', *Zvezda*, 1951, no. 2, pp. 160–2 (on *Studenty*)

Plekhanova, I. I., 'Osobennosti siuzhetoslozheniia v tvorchestve V. Shukshina, Iu. Trifonova, V. Rasputina (k probleme khudozhestvennoi uslovnosti)', *Russkaia literatura*, 1980, no. 4, pp. 71–88; on Trifonov: pp. 79–88

'Priroda nravstvennogo soznaniia v traktovke V. Shukshina, Iu. Trifonova, V. Rasputina', *Sibir'*, 1980, no. 5, pp. 82–98; on Trifonov: pp. 88–98

Proffer, E., 'Introduction', to Yury Trifonov, *The Long Goodbye: Three Novellas*, Ann Arbor: Ardis, 1978, pp. 9–16

Ravich, N., 'Podvig Andreia Zheliabova', *Literaturnaia gazeta*, 26 September 1973, p. 5 (on *Neterpenie*)

Reissner, E., 'Auf der Suche nach der verlorenen Wahrheit: Jurij Trifonows jungster Roman *Der Alte*', *Osteuropa*, 1979, no. 2, pp. 99–109

Ritz, G., 'Trifonov: Der Erlaubte Dissens. Kritische Prosa als Modell einer Abrechnungsliteratur', *Slavica Helvetica*, 33 (1989), pp. 289–313

Rogova, G., 'Itogi i razdum'ia', *Pod"em*, 1982, no. 11, pp. 135–8 (on *Oprokinutyi dom*)

Rosliakov, V., 'Utolennaia zhazhda', *Moskva*, 1963, no. 10, pp. 204–6 (on *Utolenie zhazhdy*)

Rostin, P., 'Pisatel', chitatel', tsenzor', *Poiski i razmyshleniia*, 1982, no. 1, pp. 84–9 (on *Dom na naberezhnoi*, *Starik*)

Russell, R., 'Time and Memory in the Works of Yury Trifonov', *Forum for Modern Language Studies*, 24, 1 (January 1988), pp. 37–52

'Old Men in Kataev and Trifonov', in M. Falchikov, C. Pike and R. Russell (eds.), *Words and Images: Essays in Honour of Professor (Emeritus) Dennis Ward*, Nottingham: Astra Press, 1989, pp. 155–63

Rybal'chenko, T. L., 'Zhanrovaia struktura i khudozhestvennaia ideiia (povest' Iu. Trifonova "Predvaritel'nye itogi")', *Problemy metoda i zhanra*, vypusk 4 (1977), pp. 98–105
'Formirovanie filosofskogo romana v tvorchestve Iu. Trifonova', *Khudozhestvennoe tvorchestvo i literaturnyi protsess*, vypusk 2 (1982), pp. 61–72
'Avtor v khudozhestvennom mire proizvedeniia: Povesti Iu. Trifonova i A. Bitova 70-kh godov', *Khudozhestvennoe tvorchestvo i literaturnyi protsess*, vypusk 6 (1984), pp. 157–77
Sakharov, V., '"Flamandskoi shkoly pestryi sor..."', *Nash sovremennik*, 1974, no. 5, pp. 188–91 (on *Dolgoe proshchanie*)
'"Vspominatel'naia" proza: Poteri i obreteniia. Zametki o povestiakh Iuriia Trifonova', in his *Obnovliaiushchii mir. Zametki o tekushchei literature*, M: Sovremennik, 1980, pp. 173–96
Satretdinova, R. S., *Turkmenistan v tvorchestve Iu. V. Trifonova*, Ashkhabad: AN TSSR, Ylym, 1984
Schröder, R., '"Moi god eshche ne nastupil...": Iz besed s Iuriem Trifonovym', *Literaturnoe obozrenie*, 1987, no. 8, pp. 96–8
Schultze, B., *Jurij Trifonovs " Der Tausch" und Valentin Rasputins "Geld für Maria": Ein Beitrag zum Gattungsverständnis von Povest und Rasskaz in der russische Gegenwartsprosa*, Göttingen: Vandenhoeck a. Ruprecht, 1985
Seifrid, T., 'Trifonov's *Dom na naberezhnoi* and the Fortunes of Aesopian Speech', *Slavic Review*, 49, 4 (Winter 1990), pp. 611–24
Shenfel'd, K., 'Iurii Trifonov – pisatel' chastichnoi pravdy', *Grani*, 121 (1981), pp. 112–18
Shklovskii, E., 'V potoke vremeni. Tema detstva v tvorchestve Iu. Trifonova', *Detskaia literatura*, 1983, no. 8, pp. 17–22
'Razrushenie doma', *Literaturnoe obozrenie*, 1987, no. 7, pp. 46–8 (on *Ischeznovenie*)
'Samoe glavnoe', *Literaturnoe obozrenie*, 1987, no. 11, pp. 25–34
Shneidman, N. N., 'Iurii Trifonov and the Ethics of Contemporary Soviet City Life', *Canadian Slavonic Papers*, 19, 3 (September 1977), pp. 335–51; expanded and reprinted in his *Soviet Literature in the 1970s: Artistic Diversity and Ideological Conformity*, Toronto: Toronto University Press, 1979, pp. 88–105
'The New Dimensions of Time and Place in Iurii Trifonov's Prose of the 1980s', *Canadian Slavonic Papers*, 27, 2 (June 1985), pp. 188–95
Soviet Literature in the 1980s: Decade of Transition, Buffalo: University of Toronto Press, 1989; on Trifonov: pp. 74–84
Shtut, S., 'Rassuzhdeniia i opisaniia. (Cherty literatury poslednikh let)', *Voprosy literatury*, 1975, no. 10, pp. 38–72; on Trifonov: pp. 63–70 (*Neterpenie*)

Sinel'nikov, M., 'Ispytanie povsednevnost'iu: Nekotorye itogi', *Voprosy literatury*, 1972, no. 2, pp. 46–62 (on *Obmen* and *Predvaritel'nye itogi*)

'Poznat' cheloveka...poznat' vremia...O "Starike" Iu. Trifonova', *Voprosy literatury*, 1979, no. 9, pp. 26–52

Skvortsov, Iu., 'Semeinaia drama inzhenera Dmitrieva', *Trud*, 25 July 1976, p. 4 (on Taganka theatre production of *Obmen*)

Slonimskii, M., 'Nashei partii dostoiny', *Komsomol'skaia pravda*, 18 November 1973, p. 2 (on the essay 'Sil'nee vremeni')

Smirnov, O., 'Iu. B. Trifonovu – 50 let', *Literaturnaia gazeta*, 3 September 1975, p. 4

Sokolov, V., 'Rasshcheplenie obydennosti', *Voprosy literatury*, 1972, no. 2, pp. 31–45 (on *Obmen* and *Predvaritel'nye itogi*)

Solov'ev, V., 'O liubvi i ne tol'ko o liubvi', *Literaturnoe obozrenie*, 1976, no. 2, pp. 38–40 (on *Drugaia zhizn'*)

Sozonona, I., 'Vnutri kruga', *Literaturnoe obozrenie*, 1976, no. 5, pp. 53–6 (on *Drugaia zhizn'*)

Starostin, A., Untitled introduction, in Iu. Trifonov, *Igry v sumerkakh*, pp. 3–4

Stepanenko, E., 'Tainstvo tvorchestva', *Sever*, 1985, no. 2, pp. 110–16

'Studenty o povesti "Studenty"', *Smena*, 1950, no. 22, pp. 19–20

Sukhanov, V. A., 'Roman Iu. Trifonova "Starik". (Rol' nravstvennogo samosoznaniia lichnosti v istorii)', *Khudozhestvennoe tvorchestvo i literaturnyi protsess*, vypusk 7 (1985), pp. 243–58

Svobodin, A., 'Liudi svoei sud'by', *Komsomol'skaia pravda*, 13 November 1973 (on *Neterpenie*)

Thompson, S., 'Reflections of America in Trifonov's *Oprokinuty dom*', in H. Mondry (ed.), *The Waking Sphinx: South African Essays on Russian Culture*, Witwatersrand: University of Witwatersrand Library, 1989, pp. 23–39

Tiul'pinov, N., 'Otblesk drugoi zhizni', *Zvezda*, 1976, no. 2, pp. 216–18 (on *Drugaia zhizn'*)

Trifonova, O., '"Pisat' do predela vozmozhnogo": Iz zapisnykh knizhek Iu. V. Trifonova', *Iunost'*, 1990, no. 10, pp. 4–6

Turkov, A., 'Ne o zhizni, o sud'be', *Zhurnalist*, 1967, no. 7, p. 67 (on *Otblesk kostra*)

'Byt, chelovek, istoriia', in Iu. Trifonov, *Izbrannye proizvedeniia v dvukh tomakh*, vol. I, pp. 5–20; reprinted under the title 'Chelovek, byt, istoriia', in A. Turkov, *Vechnye temy*, M: Sovremennik, 1984, pp. 123–40

'Vtoroe dykhanie', *Literaturnaia Rossiia*, 30 August 1985, p. 14

Tvardovskaia, V., 'Po povodu publikatsii pisem Iu. Trifonova', *Voprosy literatury*, 1988, no. 2, pp. 192–5

Ustinov, V., 'Esteticheskii ideal kommunizma i iskusstvo', *Zvezda*, 1964, no. 4, p. 204 (on *Utolenie zhazhdy*)

Velembovskaia, I., 'Simpatii i antipatii Iuriia Trifonova', *Novyi mir*, 1980, no. 9, pp. 255–8

Venturi, J., 'Kakim byl roman Trifonova do tsenzury', *Russkaia mysl'*, 2 May 1986, p. 10 (on *Vremia i mesto*)

Wilkiewicz, Z., 'Der Zeitbegriff in Jurij Trifonovs Roman "Vremja i mesto" ("Zeit und Ort")', in N. Franz and J. Meichel (eds.), *Russische Literatur der Gegenwart. Themen. Tendenzen. Porträts*, Mainz: Liber Verlag, 1986, pp. 205–31

Woll, J., 'Trifonov's *Starik*: The Truth of the Past', *Russian Literature Triquarterly*, 19 (1986), pp. 243–58

Inner Migrations: Iurii Trifonov's Last Two Stories, Washington: The Wilson Center, Kennan Institute for Advanced Russian Studies, Occasional Papers, 221, no date [1987]

Invented Truth: Soviet Reality and the Literary Imagination of Iurii Trifonov, Durham and London: Duke University Press, 1991

Woodward, J. B., 'The "Dotted Line"' of Jurij Trifonov's Last Novel', *Die Welt der Slaven*, 36 (1991) (N. F. 15), 1–2, pp. 330–46

Zhukov, I., 'I nakhodia istinu v poiske ... ', *Voprosy literatury*, 1976, no. 3, pp. 71–3 (on *Drugaia zhizn'*)

Zolotonosov, M., 'Muzyka vo l'du', *Ural*, 1988, no.3, pp. 167–8

Zolotusskii, I., 'Vnutri kol'tsa. O trekh povestiakh Iu. Trifonova "Obmen", "Predvaritel'nye itogi", "Dolgoe proshchanie"', *Komsomol'skaia pravda*, 17 February 1972

'Vozvyshchaiushchee slovo', *Literaturnoe obozrenie*, 1988, no. 6, pp. 23–32

Index

Abramov, F. A. (1920–83) 12, 179
Agurskii, M. 125
Akhmatova, A. A. (pseudonym of A. A. Gorenko, 1889–1966) 38
Aleksandr II, Tsar (1818–81) 126, 130, 136
Aleksandr III, Tsar (1845–95) 92, 130, 131, 132, 136
Andreev, Iu. 7, 209
Anninskii, L. A. 12, 36
Antonov-Ovseenko, V. A. (1883–1939) 123
Aptekman, O. V. (1849–1926) 123
Austin, P. 223–4

Baklanov, G. Ia., 6
Baruzdin, S. A. (1926–90) 5, 163, 214, 221
Belov, V. I. 12, 47, 210
Berdiaev, N. A. (1874–1948) 66, 73
Bespalov, I. M. (1900–37) 109
Björling, F. 215
Bocharov, A. G. 211
Brezhnev, L. I. (1906–82) 2, 47, 83, 97, 127, 138, 149, 155, 205
Brovman, G. 7, 209
Brown, E. J. 213, 214, 222
Bubennov, M. S. (1909–83) 208
Budennyi, S. M. (1883–1973) 142
Bulgakov, M. A. (1891–1940) 63, 115, 119, 179, 203, 212
Byron, Lord George Gordon (1788–1824) 124

Chagall, M. (1887–1985) 4, 86, 200
Charles IX (King of France, 1550–74) 147
Chekhov, A. P. (1860–1904) 12, 25, 74, 172, 183, 202, 212, 224

Chernyshevskii, N. G. (1828–89) 131, 221
Chukovskaia, L. K. (b. 1907) 164, 221
Clark, K. 76, 209–10, 212

Dali, Salvador (1904–90) 177, 180
Daniel', Iu. M. (1925–89) 47, 210
Danton, G.-J. (1759–94) 148
Davlet-Geray, Khan 147
De Broc, Vicomte H. 124, 148
De Maegd-Soëp, C. 211, 219
Denikin, A. I. (1872–1947) 123
Diavolo, Fra (pseudonym of Michele Pezza, 1771–1806) 130
Disraeli, Benjamin (Earl of Beaconsfield, 1804–81) 124, 216
Dolgorukii, Iu. (c. 1090–1151) 136
Dostoevskii, F. M. (1821–81) 25, 28, 78, 111, 113, 114, 115, 117, 118, 119, 131, 132, 178, 215, 216
Druzhba narodov 5
Dudintsev, V. D. (b. 1918) 33
Dumenko, B. (d. 1919) 158, 218
Dunham, V. S. 15, 209, 213
Durkin, A. 212

Efimov, I. 144, 157, 219
Egorov, A. I. (1883–1939) 123
Eisenstein, S. M. (1898–1948) 147
Eremina, S. 90, 209
Erenburg, I. G. (1891–1967) 33
Ermolaev, H. 144, 157, 219–20
Ermolova, M. N. (1853–1928) 75, 79

Fadeev, A. A. (1901–56) 38, 169
Fedin, K. A. (1892–1977) 3, 142, 169
Fet, A. A. (1820–92) 131
Feuchtwanger, L. (1884–1958) 182
Figner, V. N. (1852–1942) 123, 137

Franco, F. (1892–1975) 51
Frankel, E. R. 208–9
Frolenko, M. F. (1848–1938) 123, 134, 137

Goethe, J.-W. von (1749–1832) 115, 118, 119, 155, 203, 215
Goff, I. (b. 1928) 208
Gorbachev, M. S. (b. 1930) 1, 214
Gor'kii, M. (pseudonym of Aleksei Maksimovich Peshkov, 1868–1936) 109, 111, 113, 115, 118–19
Grekova, I. (b. 1907) 85
Grinevitskii, I. (1857–81) 131
Grossman, V. S. (1905–64) 4

Hayward, M. (1924–79) 210
Heldt, B. 96, 213
Herzen, A. I. (1812–70) 11–12, 92, 131
Homer (*c.* 8th or 9th century BC) 38
Hosking, G. A. 20, 90, 99, 210, 214
Hughes, A. C. 7, 209

Isakovskii, M. V. (1900–73) 20
Ivan IV, Tsar ('the Terrible') (1530–84) 128, 146–7, 148, 204, 221
Ivanova, N. B. 141, 210, 212, 218

Kafka, F. (1883–1924) 67, 74, 212
Kaledin, A. M. (1861–1918) 149
Karamzin, N. M. (1766–1826) 12
Kazakevich, E. G. (1913–62) 4
Khalturin, S. N. (1856–82) 131
Khrushchev, N. S. (1894–1971) 14, 30, 36, 37, 140, 199
Kletochnikov, N. V. (1846–83) 76–7, 79, 131, 136, 137, 138, 217
Kolyma 38
Kornilov, L. G. (1870–1918) 149, 154
Kosolapov, V. (b. 1910) 7
Koval'skii, I. M. (1850–78) 130
Kozhinov, V. V. 14
Krasnov, P. N. (1869–1947) 149
Krymov, A. M. (1871–1917) 149
Kundera, M. (b. 1929) 198

L. Labedz 210
Lenin, V. I. (pseudonym of V. I. Ul'ianov, 1870–1924) 2, 21, 141, 146, 219
Leont'ev, K. N. (1831–91) 66, 73

Lermontov, M. Iu. (1814–41) 12, 70
Levin, L. 208, 209, 210, 212
Literaturnaia gazeta 8
Lobanov, A. A. (1900–59) 75
Lopatin, G. A. (1845–1918) 123, 159, 221
Loris-Melikov, Count M. T. (1826–88) 131
Loseff, L. (b. 1937) 211
Lunacharskii, A. V. (1875–1933) 89, 109
Lur'e, P. 154, 218

Machiavelli, N. (1469–1527) 131
McLaughlin, S. 212, 215–16, 222, 223
Mal'tsev, Iu. 144, 157, 219
Mandel'shtam, O. E. (1891–1938?) 179
Mann, T. (1875–1955) 63
Markov, G. M. (b. 1911) 8, 107, 214
Marxism 89, 90, 119, 135, 159
Medvedev, R. A. (b. 1925) 128, 145–6, 219, 220
Meinhof, U. (1934–75) 216
Mikhailov, A. D. (1855–84) 131, 135, 137
Mironov, F. K. (1872–1921) 142, 145, 149, 158, 219
Miroshnichenko-Trifonova, O. 213
Modigliani, A. (1884–1920) 86, 180
Molotov, V. M. (pseudonym of V. M. Scriabin, 1890–1986) 141
Moro, Aldo (1916–78) 216
Morozov, N. A. (1854–1946) 77, 123
Moskovskie novosti 64
Moskovskii komsomolets 3, 168
Mozhaev, B. A. (b. 1923) 6, 12, 47–8, 209, 210, 214
Musil, R. (1880–42) 79

Narodnaia Volia ('The People's Will') 9, 76–7, 123–40, 159
Nechaev, S. G. (1847–82) 77, 131, 151, 174, 216, 217, 220
Nekrasov, V. P. (1911–87) 4
Nelina, N. A. (d. 1966) 4, 52, 212
Nietzsche, F. (1844–1900) 67, 74
Niurenberg, A. M. 4, 200, 212
Novyi mir 3, 5, 6, 47–8, 208–9

Okladskii, I. 137
Oklianskii, Iu. 87, 116, 158, 208, 210, 215, 221
Ordzhonikidze, G. K. (1866–1937) 182

Osinskii, V. (1852–79) 134–5
Ostrovskii, A. N. (1823–86) 79

Panferov, F. I. (1896–1960) 208
Panova, V. F. (1905–73) 4
Parnell, C. S. (1846–91) 129
Partridge, C. 221
Pasternak, B. L. (1890–1960) 205
Pastukhova, A. 87, 212–13
Patera, T. 211
Perovskaia, S. (1853–81) 131, 138
Peter I, Tsar ('the Great') (1672–1725) 33, 149, 191
Picasso, Pablo Ruiz y (1881–1973) 33, 66
Pisemskii, A. F. (1820–81) 131
Piskunov, V. 90, 209
Platonov, A. P. (1899–1951) 179
Plekhanov, G. V. (1857–1918) 131, 135
Plutarch (c. AD 46–119) 38
Pobedonostsev, K. P. (1827–1907) 92, 131, 132
Pokrovskii, M. N. (1868–1932) 109
Pomerantsev, V. M. (1907–71) 208
Popov, I. I. (1862–1942) 123
Populism: see *Narodnaia Volia*
Pravda 4, 154
Pribyleva-Korba, A. P. (1849–1939) 123
Pryzhov, I. G. (1827–85) 76, 79
Pushkin, A. S. (1799–1837) 12, 185

Raikin, A. 69
Rasputin, V. G. (b. 1937) 12
Robespierre, M. (1758–94) 124, 148
Roger I (King of Sicily, 1101–72) 198
Russell, R. 152, 211, 220

Sadovskii, M. P. (1847–1910) 79
Saint-Just, L. (1767–94) 130
Schröder, R. 5, 84, 212
Semeniuta, P. 134, 135, 137
Sever 47
Shafarevich, I. (b. 1923) 127, 217
Shaginian, M. S. (1888–1982) 208
Shakespeare, W. (1564–1616) 20, 25
Shatseva, R. A. 217
Shenfel'd, K. 217
Sholokhov, M. A. (1905–84) 142, 149, 218–19
Shukshin, V. M. (1929–74) 12
Sinel'nikov, M. 7, 209
Siniavskii, A. D. (b. 1925) 47, 210

Slovatinskaia, T. A. (grandmother) 3, 174
Smilga, I. T. 149
Sobolev, L. S. (1898–1971) 208
socialist realism 13, 18, 22, 26–7, 36, 42, 45, 79, 111, 124, 157, 168–9, 172
Sokolov, B. 7, 209
Solov'ev, V. S. (1853–1900) 131
Sol'ts, A. (1872–1945) 184, 189, 190, 222
Solzhenitsyn, A. I. (b. 1918) 6–7, 47, 127, 128, 209, 210, 213
Stalin, I. V. (pseudonym of I. V. Dzhugashvili, 1879–1953) 2, 3, 4, 5, 9, 11, 14, 18, 19, 20, 27, 29, 30, 32, 33, 34, 37, 38, 40, 41, 43, 48, 50, 51, 54, 58, 83, 103, 104, 127, 140, 141, 147, 149, 152, 158, 161, 166, 167, 170, 186, 191, 192, 222, 223
Starikov, S. 145, 219, 220
Suvorin, A. S. (1844–1912) 131
Svirskii, G. A. (b. 1921) 206, 224
Syrtsov, S. I. (1893–1937) 149
Sytsianko, A. 134, 137

Tendriakov, V. F. (1923–84) 12, 179
terrorism 9, 76, 77, 123–40, 148–50, 151
thaw (1953–64) 6, 14, 29, 32, 38, 45, 82, 97, 165, 169, 176, 208
Thompson, S. 223
Tolstoi, A. K. (1817–75) 38
Tolstoi, A. N. (1883–1945) 109
Tolstoi, L. N. (1828–1910) 12, 38, 71, 78, 85, 131
Torquemada, Tomas de (1420–98) 92
Trifonov, E. A. (uncle) (d. 1937) 2, 6, 183
Trifonov, Iu. V. (1925–81): biography 1–6, 75, 166, 194–6
WORKS: *Studenty* 3–4, 14–28; *Utolenie zhazhdy* 30–46; *Otblesk kostra* 140–3; short stories 29–30, 42–54; *Obmen* 54–64; *Beskonechnye igry* 64–65; *Predvaritel'nye itogi* 65–74; *Dolgoe proshchanie* 74–84; *Neterpenie* 123–40; *Drugaia zhizn'* 84–97; *Dom na naberezhnoi* 99–122; *Starik* 143–59; *Vremia i mesto* 160–80; *Oprokinutyi dom* 194–203; *Ischeznovenie* 180–93
Trifonov, V. A. (father) (1888–1937) 1–2, 6, 104, 139, 141–3, 184, 188–91, 198, 201–2, 218

Trifonova, E. (née Lur'e, mother) (b. 1904) 3, 166
Trifonova, O. Iu. (daughter) (b. 1951) 4
Trifonova, T. V. (sister) (b. 1927) 3, 5, 68, 201
Troitskii, N. A. 131, 133
Trotskii, L. D. (1879–1940) 141, 143, 191, 223
Turgenev, I. S. (1818–83) 22, 54, 70
Turkmenia 5, 29–46, 65–74
Tvardovskaia, V. 217
Tvardovskii, A. T. (1910–71) 4–7, 47, 208–9

Valuev, Count P. A. (1814–90) 131
Vasil'ev, A. 131
Vaznetsov, V. M. (1848–1926) 21, 113

Vecherniaia Moskva 157, 210
Verdi, G. (1813–1900) 105
Veresaev, V. V. (pseudonym of V. V. Smidovich, 1867–1945) 20
Vereshchagin, V. V. (1842–1904) 20
'village prose' (*derevenskaia proza*) 12–13, 47–8, 93, 128, 129
Voprosy literatury 7–8, 54–5
Voroshilov, K. E. (1881–1969) 141
Vyshinskii, A. Ia. (1883–1954) 190

Woll, J. 220
Woodward, J. B. 221

Zasulich, V. I. (1849–1919) 58, 131, 151
Zheliabov, A. I. (1850–81) 123–40, 217–18
Znamia 5, 140

CAMBRIDGE STUDIES IN RUSSIAN LITERATURE

General editor: MALCOLM JONES
Editorial board: ANTHONY CROSS, CARYL EMERSON,
HENRY GIFFORD, G. S. SMITH, VICTOR TERRAS

In the same series
Novy Mir
EDITH ROGOVIN FRANKEL
The enigma of Gogol
RICHARD PEACE
Three Russian writers and the irrational
T. R. N. EDWARDS
Word and music in the novels of Andrey Bely
ADA STEINBERG
The Russian revolutionary novel
RICHARD FREEBORN
Poets of modern Russia
PETER FRANCE
Andrey Bely
J. D. ELSWORTH
Nikolay Novikov
W. GARETH JONES
Vladimir Nabokov
DAVID RAMPTON
Portraits of early Russian liberals
DEREK OFFORD
Marina Tsvetaeva
SIMON KARLINSKY
Bulgakov's last decade
J. A. E. CURTIS
Velimir Khlebnikov
RAYMOND COOKE
Dostoyevsky and the process of literary creation
JACQUES CATTEAU
translated by Audrey Littlewood
The poetic imagination of Vyacheslav Ivanov
PAMELA DAVIDSON
Joseph Brodsky
VALENTINA POLUKHINA

Petrushka: the Russian carnival puppet theatre
CATRIONA KELLY
Turgenev
FRANK FRIEDEBERG SEELEY
From the idyll to the novel: Karamzin's sentimentalist prose
GITTA HAMMARBERG
'The Brothers Karamazov' and the poetics of memory
DIANE OENNING THOMPSON
Andrei Platonov
THOMAS SEIFRID
Nabokov's Early Fiction
JULIAN W. CONNOLLY